The Psychology of Inequality

The Psychology of Inequality

Rousseau's *Amour-Propre*

Michael Locke McLendon

PENN

UNIVERSITY OF PENNSYLVANIA PRESS

PHILADELPHIA

A volume in the Haney Foundation Series, established in 1961 with the generous support of Dr. John Louis Haney.

Published by
University of Pennsylvania Press
Philadelphia, Pennsylvania 19104-4112
www.upenn.edu/pennpress

Printed in the United States of America on acid-free paper
10 9 8 7 6 5 4 3 2 1

Library of Congress Cataloging-in-Publication Data
Names: McLendon, Michael Locke, author.
Title: The psychology of inequality : Rousseau's amour-
    propre / Michael Locke McLendon.
Other titles: Haney Foundation series.
Description: 1st edition. | Philadelphia : University of
    Pennsylvania Press, [2018] | Series: Haney Foundation
    series | Includes bibliographical references and index.
Identifiers: LCCN 2018017411 | ISBN 978-0-8122-5076-3
    (hardcover : alk. paper)
Subjects: LCSH: Rousseau, Jean-Jacques, 1712–1778.
    Discours sur l'origine et les fondements de l'inégalité
    parmi les hommes. | Equality—Psychological aspects.
    | Liberalism—Psychological aspects. | Political
    psychology—History.
Classification: LCC JC179 .M42 2018 | DDC 320.01/9—
    dc23
LC record available at https://lccn.loc.gov/2018017411

Contents

Introduction

Most people, I suspect, would be embarrassed to defend much of Rousseau's political thought outside an academic setting. In the twentieth century, Rousseau earned a reputation as both a proto-totalitarian and an oversensitive kook. Important World War II–era scholars held him responsible for the most dangerous movements in modern Europe, such as the Jacobin terrors of the French Revolution and the totalitarianism of Nazi fascism.[1] Bertrand Russell remarkably claimed, "Hitler is an outcome of Rousseau."[2] Alternatively, in some quarters, he is viewed as a flaky romantic utopist tortured by his imagination and penchant for reverie. According to these critics, he lacks the temperament to honestly and rationally evaluate modern life.[3] His emotions overwhelm his reason and lead him down an indulgent path of sentimentality and self-flagellation. This harsh reception of Rousseau in modern society, however unfair, should not be too surprising. Rousseau is perhaps the greatest critic of liberal democracy, and societies tend to scorn the ideas of their ideological enemies.

There are, however, ways to make Rousseau more respectable to our commercial and democratic age. He is much more practical and realistic than is often recognized and occasionally adopts positions that are common in the liberal tradition. For example, in book I, chapter 9, of *The Social Contract*, he defends the right to private property in terms similar to John Locke and Samuel Pufendorf. In book III, his discussion of regime design resembles Montesquieu's in *Spirit of the Laws*. In addition, scholars have frequently linked Rousseau to Immanuel Kant ever since Ernst Cassirer argued that Rousseau's concept of moral freedom is a precursor to Kant's moral theory.[4] Although Kant was sometimes a critic and "never a slavish follower of Rousseau," Kant's intellectual and personal development was profoundly influenced by him.[5] He too was principally dedicated to the freedom and dignity of the common person.[6]

At the same time, there is a danger to emphasizing Rousseau's similarities with liberal greats such as Locke, Pufendorf, Montesquieu, and Kant. By interpreting Rousseau as a modern liberal, or primarily so, he becomes far less interesting. His value to contemporary readers lies in his critique of modern society—in his ability to offend our sensibilities. To learn from him, we must be willing to entertain his claims that on the surface are too embarrassing to recite in public and are responsible for his reputation as a Nazi and a dreamer but nonetheless provide valuable insight into the nature and pathologies of contemporary life.

This book draws upon the embarrassing Rousseau. It examines his concept of *amour-propre*, which literally translates as self-love, and uses it as a means to understand and evaluate modern-day commercial democracies. Specifically, it attempts to identify the contours and texture of the modern personality as well as explain why Rousseau thinks inequality is so dangerous.

Amour-Propre Versus Rationality

At first glance, this is a strange goal for a book written in the twenty-first century. *Amour-propre* in many respects is a classical aristocratic passion. It describes humans as honor loving, glory seeking, and obsessed with superiority. Not surprisingly, in aristocratic Europe—that is, for much of the sixteenth through eighteenth centuries—numerous political theorists believed *amour-propre* to be the defining feature of human nature. As Arthur Lovejoy has convincingly demonstrated, this is true for many modern thinkers from Michel de Montaigne through Kant.[7]

As the feudal institutions died off and were replaced by liberal ones such as a commercial economy and an egalitarian democracy, however, human behavior began to change. The new order made new demands of its inhabitants. People were no longer warriors and stewards of a nation or serfs trapped in lowly social positions. They were all economic competitors fighting for wealth. More than ever before, they had the opportunity to control their fates and make their own fortunes. They had to rely on their own wits and good sense to make their way in the world. Political and social theorists, consequently, began to reconceptualize humans as strategic and calculating—as rational beings chiefly concerned with their self-interest. Although early modern natural law theorists such as Hobbes, Pufendorf, and Locke portray humans as preoccupied with satisfying their desires and survival needs, it is not until the publication of Adam Smith's *Wealth of Nations* in 1776 that the aristocratic language of glory and honor fully disappears from assessments of human nature. These natural law theorists all devote considerable attention to glory, honor, the desire for a good reputation, and envy.[8] In *Wealth*, by contrast, Smith adopts a strictly utilitarian approach. His humans are primarily strategic and calculating.[9] They do not care for glory and honor as much as they do for identifying their "advantage" and satisfying their "interests."[10] Their motives are depicted in more general and more practical terms.

It is now common to hear that sound moral reasoning involves little more than trying to satisfy vaguely defined personal preferences through strategic thinking.[11] By contrast, with a few notable exceptions, political and social theorists have stopped writing about *amour-propre*. Even among historians of political thought, it attracts comparatively little interest (though, as I will demonstrate shortly, it has recently become popular among Rousseau scholars).

The dominance of utilitarian moral language has made it difficult to even talk about *amour-propre* and the emotions and cognitive processes commonly associated with it—pride, vanity, envy, desire for honor and glory, self-consciousness, existential angst about self-worth, and notions of selfhood or identity. At best, *amour-propre* is assimilated into utilitarian analysis as one of many preferences that can be calculated as either a pleasure or a pain. That is, just as individuals would be rational if they took certain steps to purchase a home, the same would be true if they tried to cultivate self-esteem or earn honor. Such desires are merely two of countless goals that can be satisfied through strategic, rational thinking. This argument finds expression in the earliest proponents of classical utilitarianism. Jeremy Bentham, for example, includes "the pleasure of a good name" among the fourteen simple pleasures that he identifies as commonly pursued by individuals and the "the pains of an ill name" among the twelve pains most try to avoid. For him, it is no more or less important than any of the thirteen other pleasures or eleven other pains.[12]

Such truncated analysis, however, oversimplifies the passion and fails to capture its elemental nature. In many respects, *amour-propre* fundamentally differs from other preferences and involves a different set of cognitive processes. It is not like purchasing a box of cereal. On the most general level, the attempt to satisfy a preference is future oriented and relies on a strategic or calculative form of consciousness. *Amour-propre*, conversely, is more of a backward-thinking exercise that is evaluative rather than strategic. Its questions are not "How can I attain or acquire?" but "What is my value as a person?" and "Do I matter for others?" Its essence is to reflect on one's intrinsic value. If people sometimes make calculations to determine their self-worth or strategize to improve their social standing, it is nonetheless a mistake to reduce the passion solely to an object of calculation. This is why many modern theorists begin their analysis of *amour-propre* by first distinguishing it from *amour de soi-même*, or the desire for survival and well-being. The attempt to absorb *amour-propre* into utilitarian theory by treating it as just another preference thus makes a categorical mistake of confusing it with its opposite.

To be sure, *amour de soi-même* and *amour-propre* can both be at work in the same act. As Rousseau and numerous others have argued, people often try to acquire wealth as much out of *amour-propre* as *amour de soi-même*. For example, an individual may purchase a fancy car to impress his or her neighbors as well as for its superior gas mileage. Still, the motivations are analytically distinct and should not be collapsed under the general category of preference.

More negatively, some liberal and utilitarian theorists describe the passions in the *amour-propre* family—such as pride, envy, jealousy, and vanity—as impediments to utilitarian calculations and rational decision making. They are characterized as unfortunate behavioral tics that need to be overcome.[13] For example, there is an old maxim that instructs people not to let foolish pride get in the way of attaining their goals. Similarly, envy is typically viewed as counterproductive and contrary to reason. John Rawls, who writes from a neo-Kantian perspective, defines envy as a willingness to harm oneself to deny pleasure to others.[14] Conceived as such, envy appears to be a stupid emotion, or at least one that would not frequently survive a cost-benefit analysis. For instance, Harry Frankfurt argues that contemporary concerns about inequality are often laced with envy and hence are self-destructive. Too many Americans, he worries, foolishly "alienate" themselves by enviously comparing themselves to their more successful neighbors.[15] In terms of mental health, he thinks nothing good can come from such comparisons.

Finally, vanity is often viewed as a puerile superficiality that distracts individuals from pursuing more substantial pleasures. Individuals obsessed with popularity or physical attractiveness may ignore what J. S. Mill termed the "higher pleasures." In these cases, pride, envy, and vanity are ordinary, unbecoming vices that obstruct strategic thinking about what is truly best for individuals. The message is clear: "thou shalt not" experience pride, envy, or vanity, as if somehow humans would greatly improve as a species if they could expunge many of the passions and emotions that shape how they experience life.

The Limits of Rationality for Understanding Democratic Behavior

The near domination of utilitarianism, however, has been detrimental to political, social, and economic analysis precisely because its understanding of human psychology is confined to a limited set of cognitive processes. Individuals in commercial democracies are not merely calculators of preferences and advantages. They still experience pride, envy, vanity, and other passions associated with self-love. They still ask themselves existential questions of self-worth. While there is no denying the relevance and usefulness of utilitarian language in commercial democracies, there are numerous behaviors in such societies that cannot be understood exclusively through its terms. Indeed, political, economic, and social analysis is complicated business. It is doubtful whether one vocabulary or methodological approach could ever get to the bottom of it.[16] Simply because utilitarianism is helpful for understanding democratic behavior and moral psychology does not mean that other ethical vocabularies have nothing to contribute.

It is noteworthy that at the dawn of commercial democracy a few generations of liberal theorists (as well as Rousseau) thought the psychology of *amour-propre* adequate for explaining some of the workings and rhythms of the economic and political changes developing right before their eyes. There was not an immediate felt need to revamp the moral and psychological language to accommodate such changes. The old moral language, which included both self-interest and glory, seemed up to the task. Even Adam Smith, the godfather of capitalism, relies on *amour-propre* to explain economic motivations in his earlier works. In *The Theory of Moral Sentiments* he reduces the desire for wealth to vanity: "It is vanity, not the ease or pleasure, which interests us . . . the rich man glories in his riches, because he feels that they naturally draw upon him the attention of the work."[17]

Moreover, from time to time, contemporary social scientists make use of explanations and language reminiscent of the psychology of *amour-propre* to fully understand political, social, and economic behavior they observe in the United States, the quintessential commercial democracy. For example, since the Great Depression, psychologists have argued that individuals who lose their job experience feelings of worthlessness and a loss of a sense of self, which may hinder their attempts to reenter the labor force.[18] Their reflective evaluation of their social value, in other words, undermines their strategic calculations to improve their financial condition. A similar dynamic plays out in social and economic inequality. It has long been speculated that the American poor often lack a sense of self-worth. As Michael Harrington once argued, they "are pessimistic and defeated . . . and . . . are victimized by mental suffering to a degree unknown in Suburbia."[19] The mind-set of a poor person, simply put, contains much more than a series of calculations for climbing the economic ladder. They, like all people, possess a "reflective reasoning" that asks existential questions inspired by *amour-propre*, such as "Do I have value?" These considerations undoubtedly affect their economic behavior. In addition, sociologists and psychologists have successfully proved that racial or gender identity can affect academic performance. Individuals who think they will perform poorly because they are members of a historically oppressed group often do. Their attitude becomes a self-fulfilling prophecy.[20] Academic success requires confidence and a sense of self-worth in addition to intellect. Lastly, social psychologists and economists have recently published several studies identifying attitudes and behaviors that Rousseau typically associates with *amour-propre*.[21] It would be ill advised, therefore, to suggest *amour-propre* belongs to another age and is inappropriate for understanding modern life. It still has much to teach.

Rousseau's Argument in Brief:
Homeric Undercurrents in Modern Liberalism

Rousseau's own analysis is far more ambitious than those of either early liberal theorists or twentieth-century social scientists. Rather than merely describe liberalism through *amour-propre* or identify instances of *amour-propre* in liberal democratic culture, Rousseau makes a systematic argument in which he demonstrates that liberal institutions and ideologies both awaken and corrupt the passion. His argument is shocking, resting upon two controversial premises.

The first, as previously mentioned, is that *amour-propre* is a classical aristocratic passion. In ancient Greece, being *aristos* referred to either those of high birth or those who distinguish themselves as best on the basis of talent and excellence. Rousseau has little sympathy for persons of high birth; he is most interested in the latter sense of the term. He thinks that *amour-propre* becomes inflamed when it is aroused by publicly rewarding excellences and merit. Although I will not present my case for this contention until Chapter 1, for now it is worth pointing out that his discussions are replete with references to aristocratic terms such as honor and "being best." In the *Second Discourse* Rousseau describes *amour-propre* as "the genuine source of honor" and claims it results from the desire to be the best singer, dancer, orator, athlete, and so forth.[22] In addition, in the *First Discourse* his stated enemies are the intellectuals, not the nobles.

The second premise is that the desire to be *aristos* in its second meaning, as being honored for excellence, is prevalent in commercial democracies. While modern liberals praise equality and celebrate the dignity of all persons, they also fiercely compete for socioeconomic status and believe social hierarchies reflect individual merit. Commercial democracies have their own aristocrats, whom Rousseau describes as possessing many of the attitudes and psychological traits attributed to the Homeric heroes. This includes *amour-propre* as well as an inclination to cruelty and a willingness to harm the weaker and poorer members of society.

These two premises lead to a startling conclusion: modern society is more classically aristocratic than is often appreciated and produces individuals who have the same desires and concerns as their counterparts from bygone ages. Rousseau thinks that modern liberals have not created a new age of democratic equality so much as refashioned aristocracy for the commercial age. This is perhaps Rousseau at his most radical, yet also his most relevant. His analysis invites his reader to confront how deeply inequality is imbedded in modern democracies.

Recent Scholarship on Rousseau's *Amour-Propre*

This interpretation of Rousseau's *amour-propre* is at odds with much of the current literature, which seeks to revive interest in his treatment of the passion by minimizing his radicalism and assimilating it into mainstream liberalism, especially Kantianism. Contrary to earlier generations of scholars, who generally believed *amour-propre* to be mostly dangerous and destructive, today's scholars argue that it can be both good and bad. To correct for earlier one-sided, grim views of *amour-propre*, these new scholars have dedicated themselves to uncovering numerous positive uses of it in Rousseau's works. N. J. H. Dent, the godfather of this new approach, interprets Rousseau as a recognition theorist in the Kantian-Hegelian mold and contends that respect for rights and personhood originate from *amour-propre*.[23] Laurence D. Cooper argues that *amour-propre* "is a necessary condition for many good things,"[24] including familial and conjugal love,[25] virtue, patriotism, compassion, moral heroism, and, from the "Savoyard Vicar" in *Emile*, self-esteem. Adding to this list, David Lay Williams notes that in the *Dialogues* Rousseau cites it as an antidote to laziness.[26] Frederick Neuhouser, partially following Dent's Kantian-Hegelian approach, ambitiously contends that "rationality, morality, and freedom—subjectivity itself—would be impossible for humans if it were not for *amour-propre*"[27] In his account, the passion satisfies both cognitive and motivational preconditions for the establishment of the general will. Cognitively, *amour-propre* is a social and comparative emotion that allows people to view the world from other people's perspectives. With regard to motivation, it encourages people to value public esteem over individual material gain. If *amour-propre* is linked to the general will, people will be inclined to conform to the sovereign good even if it violates their individual self-interest.

There is probably little point in contesting these claims. They have been well researched and are backed up with an impressive amount of textual evidence, especially from *Emile*. A casual perusal of Rousseau's works confirms their case. Even in the decidedly negative *Second Discourse* Rousseau asserts that to *amour-propre* "we owe what is best and worst among men," though he does qualify this statement by asserting that it is responsible for "a multitude of bad things [and] a small number of good things."[28] And in *Emile* he similarly claims it "is a useful but dangerous instrument," though he again qualifies his position by stating that "often it wounds the hand making use of it and rarely does good without evil."[29] It is undeniable that Rousseau's analysis of *amour-propre* goes well beyond noxious vanity. Granted, earlier generations of Rousseau scholars were cognizant of Rousseau's claim of positive *amour-propre*.[30] The "positive *amour-propre*" theorists—Dent, Cooper, and Neuhouser—devote far more attention to it, however, and put it at the forefront of their interpretations.

To their credit, moreover, the positive *amour-propre* theorists are careful not to exaggerate the potential utility of *amour-propre* and are acutely aware of its perils. Dent concedes Rousseau "often" refers to *amour-propre* in its most perverse sense and is "sharply aware of the potential for damage,"[31] while Cooper notes "*amour-propre* never stops being dangerous—indeed, potentially calamitous—and hence needs to be sternly and thoroughly governed."[32] He also acknowledges that Rousseau's own attempt to transcend it is implausible for an overwhelming portion of the population. Neuhouser is the most cautious of the three, at least in his first book on *amour-propre*, and does not believe that Rousseau offers a credible solution to the problems created by the passion: "The highly unusual and demanding conditions that these solutions to the problem of evil presuppose—not merely a godlike legislator and an improbably wise tutor but also a complete wiping of the historical slate (in the case of politics) and total seclusion from the particular bonds of family (in the case of education)—must make us wonder exactly what kind of possibility Rousseau takes himself to be demonstrating."[33] If *amour-propre* is beneficial in many ways and an ineradicable feature of modern human consciousness, there is nonetheless little chance of limiting its dangerous expressions.

Despite this stipulation, there is something deeply dissatisfying about emphasizing the positive dimensions of *amour-propre*. By casting Rousseau as a proto-German idealist who holds that equal social standing can satisfy the emotional needs of self-respect often associated with the passion, they blunt the critical edge of his daring political theory. The central message of his various discussions of *amour-propre* is not that it is a malleable passion capable of redirection toward some social or emotional good. Rather, it is that the emerging eighteenth-century democratic and commercial order corrupts the human need for self-love. It tolerates and nurtures high levels and specific forms of inequality that, combined with *amour-propre*, often result in domination and cruelty. Indeed, it is impossible to fully understand the view Rousseau has of *amour-propre* without putting it in the context of his social and political criticism. At its core, his political thought is about inequality in liberal democracies, as is his conceptualization of *amour-propre*.

To be fair, the three positive *amour-propre* theorists are not insensitive to Rousseau's politics. Neuhouser, in particular, recognizes that the *Second Discourse* is primarily a critique of modern commercial society.[34] His discussion is largely abstract, however, and mostly involves identifying the various economic and institutional conditions that "inflame" the passion, such as leisure, luxury, division of labor, individual differentiation, and private property.[35] Neuhouser does not fully examine Rousseau's actual social criticisms and specific political enemies. His is an analytic exercise, which has considerable value but is insufficient to fully grasp Rousseau's decisively political treatment of *amour-propre*.[36] Consequently, like his fellow positive *amour-propre* theorists, Neuhouser does not appreciate the radicalness of Rousseau's criticism of commercial democracy and its tendency to overvalue individual talent.[37]

Furthermore, by focusing so much on the positive aspects of *amour-propre*, scholars disregard Rousseau's powerful critique against his contemporaries. Most seventeenth-century and eighteenth-century thinkers—such as Pierre Nicole, Pierre Bayle, Bernard Mandeville, and others—enthusiastically celebrate *amour-propre* as a cure for poverty, a catalyst for economic growth, an inspiration for intellectual development, and the emotional glue bonding society together. Rousseau was far more skeptical of *amour-propre* than his peers, rejecting most of their attempts to extract political, social, and economic value from the passion. When he argues for positive usages of *amour-propre*, it is mostly to construct healthy moral personalities that transcend the selfishness inherent in it. *Amour-propre*, in other words, can be transformative. It can create new forms of consciousness. Rousseau rarely argues it should merely be redirected to mimic virtues such as charity or promote economic growth. His utilization of *amour-propre* for positive ends is much more circumscribed than that of many of the thinkers of his age.

While the desire of the positive *amour-propre* theorists to correct for the error of earlier scholars who held too dismal a view of Rousseau's treatment of the passion is welcome, I worry that they overcorrect this problem—especially Dent and Neuhouser in his second book, *Rousseau's Critique of Inequality*. Rousseau is not Kant. Rather than try to reconcile him with liberalism, we should embrace his far-reaching social and political criticism and interpret *amour-propre* in the context of this criticism. We will learn more about him, more about *amour-propre*, and more about modern life.

The four chapters in this book trace the development of *amour-propre* from its genealogical roots in the Homeric honor culture to Saint Augustine and medieval Christianity to its rebirth among seventeenth-century French neo-Augustinians. It continues through Rousseau's debate with the *philosophes*, and finally to Tocqueville's interpretation of it as a democratic vice, though one that is ultimately harmless and occasionally useful.

In Chapter 1, I argue that Rousseau defines *amour-propre* in terms of classical notions of aristocracy and draws upon it in his critique of the *philosophe* project to become a new aristocracy.

Chapter 2 examines the religious origins of *amour-propre* through Augustine's concept of *amor sui* (translated as self-love in English and *amour-propre* in French) and traces its development through seventeenth-century neo-Augustinians and early Enlightenment thinkers such as Mandeville. Augustine's treatment of *amor sui* is varied and wide-ranging. Augustine offers, however, two narratives of the passion that are of supreme importance in modernity. The first is democratic and seeks to identify instances in which *amor sui* can be manipulated for some societal benefit. The second is aristocratic and identifies a process in which *amor sui* degenerates into a more destructive passion—*libido dominandi*, or lust for domination and control. Surprisingly, most neo-Augustinians hold a more modern, utilitarian interpretation of *amor sui* and downplay Augustine's own warnings that it tends to become a gateway emotion to the lust for domination. Instead, they emphasize its social utility in the city of humans, or *civitas terrena*.

In Chapter 3, I contend that Rousseau's narrative in the *Second Discourse* closely mirrors Augustine's treatment of *amor sui* as a gateway to domination and despotism. Furthermore, I examine his various solutions to *amour-propre* and conclude they all are designed to eliminate the aristocratic and commercial conditions most responsible for its most dangerous expressions.

Finally, in Chapter 4, I argue that Tocqueville implicitly challenges Rousseau's thesis that *amour-propre* results from aristocratic psychology and is dangerously inflamed by commercial capitalism. While he accepts that "inflamed" *amour-propre* is most common in commercial societies that sustain social-class fluidity, he also believes the passion to be essentially democratic rather than aristocratic. That is, it results from the commitment to equality more than from the rewarding of excellences. Tocqueville is also less pessimistic than Rousseau and rejects his argument that it degenerates into a desire to dominate and tyrannize over one's neighbors. The most dangerous tyrannies of the modern age, he thinks, are inspired by weakness and mediocrity, not the excellences of the talented.

Chapter 1

Being *Aristos* and the Politics of Aristocracy

Rousseau undertakes his initial inquiry into *amour-propre* early in part II of the *Second Discourse*. His first step is to connect it to aristocracy. In his anthropologic natural history, he describes early humans settling into villages for the first time. These new social living arrangements forever change the consciousness of the species and create a powerful new desire: that of being *aristos*, or "being best." Rousseau writes,

> It became customary to assemble in front of the Cabins or around a large Tree: song and dance, true children of leisure, became the amusement or rather the occupation of idle men and women gathered in a crowd. Everyone began to look at everyone else and to wish to be looked at himself, and public esteem acquired a price. *The one who sang or danced best; the handsomest, the strongest, the most skillful, or the most eloquent came to be the most highly regarded,* and this was the first step at once toward inequality and vice: from these first preferences on one side were born vanity and contempt, on the other shame and envy; and the fermentation caused by these new leavens at last produced compounds fatal to happiness and innocence.[1]

Granted, Rousseau does not explicitly use the term *amour-propre* in the passage (hereinafter referred to as the "competition for esteem"). Many scholars, however, are comfortable with Victor Goldschmidt's contention that Rousseau's village residents are experiencing an emotion, if not the same as *amour-propre*, at least resembling it and represent a harbinger of things to come.[2] Like civil humans, as most scholarship acknowledges, the village inhabitants are both self-conscious and competitive. Self-consciousness, in fact, results from competitiveness. The villagers become aware of themselves as individuals and form an identity through repeated comparisons with their peers. As Jean Starobinksi observes, it is the first time in which there is an "active division between *self* and *other*."[3] In the process, the villagers develop a social consciousness in which they learn to view themselves through the perspective of others. That is, they learn to think of themselves in the third person. Surprisingly, however, little attention is paid to the language of being *aristos* in the "competition of esteem" passage—even though such language is clear and obvious. The members of Rousseau's little society all want to be the best at something: singing or dancing, intelligence, and so on. Importantly, they do not want merely to be appreciated for their finer qualities or recognized as a person worthy of respect. They do not even want to be better than their neighbors. They want to be *aristos*, or to "claim first rank as an individual."[4] They desire a level of superiority that is not easily satisfied and leaves little room for the success of others. Most scholars, however, ignore this language and interpret it as either a proxy for the competitive nature of civil society or diminish it to a superlative desire for a higher relative rank. Almost no one takes seriously that Rousseau actually means in the passage "being best."

The three "positive *amour-propre*" theorists—Dent, Cooper, and Neuhouser—interpret the competition for esteem in this manner. Dent is decidedly unimpressed with the passage. He dismisses it as "an attractive tale" noteworthy only for its vagueness: "Little explanation is given of why they wish to consider and be considered should emerge; nor of why once it has, it should come to dominate and shape the individual character and human relations so pervasively."[5] Tellingly, Dent reads being *aristos* right out of the passage and reduces it to a desire to "be considered." Cooper's analysis of the competition for esteem is brief and mostly addresses cognitive developments.[6] Insofar as Cooper is interested in the link between talent, being *aristos*, and *amour-propre*, it is, following Dent's lead, to demonstrate that Rousseau does not believe that aspirations for achievement necessarily lead to zero-sum competitions in which everyone wants to dominate others. Eager to capitalize on the positive aspects of *amour-propre*, he makes much of the pride and vanity distinction from *Corsica* and argues that there are nonrelational forms of *amour-propre*.[7]

Neuhouser is of two minds about this issue.[8] In his first book, *Rousseau's Theodicy of Self-Love*, he contends that being best is the most primitive expression of *amour-propre* and is its default setting. He also expresses reservations about reading Rousseau as a proto-Kantian, arguing that self-esteem and being recognized as worthy of equal rights are not the same thing.[9] In his

second effort, *Rousseau's Critique of Inequality*, he appears to reverse his position. He rarely mentions the aristocratic language of being best and is most
interested in the relational or positional aspects of *amour-propre*. He writes:
"The relativity of *amour propre* contrasts sharply with the absolute, or non-
comparative, character of *amour de soi-même*."[10] Elsewhere, directly citing the
lines about being best, he downgrades it to a desire to be more esteemed than
others.[11] In addition, he moves closer to a traditional Kantian interpretation
of Rousseau's *amour-propre* by accepting Dent's claim that equal social status
can satisfy the urges for recognition born of *amour-propre*, though he is more
interested in Joshua Cohen's version of the argument.[12] As evidence, he cites
the paragraph immediately following the competition for esteem, in which
Rousseau states that "as soon as men had begun to appreciate one another and
the idea of consideration had taken shape in their mind, each one claimed a
right to it, and one could no longer deprive anyone of it with impunity. From
here arose the duties of civility . . . and from it any intentional wrong became
an affront."[13] Consistent with his Kantian interpretation of *amour-propre* as a
form of recognition, Neuhouser construes "duties of civility," questionably I
think, as referring to objective standards of respect that everyone ought to
enjoy equally. They represent a form of self-esteem that is absolute rather than
relative.[14]

Dent, Cooper, and Neuhouser in *Rousseau's Critique of Inequality* are not
wrong to focus on the relational nature of *amour-propre*. Being best is by definition comparative, and Rousseau often writes of *amour-propre* without men-
tioning the desire to be best. He even uses the term "consideration" as a
descriptor for the passion. They are also on safe ground in arguing for nonrelational forms of *amour-propre*. Nonetheless, the aristocratic-laden language is
eye-catching and prominent in the text. It should not be casually dismissed or
ignored.

There is a second interpretative approach to *amour-propre* also common
in the literature. Numerous scholars maintain that Rousseau develops the
concept primarily to criticize commercial society. Some make general claims
that Rousseau is addressing either the harmony-of-interests model popular
with defenders of the emerging capitalist order or simply the inequality of
conditions in modern Europe.[15] One Rousseau scholar, Helena Rosenblatt,
contends that *amour-propre* is partially designed to shed light on the political
corruption of the patrician classes in Rousseau's hometown of Geneva.[16] In
her novel interpretation, Rousseau takes the side of the bourgeoisie against the
aristocracy of high birth. Other scholars, including Neuhouser, make analytic

arguments to demonstrate that commercial economic activities themselves corrupt *amour-propre*. As a consequence of the competitive and zero-sum nature of commercial economies, they contend, the desire for recognition transforms into a desire for superiority.[17]

As with the Kantian-Hegelian approach, there is much to be said for these economic interpretations. In the *Second Discourse*, Rousseau links the innovations mostly commonly associated with the rise of commercial society, including division of labor and technological developments such as the use of metallurgy, to the bad forms of *amour-propre*. Furthermore, these economic interpretations rightly highlight the political critique underlying Rousseau's anthropology. Whatever pretenses Rousseau has to providing an accurate natural history, his intention is to do social criticism.[18] In addition to the "Preface," in which he explicitly states that his natural history is designed to assist the reader in "judging our present state,"[19] the final two paragraphs of the essay make clear that his comparison between natural and civil humans is designed to highlight the corruptions of his age. The discourse is plainly meant to be more than a naturalist screed against civilization.

The "commercial *amour-propre*" theorists, however, also wrongly ignore Rousseau's reference to being *aristos*. In many of their accounts, *amour-propre* is downgraded from a desire to be best to a desire for praise and recognition.[20] On the surface, it makes perfect sense that these scholars would disregard Rousseau's aristocratic language. If Rousseau is criticizing Europe's present state, then it would seem that condemnations of aristocracy are anachronistic. By the mid-eighteenth century, Europe was transitioning to democracy and capitalism. The courtly aristocracy was in retreat and slowly being supplanted by a new upstart class composed of men of commerce, legally trained administrators, and intellectuals—even if the nobles in some nations retained considerable power through World War I.[21] Few, after all, would consider the eighteenth century the "Age of Aristocracy." Furthermore, the commercial values of the age, at least upon first inspection, appear antithetical to aristocratic ones. The new moneyed and administrative classes subscribed to economic and bureaucratic values of profit and orderliness in place of honor, and they championed a form of equality premised on the idea that everyone ought to have equal opportunity to amass societal rewards. They viewed *les grands* as their chief rivals.

This surface dismissal of Rousseau's aristocratic language only makes sense, however, if aristocracy refers to the aristocracy of high birth—the modern European feudal nobility defined by hereditary titles, taxing and hunting privileges, special political dispensations, and refined mannerisms. If aristocracy is conceptualized as being best in terms of merit and excellence, then Rousseau's intentions become clearer. Indeed, the aristocratic language provides an essential clue as to how Rousseau wants the reader to judge "our present state." In surveying the emerging commercial societies, as argued in the "Introduction," he seems to think that important elements of the aristocratic value structure thrived. Rather than view Europe as transitioning from aristocracy to democracy, he sees a reassertion of classical aristocratic values. To prove the claim that the values of modern commercial life overlap with those of classical aristocracy, he makes use of rather unorthodox evidence. He analyzes the psyche of the new commercial, administrative, and intellectual classes and portrays it as similar to that of the heroes of epic poetry. *Amour-propre*, an emotion born of the desires for excellence and honor, is the lynchpin in his damning portrayal.

Although this interpretation may seem strange and counterintuitive, it is consistent with the philosophical analysis Rousseau offers of *amour-propre*, the political development of modern Europe, and his experiences of these political developments while living in Paris. That is, philosophy, politics, and biography all point to such a conclusion.

Philosophical Evidence: Sophocles and the Classical Aristocratic Personality

Sophocles provides an especially helpful analysis of the classical aristocratic personality in his tragedy *Ajax*. He was fascinated by Homer and, as Jennifer March claims, "was known in antiquity as 'the most Homeric' tragedian, and certainly the *Ajax* can justifiably be considered the most Homeric of his extant plays."[22] Among other things, *Ajax* is a about the political and social world, in particular the transformation in fifth-century Athens from an aristocratic worldview to a democratic one.[23] To capture this change, Sophocles constructs a dichotomy between aristocratic and democratic psyches that is more analytically succinct than anything found in Homer's celebrated poems. Like many in his age, he was acutely aware that the rise of democracy dramatically altered human consciousness. Democrats apprehend the world in ways fundamentally different from those of their aristocratic counterparts. The insights Sophocles dramatizes here remain relevant. His dichotomy between aristocracy and democracy has shaped much of the thinking on the subject and continues to structure scholarly opinion. As we will see in chapter 4, it is the starting point of Tocqueville's analysis of American democracy.

In brief, Sophocles understands aristocrats to be honor loving, democrats to be prudent and calculating. His character of Ajax, who represents the aristocratic ethos, is a hulking warrior who cares only for honor and glory and fears nothing more than shame.[24] His devotion to these values is so complete that he commits suicide after being disgraced by the goddess Athena, who tricked him into slaughtering cattle rather than the Greek leadership he held responsible for awarding Achilles' armor to Odysseus rather than himself. Ajax proclaims, "Honor in life or in death: a man is born noble, he must have one or the other."[25] Conversely, Odysseus, who is a stand-in for democratic humans, looks after only his personal well-being, and does so in a meticulous and strategic way. As called for by the democratic world in which he lives, he carefully weighs and balances his options, looks to the future, and exhibits a flexibility utterly absent in Ajax. At times, he exhibits little fidelity to ideals or principles and does not look at himself or the world in exalted terms. It is a place that must be carefully navigated, which requires negotiation and compromise.[26] For example, regarding honor, Odysseus is willing to sacrifice much to avoid disgrace, as evidenced by the fact that he agrees to bury Ajax because he too will face the same need in the future and does not want to make enemies who might deny him last rites. He sees sacrifice in practical terms. Unlike Ajax, he does not wish to be great and has no need to make statements to the world. His drive for honor is moderated by prudence; he hedges his bets and opts for "not disgrace." Likewise, he is not strongly attached to moral principle. Paul Woodruff, who writes a persuasive defense of Odysseus, concedes his "values slide around to suit his needs" and that "you can depend on him to look after himself."[27] In the play, he readily admits that his well-being represents his overriding concern and that his compassion for Ajax's humiliating death stems from his fear that he might share in the same fate.[28] The question of whether Ajax deserves burial is secondary to his own desire for a respectful funeral. Presumably, if some moral ideal disrupts Odysseus's calculations of self-interest, then it can be ignored or rationalized away. Aware of this moral reasoning, Ajax complains Odysseus will do anything if it leads to personal benefit. Sophocles tidily sums up Odysseus's attitude through one simple exchange with Agamemnon. When Agamemnon questions his unprincipled, individualistic ethic by snidely asking, "It's all one, then, and each man works for himself?" Odysseus quickly retorts, "There is reason in that. Who else should I work for?"[29]

To be sure, Sophocles' Odysseus seems to be motivated by more than his own self-interest. At both the beginning and the end of the play, he appears to show genuine compassion for Ajax and demonstrates the ability to empathize with the loss of life and humiliations of others. For this reason, he has attracted some sympathy from scholars. Woodruff calls him a man of "deep compassion" and "deep reverence," and March suggests that the pity Odysseus has for the dead is reminiscent of the more appealing portrayal of him in Homer's *Odyssey*.[30] While his compassion is still selfish,[31] it amounts to more than a shrewd attempt to tangibly improve his lot. It comes from a recognition of the precariousness of human fate. Tragedy is around the corner for everyone, Odysseus realizes, himself included. In addition, he makes an appeal to justice and natural law, arguing that both compel him to bury Ajax.[32] This, too, implies that he is willing to stand on some moral principle or impulse that is not directly tied to his interests. By including compassion and justice in his moral reasoning, Sophocles complicates his moral psychology and makes it difficult to interpret Odysseus simply as a crass moral opportunist. If he works for himself, he can work for others as well.

At the same time, however, Sophocles' nuanced portrayal of Odysseus's moral impulses contains an obvious tension. Self-interest and justice do not always lead to the same conclusion. Sometimes, following justice requires that we work against ourselves. All this begs the question: Would Odysseus agree to bury Ajax if he believed it would harm his self-interest? For example, what if burying Ajax threatened his high standing and reputation among the Greeks or even the chance that he might receive a proper burial? There is no direct evidence in the text that answers this question. By presenting Odysseus's self-interest as coinciding with justice—that is, both point to honoring Ajax in death—Sophocles avoids the tensions in Odysseus's moral reasoning.[33] Accordingly, it might be presumptuous to contend that Odysseus is either opportunistic or compassionate and just. It might be argued that his willingness to utilize contradictory forms of moral reasoning confirms suspicions that he is a slippery, unprincipled opportunist who will say anything to further his interests. On this interpretation, Odysseus appeals to justice and natural law only as rhetorical device. If other people are moved by such considerations, then it makes sense to refer to them. It is just as plausible, however, to adopt Woodruff's and March's softer stances. The text cannot rule out either interpretation. Perhaps Sophocles only means to suggest that justice and natural law can find space to operate in the democratic consciousness and are not fully eclipsed by self-interest.

In any event, there are a few aspects of Sophocles' dichotomy between aristocratic and democratic worldviews that are worthy of elaboration. First, the portrayal of Odysseus in *Ajax* as fundamentally prudent is slightly out of step with the more common view of him as cunning, artful, and clever. In Homer's *Odyssey*, the reader is meant to marvel at his resourcefulness and sense of élan, which gets him out of numerous life-threatening predicaments. The Odysseus of the *Ajax*, by contrast, comes off as a somewhat meek and risk averse. His reasoning is not fantastical or unduly clever (unless his appeals to justice and natural law are more cynically interpreted as a function of his self-interest). At best, it is reminiscent of the reasoning in the "veil of ignorance" from Rawls's *Theory of Justice*—a classic hedge to avoid the worst possible outcomes.[34] In addition, the submissive attitude of Odysseus toward Ajax at the end of the play arguably undermines the suspicion and distrust that many Greeks allegedly had of him. If he is often unprincipled, he is not conniving and deceptive. He is not the liar that he is sometimes made out to be in the literature. Indeed, his behavior is entirely predictable once his conservative orientation is understood. His selfishness is petty and ordinary, and more likely to inspire contempt than wariness.

Second, it is easy to overstate the differences between the aristocratic ethic and the democratic one. It is not as if aristocrats do not calculate or have no interest in money, just as it would be wide of the mark to suggest that democrats are indifferent to honor and sacrifice. Even Sophocles blurs the line between aristocrats and democrats. Every bit as self-centered as Odysseus, Ajax too works for himself by *calculating* that suicide can restore his honor and secure his destiny as a great warrior, whatever the consequences for anyone else. On the other side of the ledger, Odysseus still values honor. To reiterate, he elects to bury Ajax so as to not make enemies who might seek to shame him by denying him a proper burial. While his selfishness is noteworthy because it is enlightened and encourages compassion toward enemies, it is does not fully abandon the central value of aristocratic ethics.

Still, the two men reason from entirely different places. Ajax is narrowly focused on the value of his identity. He cares only about his *aristeia*, his being best on the battlefield, and defines himself solely by being superior to his peers. This superiority is his essence. It is, to borrow an epigram from Pindar, who Ajax is.[35] In the text, it is described as his destiny. If he holds a "great deeds" ethic, the emphasis is on "deeds" plural. His superiority is not based on one flash-in-the-pan achievement; it is sustained superiority rooted in his superior nature. The idea is that he is great, not merely that he does great things.

This is why he can only interpret his defeat to Odysseus as an insult and cannot negotiate or bargain with the Greek leadership to lessen his humiliation. When the leaders of the Greek army judge him less worthy of Achilles' armor than Odysseus and Athena tricks him into slaughtering cattle instead of the leaders, they do more than defeat him in a contest or make him look silly. They insult his nature and debase his identity. Ajax is no longer a great warrior but rather a laughingstock; he is fit for shame, not honor. It is all the worse that he loses out to faithless Odysseus, who values expediency over nobility and represents a society that mocks his aristocratic values.[36] The issue of identity is crucial, as it directly shapes how people experience honor and shame. As Bernard Williams observes, Ajax's suicide is impossible to comprehend without understanding his identity as a hero. He is done in by his expectations of the world and its expectations of him.[37] His whole identity is predicated on the idea that he is not supposed to experience shame. When he does, he ceases to be who he is. This is why Odysseus feels compassion for him, and why many of his supporters in the play are perplexed by his behavior. The former knows all too well the burdens of superiority while the latter do not.

Furthermore, the concerns Ajax has about his identity have implications that extend beyond his immediate community. His aim is not merely to attain glory but to attain eternal glory. True to the Homeric code, he desires *kleos*, or the glory that earns him the privilege of being sung about by the poets in a thousand years. Achieving *aristeia* promises immortality or at least some version of it. What matters is not so much how he fares in this world but how he is remembered by future ages. The temporal considerations of immortality escalate the importance of his identity, which lead him to one inescapable conclusion. By taking his own life, Ajax can erase his final days and reclaim who he is. He can fulfill his destiny. His premise is that he has been dishonored and shamed in this life. If he continues to live, he will always be dishonored. So, by killing himself, he reasons he can reclaim his honor. Once dead, provided that he receives a proper burial, he will be defined not by his interactions with Odysseus and Athena but by his true nature. He will be remembered as a great warrior, a noble soul who restored his identity by courageously confronting and conquering his disgrace. While his reasoning may seem strange to the modern mind and indeed to the democratic ethics of fifth-century Athens, it is perfectly consistent with his worldview.

Finally, the natural superiority Ajax displays paradoxically compels him to accept the limits of human agency in the earthly world. To further diminish his defeat to Odysseus and subsequent humiliation by Athena, he endeavors to disavow as much personal responsibility for his downfall as possible by blaming it on fate. There is in the play a curious distinction between destiny and fate: if his destiny is to be immortalized as a great warrior, his fate is to have an unhappy ending in earthly life. His destiny is who Ajax is, or his essence; his fate is what is predetermined to happen to him during the course of his life. He assumes his suffering at the hands of Odysseus and Athena was prescribed by fate, even though his arrogance invited Athena's wrath. In fact, upon reflecting on his disgrace, he realizes that his name, *Aias* in Greek, means "lament." Sure enough, his final hours on earth could only be described as lamentable. His destiny and fate are at thus at cross purposes. It is through suicide that Ajax preserves the former from the machinations of the latter. Destiny, then, protects Ajax against the vicissitudes of life and ensures that his failures do not undermine his claim to *aristeia*. It insulates him from the uncertainties of actual competitions and in its own way is a hedge against the possibility of failure.

By contrast, Odysseus's motives and primary loves lack such specific content. All we know about Odysseus is that *timé* and *kleos* are not his overriding desires. He willingly sacrifices them to avoid their inverse. He seeks to protect his well-being and shuns disgrace, even if it lessens the value of his personality. But, the reader acquires little insight into his values other than that his preeminent concern is not how others view him or whether he will be glorified by future ages. Similar to classical utilitarianism, *kleos* is presumably just one of many preferences that he may wish to pursue. Consistent with the democratic ethic, he still honors things. He honors useful things, however, which may or may not include *aristeia* and *kleos*. Other than his dedication to self-interest, there is no absolutism in his thinking. He is simply prudent and calculating and is not uniformly focused on one good or desire. It is implied that he is sensitive to his various needs and weighs and balances them as situations require. If this means he cannot have eternal glory, he at least takes comfort in avoiding eternal disgrace. It is safer to go unsung. Furthermore, Odysseus rejects Ajax's fatalism and the idea that either his destiny or his fate is predetermined. He defines himself solely by his earthly interactions and takes full responsibility for the meaning of his existence. If he cannot fully control his life, he nonetheless can influence how he is perceived and how the world treats him.

Odysseus and Amour de Soi-Même, *Ajax and* Amour-Propre

The similarities between Odysseus's "work for himself" ethic and Rousseau's *amour de soi-même* are obvious enough, especially if the former is compared to Dent's expansive interpretation of the latter. According to Dent, *amour de soi-même* "signifies a concern, a care, to look to, guard, preserve and foster one's own personal well-being, guided by a true and clear sense or idea of what the well-being of oneself comprises and requires."[38] Notably, it takes both nonreflective and reflective forms. The former is more primitive and represents an instinctual desire to survive. It lacks social awareness of and typically does not take into account other persons unless they are an immediate threat to survival. Reflective *amour de soi-même*, conversely, entails a deliberative attempt to ascertain well-being and does so in the context of one's environment and how a person can thrive in that environment.[39] It calculates well-being with reference to others. The only concern of Odysseus, of course, is his well-being. His concession that Ajax is his superior to him with regard to his *aristeia*, in fact, can be interpreted as an expression of reflective *amour de soi-même*. Odysseus understands that he must grant Ajax his due if he is going to secure his own well-being.

Dent's distinction between unreflective and reflective *amour de soi-même* is also helpful for explaining why Rousseau would not be favorably disposed toward Odysseus. Rousseau knows that he cannot recreate the unreflective *amour de soi-même* of primitive humans and understands that the desire for well-being is too thin to serve as a moral psychology to support freedom in the modern world. If selfishness is relatively harmless in a life of solitude, it raises numerous problems in collective social living. Indeed, *amour de soi-même* is just as likely to encourage someone to injure or coerce his or her neighbors as to assist them. As Sophocles' portrayal of Odysseus demonstrates, individuals who "work for themselves" show compassion only when they reason from a position of weakness. Odysseus agrees to bury Ajax because he can imagine suffering the same disgrace in the future. From a position of strength, however, the same individuals might callously ignore or even directly harm their neighbors if they believed it would promote their interests. Accordingly, *amour de soi-même* is too unreliable to promote freedom and inspire people to adhere to the general will. It promotes sociability and concern for others only under certain conditions that likely will not exist on a permanent and universal basis. Presumably, by working for himself Odysseus would be one of the free riders that Rousseau must "force to be free." He is too calculating to consistently submit to the common good and would depart from it if he could identify some private interest that contradicts it. To sustain the general will, people need not only affective ties to their community but also to dedicate themselves to right and justice; virtue must take the place of natural goodness. Petty selfishness will not suffice. This is why Rousseau scolds Enlightenment thinkers: "For vices that show courage and vigor, you have substituted those of small souls."[40]

Granted, in *Emile* Rousseau does make an argument that appears to correspond to Odysseus's mind-set: "It is man's weakness that makes him sociable."[41] Compassion and empathy of the sort exemplified by Odysseus, in other words, are crucial for a well-functioning, harmonious society. It is probably best, however, not to read too much into this general similarity. Other than their shared sense of compassion, Emile and Odysseus have nothing else in common. His sense of his vulnerability is supposed to form in Emile a species-based identity rather than an individualistic one. More to the point, his moral psychology is based on *amour-propre*, not *amour de soi-même*. It is more aristocratic—it is driven by a sense of who he is rather than how he might satisfy his well-being.

On the other side of the ledger, the aristocratic values Ajax has—to have his superior abilities, or his *aristeia*, eternally recognized by the species and to establish his identity as a great hero—overlap with the spirit of Rousseau's *amour-propre*. This comparison plays out on several levels. First, as previously mentioned, Rousseau in the *Second Discourse* immediately connects *amour-propre* to both honor and being *aristos* in the competition for esteem. That is, everyone wants to be recognized as being the best at something. As in the Homeric honor culture, being best is linked to some socially relevant ability.[42] Granted, there is a wider array of talents through which to distinguish oneself for Rousseau than among the classical aristocratic warriors, who care only for military might. Rousseau's individuals care for being *aristos*, not the narrower desire for *aristeia*, and compete to be best based on such traits as physical strength, agility, physical attractiveness, and intellectual skill. Rousseau, of course, is alive in an age of commerce and intellectual advancement, not constant warfare, and identifies traits consonant with success in those activities. Heroes in commercial societies do not wield swords. Nonetheless, in both accounts, people seek to be honored for being best.

Second, Ajax's preoccupation with the value of his identity also lies at the center of Rousseau's notion of *amour-propre*.[43] Individuals in the competition for esteem become defined by their talents and abilities. They shape the core of a person's identity. People are what they achieve. They are not merely sing-ing and dancing; they wish to become great singers and dancers. Although Rousseau does not provide detailed philosophical analysis for his assumption that *amour-propre* involves the process of identity construction,[44] a case can be made for it using clues from the *Second Discourse* as well as statements from his other writings. In the discourse, *amour-propre* emerges only in social set-tings in which people have constant contact with individuals who are not part of their family. In such an environment, people are accustomed to seeing oth-ers and being seen by them. They cannot help but compare themselves to them. Importantly, their comparisons are not onetime evaluations. They are made repeatedly and form a pattern that allows people to develop conceptions of their neighbors. In other words, their observations of their peers are cumu-lative and hence give rise to public identities. In contrast to primitive humans who made few comparisons and probably forgot them upon making them, social humans come to have a defined sense of their neighbors as individual selves. In turn, people define themselves according to how they stack up against their peers and what is reflected back to them by their social interac-tions. They develop a social persona—they become someone. More simply put, they construct a narrative of their life based on their repeated peer com-parisons. This narrative is how they come to know themselves and reflect upon the value of their existence. Rousseau even develops terminology to ex-plain this phenomenon. At the end of the *Second Discourse*, he calls it "the sentiment of existence" and negatively describes it as tainted by *amour-propre*.[45] In *Emile*, he more appropriately terms it the "sentiment of identity" and neutrally describes it as a function of memory: "Memory extends the sentiment of identity to all the moments of his existence; he becomes truly one, the same."[46] Or, from the same passage, it is the process by which a per-son "gains consciousness of himself."[47] Thus, cognitively, *amour-propre* is a self-conscious reflection of a person's public identity, which is based on so-cially recognized superior abilities.

Third, both Ajax and Rousseau view social life and identity as a zero-sum competition. One person's success is by definition another person's defeat. There is only one best. Everyone else suffers by comparison. Ajax takes no sol-ace in being a great warrior. He needs recognition that after Achilles he is the best and cannot share this honor with Odysseus or any other warrior. Likewise, at the conclusion of the *Second Discourse*, Rousseau claims members of the aristocratic classes will fall into the lower ones until only one all-powerful ty-rant remains. While such competitiveness need not necessarily undermine the felt need for respect and recognition, it nonetheless is a rather high hurdle in cultures with a strong sense of honor and shame.

Fourth, Rousseau holds a watered-down version of Ajax's notion of destiny, arguing that an individual's lot in life is largely predetermined. Nature endows individuals with certain talents and abilities, and there is little one can do to alter where one winds up on the social ladder. Only a few have a realistic chance of being best. This does not mean that identities can never change, as Rousseau thinks that people will always harbor hope that they can find their way to the top: "Remember that as soon as amour-propre is developed, the relative *I* is constantly in play."[48] Still, once identities are formed, they are difficult to alter. Talents and physical appearance tend not to change much—they are something into which people are born. As Rousseau observes in "Preface to *Narcissus, or the Lover of Himself*," "Men are rewarded only for qualities which do not depend on them: for we are born with our talents."[49] To alter one's identity may very well require moving to a new community and acquiring a new peer group. Even then, a person is still defined by his or her natural abilities and personal achievements that stem from them. Granted, Rousseau's "fatalism" is less mystical than Ajax's. He has no corresponding notion of Ajax's fate. Misfortune in this life results mostly from a person's destiny—of who the person is. If Bernard Williams is right that Ajax's suicide is prompted as much by his identity as a great hero as by Athena's tricking and hence disgracing him, there is no particular reason why Rousseau's common person would contemplate suicide because of public shame. Common persons have no higher self to reclaim, and they enter society with much lower expectations they will be honored, or even appreciated, by their peers. Presumably, most silently endure their humiliating lot in life—one in which they are cruelly forced to compete in activities at which they can never win. If they commit suicide, it is probably because their constant shame becomes too much to bear or they tire of not mattering and having no meaningful expectations to live up to. The same lesson applies to fallen elites in Rousseau's world. If they commit suicide, it is because they cannot endure the shame of their declining fortunes or public disgrace. There is nothing redemptive about suicide in the modern age. It is simply a means to eliminate pain.

Finally, Rousseau even claims that modern humans resemble Ajax in their desire for immortality. At the end of the *Second Discourse*, he states that "the Citizen, forever active, sweats, scurries, constantly agonizes in search of ever more strenuous occupations: he works to the death, even rushes toward it in order to be in a position to live, or renounces life in order to acquire *immortality*."[50] The moderns, alas, also wish to be sung about.[51]

Rousseau Contra Sophocles

There are, of course, good reasons not to overstate a Rousseau-Sophocles linkage, though none rises to the level of making such a comparison indefensible. First, there is no direct textual evidence connecting Rousseau's *amour de soi-même* and *amour-propre* distinction to the clash of values in fifth-century Athens that inspired Sophocles to write *Ajax*. Although Rousseau was familiar with both Homer and Sophocles, as demonstrated by the fact that he refers to them more than a dozen times in his published and unpublished works, he only once connects Homer to either *amour-propre* or being best and never mentions Sophocles' *Ajax*.[52] Both poets are mostly background noise cited for relatively minor arguments and concepts that at best play a supporting role in Rousseau's philosophy. Still, as previously argued, the conceptual similarities between Sophocles' distinction between democratic and aristocratic personalities and Rousseau's *amour de soi-même* and *amour-propre* are conspicuous. Even if it is conceded that Rousseau did not directly borrow from Sophocles, the analytic similarities between the two distinctions are obvious enough. As I argue in Chapter 2, Rousseau's entry point into the aristocratic mind-set comes from one of its critics, Saint Augustine.

Second, Rousseau is far less admiring of the Homeric honor culture than is Sophocles.[53] On the surface, this may not seem to be the case. In the one passage in which he discusses the content of Homeric ethics, he endorses it as necessary and good, at least for certain peoples. In *Considerations on the Government of Poland*, he tries to revive Polish patriotism and identify a suitable ruling class through *agonistic* games and events that reward the most talented and manly. These games, he proposes, should be modeled on "Homer's heroes," who "were all distinguished by their force and skill," as well as "Knights' tournaments," in which men "were . . . avid for honor and glory."[54]

The purpose of such games, however, is not Homeric. They are not designed to provide source material for poets. Rather, they are a means to much more important ends: promoting patriotism and ensuring the safety of the state. Patriotism is achieved by increasing the "pride and self-esteem" of the participants, which is redirected to promote love of country and a common

Polish identity through reminiscences of past national glories.[55] It is common among Rousseau scholars, in fact, to cite this passage as proof that *amour-propre* and honoring talents can be manipulated for positive purposes, such as the promotion of civic virtue. The latter goal of ensuring state security is attained through the selection and establishment of a manly aristocratic class capable of mounting an effective military defense against invaders. The Homeric games and knights' tournaments are specifically tailored to address Poland's geopolitical vulnerabilities. Rousseau worries that Poland is too decentralized and underpopulated to fend off military threats from its more powerful and despotic neighbors, such as Russia. If Poland is to prevent foreign invasion, it needs to become a unified nation guided by powerful military leadership. Thus, unlike Ajax and Achilles, Rousseau seeks to promote the glory of collective identities rather than individual ones and does so in service to *amour de soi-même* rather than *amour-propre*. Sensibly, Rousseau views Homer's martial ethic as an asset for a people facing military dangers. In a world of nation-states, patriotism and a warrior class have their uses and must be cultivated. Homeric practices and attitudes are for him a means to a different end and do not imply an endorsement of aristocratic values.

Sure enough, absent such geopolitical concerns, Rousseau presents a much more mixed picture of classic aristocratic values. In "Discourse on Heroic Virtue," he provides a modest defense of heroism and heroes. Love of glory, he claims, is responsible "for innumerable goods and evils."[56] The formulation here is more balanced than his earlier descriptions of the utility of *amour-propre* in the *Second Discourse* and *Emile*, which are more skewed toward inevitable evils. But it is hardly a ringing endorsement. Moreover, Rousseau portrays martial glory as a poor substitute for virtue. True heroes are wise men who desire virtue and the happiness of their fellow citizens, not warriors trying to kill their way to eternal glory. And heroes for him are hardly the best of men. Rather, they are "a composite of good and bad qualities that are beneficial or harmful depending on circumstances."[57] While the essay is not all that helpful—Rousseau begins it by conceding "this piece is very bad"[58]—this last point about circumstance is crucial for understanding his critique of *amour-propre* and love of glory and why his endorsement of Homer in *Considerations on the Government of Poland* is not generalizable to other societies.

In the context of Enlightenment Europe, as evident from the first two discourses as well as later writings, Rousseau thinks the concept of the hero or the existence of a superior class of individuals is positively dangerous. In such environments, love of glory serves neither the collective good nor *amour de soi-même*. It becomes solely a means for self-aggrandizement. People will want to be best for the sake of being best, and hence will develop the worst sorts of *amour-propre*. In all likelihood, they will cause untold amounts of evil. The great, in other words, become a grave threat to the good. When writing of Paris and Enlightenment Europe, Rousseau dedicates himself to equality and promotes the virtues of the common person. He sees it as his duty to protect the dignity of such people against the superior personalities or heroes in their community.

When Rousseau writes in this vein, few would dispute that he is the "anti-Homer" or, as Judith Shklar once wryly referred to him, "the Homer of the losers."[59] Nietzsche's characterization of Rousseau as committed to "an ideal born of *hatred for aristocratic culture*" likewise gets to the core of Rousseau's motivations.[60] Although Nietzsche has been accused of being unfair and simplistic toward his Genevan predecessor,[61] a charge that is probably true, his bird's-eye view of Rousseau nonetheless manages to identify the topical thread that ties together so many of Rousseau's writings. Nietzsche's Rousseau views genius and being best as a social problem in need of a solution.

Third, and most important, Rousseau blurs the aristocrat-democrat distinction that structures Sophocles' *Ajax*. The modern Europeans whom he so persistently criticizes— the urban ones committed to the Enlightenment and commerce—are a strange amalgam of both the aristocratic and the democratic personalities. They are one part Odysseus and one part Ajax. They are strategic, calculating, and materialistic and yet supremely consumed with honor, the value of their identity, and ability-based superiority. In some cases, they even strive for immortality. If they speak the language of utilitarianism, they are still dedicated to being *aristos* and, as will be demonstrated, seeking societal dominance to complement their perceived excellences. They do more than work for themselves in the prudent, flexible way that is exemplified by Odysseus. There is a good deal of Ajax in them, even if they lack the vocabulary to account for it.

It requires little effort to reconcile the seemingly disparate democratic and aristocratic values of modern bourgeois Europeans. Their "democratic" commitments to utility and practicality are easily assimilated into the aristocratic value structure. They become yet another criterion for being *aristos*. Once utility and practicality are established as a dominant set of values, those who best exemplify such traits plausibly can demand membership among the *aristoi*. This is even true of Odysseus. He wins Achilles' armor because he successfully argues that his intelligence is more useful to the Greek war effort than Ajax's brute strength. As Woodruff points out, after nine years of war it was clear to everyone that brute strength was not going to win the war. It took Odysseus's idea of the Trojan horse to finally secure victory.[62] Rousseau essentially argues that the new bourgeois elite echoed Odysseus's claim to being *aristos* and called for the establishment of an "Odyssean" aristocracy. The members of the elite argued that their ability to administrate the world, produce wealth, and invent knowledge ought to define new criteria for being best—that the useful and the clever ought to rule.[63]

Publicly at least, these new bourgeois heroes did not speak like ancient heroes. Their vocabulary consisted of such terms as equality, popular sovereignty, and liberty. Rousseau, however, sees this as little more than hypocrisy and ideology, and he warns his readers not to be fooled. The new upstart men of commerce and administrators (and to a lesser degree intellectuals) supported opening up the political system and other democratic measures only to the extent that the new measures would weaken their perceived enemies and promote their own ambitions.[64] If they championed equality, it was only in a form such as equality of opportunity, which would not get in the way of their aristocratic ambitions.[65] They knew that if they were to attain their goals of becoming the new *aristoi*, they had to subvert the old powers. They had to delegitimize, in short, the courtly aristocracy and the church. If democratic language was suitable to this purpose, they were more than willing to use it. Thus, like Odysseus, their values slid around to meet their desires, which paradoxically were aristocratic.

It is therefore sensible to conclude that Rousseau interprets the great social-class battles of the eighteenth century as an ideological scrum between competing aristocratic factions rather than between democrats and aristocrats. The contest between Ajax and Odysseus is not between two separate worldviews so much as between competing claims to the same prize. While the old and new aristocrats fought for dominance, Rousseau worried about the common people. In his view, they were merely pawns in this upper-class competition, to be used, abused, and demeaned for someone else's ends. Throughout his writings, he tears off the democratic clothing of Europe's emerging elite and attempts to protect the masses against the elite's scheming and maneuvering for dominance.

Political Evidence: Elias's *Civilizing Process* and Elite Politics in Modern Europe

Rousseau's intuition about the nature of eighteenth-century politics draws support from important historical scholarship. In particular, Norbert Elias's *Civilizing Process* perfectly frames Rousseau's narrative. According to Elias, the medieval era in Europe is at first dominated by a warrior aristocracy of landowning knights who, like the ancient Greek aristocrats, earned their superiority on the battlefield. It was a violent, almost anarchic age in which those with official power were unable to monopolize authority. The nobility could share in ruling, provided that they had "the power to command and punish, to coerce."[66] In a violent age, naturally enough, the especially violent will dominate and have a strong claim to being best. True to classical aristocracy, these knights did not view their power simply in realpolitik terms. They obsessed about honor and glory and desired to be remembered and lauded by subsequent generations. The knightly aristocracy differed from their Greek counterparts in one crucial respect, however: they were also dedicated Christians and combined martial virtue with moral virtue.[67] They were firmly committed to ideals of compassion and justice, and believed it was their duty to protect the weak. This knightly ideal meant that warriors could not merely work for themselves. They had to think about others as a matter of principle and not just when they believed it to be beneficial. Interestingly, in this Christianized aristocracy, knights were receptive to the idea that members of the peasant classes could earn glory and honor. According to Johan Huizinga, "The passionate defenders of the ideal of knighthood at times intentionally list the deeds of peasant heroes . . . to show they had great courage."[68] It was not unheard of for peasants themselves to try to immortalize themselves through great deeds. For example, Keith Thomas writes of Michael An Gof (a.k.a. Michael Joseph), a blacksmith who in 1497 led fifteen thousand Cornish tax rebels to London in the hope for "a name perpetual and a fame permanent and immortal."[69] Unfortunately, An Gof was hanged for his crimes. To be sure, there is a rather wide gap separating the Christian ideals espoused by the knights and their actual behavior. While the knights believed themselves to be defenders of beauty and virtue and were of inestimable social value, critics tend to dismiss them as little more than a self-serving elite scrambling for power and glory. Indeed, "seen from a truly spiritual view, all the noble life was nothing but open sin and vanity."[70]

It was not hypocrisy that did the knights in, however. The anarchic political system could not last forever. Monarchical families emerged, as knights engaged in zero-sum competitions for land that increasingly concentrated power in a few hands until one family claimed victory and became the ruling family of the nation. Kings would slowly establish absolute power in England, France, and the Hapsburg territories. These structural changes led to the demise of the knightly aristocracy, as their abilities on the battlefield were not only unnecessary but also an unambiguous threat to these new absolutist kings. Warrior aristocrats simply could not be tolerated. At the same time, the new monarchs required capable administrators to govern their vast territories. Accordingly, universities became much more important, as they churned out a new socioeconomic class of lawyers and specialists capable of filling the monarchical need for rational administration. This new class of trained administrators was joined by a class of financiers and bankers, who learned to make money in the emerging commercial economy, and eventually a class of intellectuals, who taught in the universities and populated Europe's urban centers. Combined, these new classes successfully challenged the old landed knightly nobility for social preeminence. Unsurprisingly, this struggle did not resolve itself quickly. The decline of the old knights was a slow process, as many could make money from their lands and remain powerful in the new age. Although they were, as Elias notes, a "functionless" social class and no longer had a claim to being best, they did not quietly disappear.[71] Still, they slowly lost ground to the new administrative and commercial classes and by the beginning of the seventeenth century could no longer be considered the dominant social class.

For a time, the monarchs greatly benefited from this aristocratic turmoil. The two groups that posed greatest threats to their sovereignty were consumed with one another. As the new middle-rank lawyers, businessmen, and administrators increasingly gained the upper hand in their struggles against the old knightly aristocracy, however, the monarchs realized they could not afford to let these upstart classes vanquish the landed nobility. They surmised that a victorious middle rank would set its sights on political power next and try to supplant monarchy itself. So, they made every effort to string along class warfare as long as possible. To that end, the kings tipped the scales in favor of the old knightly aristocracy by awarding it tax exemptions, taxing powers, positions at court, and other important privileges in the hope of creating a roughly equal balance of power between the old knights and the new lawyers and bankers. The hope was that if the old knights could not compete monetarily with the upper strata of the upstart middle classes, at least they could claim to be the true aristocratic class.

Monarchical privileges alone, however, were not enough to merit the claim of being best. The old knights needed a new justification that would allow them to assert their superiority and define themselves as the true aristocracy. This was no simple task. The most obvious criteria for being best—superiority on the battlefield and wealth—were unavailable (though they would continue to subscribe to martial values even if they were rarely called upon to use them.) They would eventually settle on *civilité*. That is, they would distinguish themselves based on "fine dress, elaborate manners, and elegant speech."[72] They were, in short, members of a courtly aristocracy who were refined and polished, in contrast to the simple and vulgar or "rude" lower classes. This new aristocratic code of manners was not as petty as it sounds. It included civic virtue and was meant to publicly signify true superiority inherited from one's ancestors. The nobles saw themselves as worthy of honor or public recognition for their distinctive genetic quality and felt obligated to behave in accord with their supposed superior nature. Nonetheless, whatever lip service was paid to love of country and virtue, courtly life was far from idyllic. Refined and polite mannerisms often did not lead to elevated behavior, even if there was little possibility of physical violence. The courtly aristocrats were cliquey and vigorously competed in what was a never-ending game for superior social status. Elias compares it to a stock market: "As in every 'good society,' an estimate of the 'value' of each individual is continuously being formed."[73] Successful courtiers became experts at expressions, suppressing emotion, disguising passion, and any other dissimulations to conceal views or feelings that might detract from their public reputation. Thus, they were judged neither by talents nor achievement, nor even their wealth, but by how well they earned the favor of the monarch and how well they conformed to increasingly refined standards of taste and manners.

Elias, to be sure, has his detractors. C. Stephen Jaeger, for example, argues that courtliness originated much earlier in the clergy and later shifted to the secular nobility.[74] Jonathan Dewald contends that the knightly aristocracy was far more resilient and flexible than Elias assumes, and in large measure adapted to the new bourgeois standards of excellence. Many attended university and learned the art of administration so prized by ascendant monarchs. Others figured out how to succeed in the new commercial economy and retained or even grew their wealth. As a class, they managed to remain powerful in some nations into the twentieth century. In addition, a good number were neck deep in the new intellectual trends and helped shape the new bourgeois culture. The salons, which represented the physical space in which the Enlightenment developed in France, were funded by aristocrats. And, whatever role they played in advancing the social status of intellectuals, they still were governed by the rules of courtly aristocracy.[75] As Antoine Lilti notes, aristocratic hosts insisted that guests show "respect for the rules of civility and politeness, rules that governed both access to the salons and the attitudes of those who attended them."[76] Rousseau, who was allowed some petty rebellions against the rules of *civilité*, is the exception that proves the rule. For their part, many bourgeoisie took advantage of every available opportunity to enter the nobility by purchasing titles from kings eager for cash. Dewald undoubtedly is correct in contending that the line separating the bourgeois classes and the nobility is much blurrier than Elias lets on. Nonetheless, the essential core of his narrative holds up. The knightly aristocracy gave way to competing bourgeois and courtly aristocracies in the seventeenth and eighteenth centuries. Being *aristos* did not have coherent meaning.

Personal Evidence: Rousseau Contra the *Philosophes*

The problem of a bifurcated aristocracy would resolve itself in the eighteenth century, as the bourgeois classes would win something of a cultural victory. When they were finally confident enough to challenge the courtly aristocracy for social supremacy, the new bourgeois upstarts had little difficulty identifying their vulnerabilities. The courtly aristocracy, they argued, were not legitimate aristocrats and had no plausible claim to being best. Their supposed superiority—*civilité*—was not a true superiority. In place of *civilité*, the rising bourgeois classes strenuously asserted that only those who possessed talent, or more specifically, some form of intellectual ability, ought to be considered elite members of society. Thomas Paine may very well have summed up their line of attack with one acerbic quip: "Nobility equals no ability."[77]

As has been well established, Rousseau had a front-row seat to this cultural skirmish through his experiences with the *philosophes*. Although he also is critical of the economic elite and employs *amour-propre* against the wealthy, he begins with the intellectuals.[78] Like the administrators and bankers, the *philosophes* vigorously argued that they, the men of letters, were the most socially valuable members of society and hence ought to occupy the highest rungs of the social ladder. They had the most legitimate claim to being best.

Many followed Voltaire in his "desire . . . to lift the status of the men of letters to the highest rank of society."[79] Rousseau was plainly aware of this project, complaining in "Preface to *Narcissus*" that his intellectual friends "cared more about the interests of the men of letters than about the honor of literature."[80]

Rousseau, in fact, was a full-fledged participant in eighteenth-century aristocratic politics and was for a time probably supportive of his friends' claims.[81] In "Preface to *Narcissus*," he concedes that he was "seduced by the prejudices of my century."[82] Like so many young provincials, his adolescent ambition, as detailed in *The Confessions*, was to become a celebrated man of letters.[83] Rousseau also grew up with little love for the courtly aristocrats and was contemptuous of the humiliating relationship between the peasants and their so-called superiors. His father, after all, was chased out of Geneva after a tiff with a local aristocrat involving hunting privileges. Both attitudes encouraged a restlessness and an eagerness to climb the social ladder, which eventually drew him to Paris.[84] Although he received little formal education and did not exhibit any intellectual ability during his childhood, he arrived in Paris aged almost thirty and ready to distinguish himself as both a musician and a playwright. In *The Confessions*, he describes his attitude as one perfectly consistent with those of his *philosophe* friends—talent was to be his ticket to a better life. He recounts thinking during his journey to the capital of the Enlightenment: "A young man who arrives in Paris with a passable appearance and who is heralded for his talents is always sure of being welcomed."[85] Moreover, Rousseau admits that he was driven by the desire to be *aristos* and would do anything and everything to earn fame. In reference to his attempt to become a chess master, he writes, "I said to myself, 'Whoever excels in something is always sure of being sought after. Be first, then in anything at all; I will be sought after; opportunities will present themselves, and my merit will do the rest.' "[86] It is easy to connect both of these recollections to the competition for esteem (or perhaps the "competition for excellence") passage in the *Second Discourse*. The imagery of leisurely singing and dancing, of course, is clearly not a reference to Paris. Scholars think it refers to the village Maypole feast[87] or the naturalistic works of Joseph-François Lafitau or John Brown, which took American Indians as the model.[88] The competition aspect, however, arguably refers to Paris. Recall from the passage on competition for esteem that the two criteria by which people wish to distinguish themselves are talents and physical appearances: "The one who sang or danced best; the handsomest, the strongest, the most skillful, or the most eloquent." Aside from "the strongest," all of these refer to intellectual or musical abilities and good looks—the same two criteria Rousseau claims would help him find acceptance in Paris in *The Confessions*. The second passage, with its reference to "being first," is even more remarkable, as it directly links his own attitudes to the "being best" language in the competition for esteem that is generally ignored by scholars.[89]

In any case, Rousseau eventually soured on Paris as it became clear that life as a man of letters was much harsher than he had supposed. His talents were not immediately welcomed, and he was never fully comfortable making them the core of his identity. His first try at fame, which came in the form of a submission of a musical notation system to the Academy of Sciences, revealed a spiteful side to him that seems almost unimaginable in his younger self. Although the committee ultimately rejected the system, he was congratulated for a fine effort and encouraged to pursue further study in the field. He managed, in short, to attract favorable consideration. Rousseau, however, saw no silver lining in the committee's decision, and his reaction was bitter. Aside from one objection from the famous composer Rameau, Rousseau dismissed the criticisms of the committee members as nonsense and remained angry at them at least until he wrote *The Confessions* some twenty-five years later.[90] If his goal was to be *aristos*, then any sort of failure must have been completely unacceptable. His experiences did not improve much in this regard, and the next seven years proved frustrating.

To be sure, Rousseau did have some positive experiences in Paris. He was accepted in the salons, where his rustic mannerisms and creativity were appreciated as colorful. He also managed to make several friends among the *salonistes* and contributed several articles on music and one on political economy to Diderot and d'Alembert's *Encyclopedia*. Yet he was never comfortable in Paris and eventually succumbed to intense feelings of alienation and self-loathing. It was only a matter of time before he rejected the ideological claims of the *philosophes* to become the new aristocracy. By late 1740s, he had already emotionally divorced himself from Paris and expressed an irritation at its intellectual culture that began to show up in his writings. In a 1749 letter, he blasts Paris as an arrogant, snobby, inauthentic city that, tellingly, "crushes humble talents."[91]

The First Discourse

The *First Discourse* gives philosophical expression to Rousseau's discontent and systematically challenges the pretensions of the *philosophes* that they are the true aristocrats. In the essay, Rousseau makes three basic arguments. The first criticizes the *philosophes* on their own terms—that is, through an "Odyssean" or democratic category—by minimizing any possible social *utility* of the arts and sciences. Whatever social benefits that might be attributed to them are more than offset by the moral corruptions they induce. As he puts it in "Preface to *Narcissus*," "A craving for distinction necessarily engenders evils infinitely more dangerous than all the good of letters is useful."[92] If it is possible to provide specific examples in which arts and sciences make genuine contributions to the well-being of society, and Rousseau plainly accepts that at least science is good at what it does,[93] he nonetheless urges his audience to consider the disastrous cultural consequences of the Enlightenment. The old moral system, he insists, was fully discredited by the new arts and sciences. Religion and patriotism in particular suffered badly: "They [the men of letters] smile disdainfully at such old-fashioned words as Fatherland and religion."[94]

Rousseau also attacks the most obvious benefit of the arts and sciences: their economic advantages. The Scottish theorists were particularly adept at identifying the processes by which this occurred. As David Hume observes in "On Commerce," knowledge makes people more productive, which in turn leads to the creation of a manufacturing and luxury economy. Driven by the desire for new creature comforts, people work both harder and more shrewdly—they sweat and scheme to get their hands on the finer things in life, which leads to even more wealth and more production.[95] Rousseau is unimpressed, however, arguing that this alleged virtue is really a vice that makes people more miserable. Luxury, he contends, sets in motion a perverse trinity of hypocrisy, effeminacy, and idleness.[96] Appearance becomes all important, and people strive hard to remove labor as a condition of life and live in complete opulence. As a result, they become lazy and effete.[97]

In addition, Rousseau fires a warning shot over his fellow intellectuals that they would not fare so well in the commercial world. While Voltaire heaped praise on the English in his *Philosophical Letters* for financially rewarding the merit of its writers,[98] Rousseau argues they are in a catch-22 situation. Either they are corrupted by the desire for success or they fail to profit from their endeavors. On the one hand, the desire for fame and glory encourages writers to dumb down their works and pander to public opinion.[99] Truth does not easily find a home among these new intellectual aristocrats, as it takes a back seat to personal ambitions. When people work for themselves, they are apt to ignore inconvenient truths that get in the way of their own aggrandizement.[100] The best thing that could happen to genius, Rousseau argues, is for it to be left alone to develop free from all the temptations of society. On the other hand, he accepts that most of the artists and scientists of his day are not financially thriving. Unlike the new class of bankers and financiers, they are anything but lazy and rich. For Rousseau, this only proves how inequitable the new economy actually is. The artists and scientists who create wealth have no share in it and wind up supporting the lavish lifestyles of the shrewd, slothful, and greedy.[101] Lastly, Rousseau acknowledges that intellectual life is home to all sorts of unproductive rivalries and conflicts. In his "Letter to Beaumont," he even claims that books themselves are the great cause of conflict; they "are sources of inexhaustible disputes."[102]

The second and third arguments shift away from disutility to aristocratic categories of vanity, identity, and natural superiority. Rousseau denigrates intellectuals as driven by nothing more than glory and ambition—by a desire to be publicly celebrated and socially important. Their motives resemble those found in Ajax. Artists and scientists are creatures of ego, more concerned with their own glory than any social good that might result from their pursuits.[103] At best, a few great scientists and philosophers can practice their trade without being corrupted by it: "Science is not suited to man in general."[104] His soon to be former friends, he believed, were nothing more than self-serving phonies who managed to create a mean-spirited culture that made Socrates' treatment by Athens seem tame by comparison.

Rousseau's third argument continues this theme but considers it from the opposite side of the social spectrum. Rather than focusing exclusively on the winners, as did the ancient Greeks, Rousseau contends that the social esteem accorded to intellectual talent and genius demeans the overwhelming mass of ordinary citizens. In this new world of the arts and sciences, the basis of individual identity is dramatically altered, as identities based on moral character and citizenship give way to ones based on talent. In one passage, he laments that "we have Physicists, Geometricians, Chemists, Astronomers, Poets, Musicians, Painters; we no longer have citizens; or if we still have some left, dispersed in our abandoned rural areas."[105] In another, he complains that "people no longer ask about a man whether he has probity, but whether he has talents."[106] For the ordinary working-class and peasant citizens, Rousseau believes this shift is psychically catastrophic, as they can only be demeaned by this new value structure. Those "to whom Heaven has not vouchsafed such great talents and whom it does not destine for so much glory" will find life frustrating and demoralizing because they will be encouraged to think they are valuable only if they are engaged in the arts and sciences.[107] They will thus be judged by traits they lack: "Someone who all his whole life will be a bad versifier or an inferior Geometer, might perhaps have become a great clothier."[108] Or, again from "Preface to Narcissus," "men are rewarded only for qualities which do not depend on them: for we are born with our talents, only our virtues belong to us."[109] And Rousseau worries that they could not help but feel bitter, resentful, and envious: "Let us know how to rest content . . . without envying the glory of those famous men who render themselves immortal in the Republic of Letters."[110] Outside the great urban intellectual centers, Rousseau argues, people are judged by their own good character and patriotism, which are things everyone can develop. In Paris and others cities in which talent replaces virtue as the standard for what it means to be an excellent human being, most people will come to loathe themselves and think they are of no value.[111] Societies that overvalue intellectual talent thus contain within them a bizarre and existentially troublesome contradiction. They still require farmers, clothiers, watchmakers, and others but refuse them the social basis for self-respect.

Thus, Voltaire's project to elevate the men of letters to an aristocratic station would result in a modern form of the Homeric honor culture. Rousseau was well aware of how the common person fares in such a world. He fought against it throughout his career and consistently warned his fellow Europeans against talent-based public identities. "In a well-constituted State," he writes in "Preface to *Narcissus*," "all citizens are so equal that no one is preferred to others as being neither the most learned nor even the most skillful."[112] In *Emile*, he directs his tutee to "desire mediocrity in everything, without excepting even beauty."[113] And, in unpublished notes, he approvingly cites the lack of stature of great writers in antiquity. Neither Homer nor Virgil, he claims, were considered great men despite their considerable ability. Agreeing with his ancient counterparts, he asserts that if "it is not impossible for an author to be a great man, it is not by writing books either in verse or in prose that he will become such."[114] On the other side of the coin, he also makes sure to hold up the working classes as the salt of the earth. He portrays them as the beacon of humanity and idealized their traits of simplicity, moderation, hard work, and authenticity as universal virtues to which everyone should aspire. In "Letter to d'Alembert on the Theater," he praises "provincial men" as possessing "more original spirits, more inventive industry" and being "less imitative" than their Parisian counterparts. And, of course, rural genius "compares itself to no one."[115] His message to his Parisian colleagues is clear: do not take being an intellectual too seriously.

Rousseau and Adam Ferguson

Rousseau's narrative shows up in a more economic form in Adam Ferguson's *Essay on the History of Civil Society*. In the *Essay*, Ferguson echoes Hume's view that increased productivity fuels a luxury economy, which in turn gives rise to new and more cognitively challenging occupations in such fields as banking and law. He follows Rousseau, however, by contending that these economic developments lead to a psychically bruising preoccupation with talent-based identities. In the new luxury economy, the identity of a person is a function of his occupation: "Each individual is defined by his calling."[116] Naturally, those with more intellectually challenging jobs are able to garner more social esteem. Led by "applause as well as profit,"[117] the so-called best and brightest flocked to careers in law and finance in order to occupy a social status as high as possible. By contrast, the vast majority of workers, who remain in the older professions, the mechanical arts or farming, occupy the lower rungs. There is, moreover, a new class of factory workers that have even less challenging jobs. Because of the division of labor and industrialization, these individuals spend all their days performing mindless repetitive tasks. Accordingly, they are deprived of any intellectual stimulation and likely become dullards. They are mere cogs in machines: "Manufactures, accordingly, prosper most, where the mind is least consulted, and where the workshop may, without any great effort of imagination, be considered an engine, the part of which are men."[118] Adam Smith observes this phenomenon before Ferguson and more bluntly calls such workers "stupid." In *Lectures on Jurisprudence*, he proclaims: "It is remarkable that in every commercial nation the low people are exceedingly *stupid*."[119] He repeats the charge in *The Wealth of Nations*, asserting that the average worker "naturally loses . . . the habit of exertion, and generally becomes as *stupid* and ignorant as it is possible for a human creature to become."[120] Presumably, those on the assembly line become the dregs of society, invariably demoralized and ashamed of themselves. Individuals in more elevated professions—ones that require study and skill—look down on them and view them as men viewed slaves and women in earlier "rude" ages. As in Rousseau's passage on the competition for esteem, the winners become vain and contemptuous of those below them, and the losers become envious and self-loathing. Ferguson's conclusion is likewise Rousseauian: "In every commercial state, notwithstanding any pretension to equal rights, the exaltation of the few must depress the many."[121]

Ferguson buttresses his case by contending that this problem is specific to modern commercial societies. The old aristocracies in "rude" civilizations, strangely enough, were far less enamored of talent and ability and maintained a general egalitarianism. Ferguson grants that during such ages some people might have been better warriors or had some special talents and that natural inequalities were ubiquitous. They were only recognized, however, during a hunt or whatever activity was taking place: "In times of relaxation," which was most of the time, there was "no vestige of power or prerogative."[122] Thus, inequality was confined to certain times and did not become the core of a person's identity. It is the rise of commerce that led people to answer the questions "Who am I?" and "What is my self-worth?" with "What can I do?"

Ferguson, of course, is not a full-fledged Rousseauian. Despite this glum portrait of commercial life, he remains committed to commercial capitalism. Still, the similarities between his analysis of the psychological effects of inequality in commercial life and Rousseau's are striking. Both men view inequality as not merely an economic problem but a psychological and existential one that touches on people's sense of their innate self-worth.

A Hesitant Debate

In any event, given the success of the *First Discourse* and the widespread attention it attracted, it was inevitable that Rousseau found himself in a spirited debate with his then friends. It took a while, however, for the debate to get off the ground, as both parties to the dispute had good reason to avoid it. The *philosophes* were surprised and disappointed by their friend's apparent rejection of the Enlightenment after willingly contributing several entries to their *Encyclopedia*, and they had every reason to think they were innocent of the charge that they denigrated the working classes. Had they not, after all, made a special effort to afford the mechanical arts a prominent place in the *Encyclopedia*? Accordingly, they spent as much time downplaying their disagreement with Rousseau as they did defending their alleged aristocratic ambitions. Rousseau had his own problems. He very much wanted to remain an author yet had potentially undermined his literary credibility through his aggressive takedown of the arts and sciences in the *First Discourse*. Critics immediately seized on this paradox, noting that the great critic of the arts and sciences was himself an intellectual who used a public competition to make his case. Rousseau had tensions that had to be relaxed. He needed to distinguish himself from his Parisian friends, which required carving out some social space for arts and sciences that did not demean the lower classes.

It did not take much effort for Rousseau to solve his problem. All he had to do was to construct a new model of authorship that avoided all the perversities characteristic of urban intellectual life.[123] He did so by identifying a variety of traits that transformed writing books into a virtuous activity. According to Christopher Kelly, this included publishing material that promotes the common good and taking responsibility for what one publishes—writing in a manner that involves both discretion and openness.[124] Robert Darnton makes a similar point, though he argues that Rousseau also attempts to transform the nature of reading so that his audience would not be corrupted by intellectual values.[125] To read his novel *Julie* and glean its truths, Rousseau contends in its "Preface," it is necessary to adopt the standpoint of a provincial, a foreigner, or a child.[126] And, with this problem out of the way, he was free to fully engage his former friends and challenge everything they stood for.

The issue of Rousseau's apparent heresy raised in *philosophe* circles proved more difficult to resolve. D'Alembert, Diderot, and others employed several rationalizations and strategies to deescalate the conflict between them and their supposed fellow traveler. First, they denied Rousseau was repudiating the Enlightenment. As several scholars have noted, d'Alembert argues in his *Preliminary Discourse* that Rousseau's very participation in the *Encyclopedia* confirmed he was a friend of the project and did not mean to include it in his critique of the arts and sciences.[127] More generally, the *philosophes* just assumed that Rousseau was being clever in an attempt to win a contest. Diderot, in fact, boasted that he provided Rousseau with the insight that the arts and sciences were corrupting and insisted it was merely an attempt to distinguish his essay from the essays of competitors.[128] He also encouraged his friend to use the discourse as a springboard to attain the fame all the *philosophes* sought by publishing it. When this happened and the discourse catapulted Rousseau into Europe's collective consciousness, Diderot eagerly congratulated his friend: "*It is succeeding beyond the skies; there is no precedent for a success like it.*"[129] Some scholars, such as Rousseau biographer Raymond Trousson, interpret such congratulations as evidence that the *philosophes* were not threatened by Rousseau's essay and did not "take offense neither at the thesis of the Discourse nor the responses."[130] For his part, Rousseau was mildly irritated at the eagerness of his friends to explain away the *First Discourse* as well as their claims that he did not believe a word he wrote.[131] This annoyance, however, did not immediately lead to breaking off his relationships.

Second, both Diderot and d'Alembert cast themselves as defenders of the artisan classes. In the *Preliminary Discourse*, d'Alembert goes out of his way to criticize the low esteem in which artisans are typically held: "But society, while justly respecting great geniuses for enlightening it, ought not to degrade the hands by which it is served."[132] At the end of the discourse, moreover, he chastises Ephraim Chambers, whose *Cyclopedia* was the model for his and Diderot's own project, for his mediocre entries on the mechanical arts and his failure to take them as seriously as the liberal arts.[133] Diderot, whose father was a successful cutler, likewise calls on society to hold artisans in higher regard in some of his *Encyclopedia* entries. In "Art," he laments that the distinction between liberal and mechanical arts has degraded people who are "estimable and helpful," and "has given a low name to people who are worthy and useful."[134] Such sympathies are also evident is in some of Diderot's literary works and "bourgeois tragedies."[135] Granted, d'Alembert and Diderot's concerns about the dignity of the laboring classes were not unique among the *philosophes* and cannot with certainty be attributed to Rousseau's criticisms of their elitism. The issue was in the air before Rousseau penned his dissident discourse. For example, in his 1747 *Man a Machine* the provocateur Julien Offray de La Mettrie, who can hardly contain his pride in his talents as a scientist and doctor, encourages "those on whom nature has piled her most precious gifts" to "pity those to whom these gifts have been refused."[136] To avoid wounding the less talented, he counsels against false modesty, as it would only inflame their resentment. Still, given the developing tiff between Rousseau and Diderot, and others, it is sensible to interpret the aforementioned passages as attempts to assuage their friend's fears of the Enlightenment.

Third, d'Alembert and Diderot's defense of the mechanical arts includes concessions to Rousseau's contentions that the arts and sciences could be corrupting and that intellectual achievement is motivated by a desire for glory and public esteem. In his *Preliminary Discourse*, d'Alembert grants that "letters certainly contribute to making society more amiable; it would be difficult to prove that because of them men are better and virtue is more common."[137] And in a private letter to Rousseau, he accepts the argument that artists and scientists are driven by vanity: "Public esteem is the principal goal of every writer."[138] He knows intellectuals can be foolish, self-important, and prone to unproductive factious rivalries. Again from his *Preliminary Discourse*: "Men of letters ordinarily have nothing in common, except the lack of esteem in which they hold each other."[139] Poets, for example, think little of engineers, and vice versa. Diderot takes a similar tack in his *Encyclopedia* entry on encyclopedias from the fifth volume, entitled, appropriately enough, "Encyclopedia." He too accepts that enlightenment and virtue are not perfectly compatible. The *Encyclopedia* should thus aim to teach humans to be virtuous as well as provide accessible knowledge, "because," he writes, "it is at least as important to make men better as it is to make them less ignorant."[140] To that end, he encourages people to record all the great deeds of virtuous behavior and inscribe them on a publicly displayed marble column to inspire virtuous behavior. He proposes that as the old monarchs are immortalized through public effigies, statues, or busts, private individuals should be honored in a similar way if they perform extraordinary acts of virtue. If there is any lingering doubt as to whom Diderot is addressing, he makes clear his audience by naming names: "Oh, Rousseau, my dear and worthy friend! I have never been able to refuse the praise you have given me, and I feel that it has increased my devotion to truth as well as my love of virtue."[141]

Furthermore, Diderot acknowledges that the scholars who populated France's various intellectual academies and societies were driven by glory.[142] Tellingly, he describes them in unmistakably Homeric terms. Authors, he claims, "should strive for immortality by writing books."[143] He even admits it is part of what drives him and d'Alembert: "And that posterity, while raising to immortality the names of those who will bring man's knowledge to perfection in the future, will perhaps not disdain to remember our own names."[144] While he assures his readers that the editors and contributors are self-sacrificing humanists who want to better humankind, his frank acknowledgment of his own vain ambitions and his explicit reference to the Homeric honor culture seem designed to mollify Rousseau by conceding his criticisms.[145]

The Philosophes *Strike Back*

Nonetheless, no matter how heartfelt these concessions, there were limits to how far Diderot and d'Alembert would go in ameliorating Rousseau's concerns.[146] D'Alembert in particular refuses to concede Rousseau's argument that knowledge undermines virtue, contending that vice is much more dangerous when combined with ignorance.[147] Moreover, both d'Alembert and Diderot denigrate the mechanical arts in the very same essays in which they defend them. D'Alembert contends that the mechanical arts require little ability, as most have been simplified to a "routine" that most people can easily master.[148] As a consequence, jobs in the mechanical arts usually attract individuals from impoverished backgrounds. For his part, Diderot argues that progress in the mechanical arts is hampered by an irrational, almost superstitious, obsession with guarding trade secrets, which hampers progress. The mechanical arts, he thinks, also need the assistance of the natural sciences if they are to progress and develop. So, even as they go out of their way to defend the mechanical arts, d'Alembert and Diderot cannot help but belittle them. In other writings, they can be downright contemptuous of provincials and the working classes. In defending Voltaire's attempt to establish a theater in Geneva, d'Alembert condescendingly asks: "Why begrudge men, destined almost exclusively by nature for crying and dying, some recreational diversions that help them bear the bitterness or the insipidity of their existence?"[149] Diderot likewise was not above making mean-spirited comments. In one of his nastier remarks, he wrote in a letter to his lover Sophie Volland that "mediocre men live and die like brutes."[150] "The sense of the inequality of men," one commentator observes, ". . . was deeply rooted in him."[151] Even some of his sympathizers concede that when Diderot tries to be complimentary toward the peasants in his plays, his portrayals are less than compelling and betray "a wide gulf between observer and observed."[152]

Beyond their deep-seated contempt for ordinary Europeans, the *philosophes* refused to back down from their insistence that they were the true aristocracy. Like the leading men of the Renaissance, they constructed a narrative in which they were the most important social class in modern Europe.[153] As Darnton has established, they defined knowledge such that the whole of human history was a product only of great kings and great geniuses.[154] Naturally, they had no doubt that they belonged in the latter category and believed that they alone were responsible for the progress of the species.[155] Mere months before Rousseau wrote the *Second Discourse*, d'Alembert penned an essay, entitled "Essai sur la société des gens de lettres et des grands," that specifically tried to make this case. Early in the essay, he beseeches the courtly aristocracy to recognize the superiority of the men of letters and encourages his fellow intellectuals to assume their rightful place at the top of the social and cultural ladder (though he sternly advises them to avoid politics).[156] At times, d'Alembert aggressively challenges the status of the courtly aristocracy. He was particularly incensed at the paternalistic relationship between the men of letters and the nobles, and followed his good friend Voltaire by reminding the aristocrats they were not superior to the men of letters but, indeed, were indebted to them. He writes: "The wise man does not forget that if there is an external respect which talents owe to titles, there is another and more real one which titles owe to talents."[157] Moreover, in the preface to volume three of the *Encyclopedia*, d'Alembert mockingly informs princes and nobles that they will find themselves included in the *Encyclopedia* only if they earn inclusion, "because the *Encyclopedia* owes everything to talents, nothing to titles, and that is the history of the human spirit and not the vanity of men."[158] The other *philosophes* fully embraced this project. Voltaire echoes d'Alembert's call in a 1755 entry for the *Encyclopedia*, "Men of Letters," in which he repeats the narrative from the *Preliminary Discourse* that the *philosophes* were anointed successors to the Renaissance and were charged with instructing and refining the species. Diderot, Rousseau's best friend among them, also repeatedly calls for the elevation of the intellectuals in French society.[159] Furthermore, in a famous passage of *Le fils naturel*, he links this glorification of the talented to civic virtue, arguing that the talented have a unique obligation to serve society. In the play, Constance tells Dorval: "You have received the rarest talents, and you must render them to society. Let the useless move about without object, embarrass society without serving it, and distance themselves from it. They can. But you, I dare say, cannot without it being a crime."[160] Notably, Dorval is instructed to serve society, not the government. His responsibility to humanity is much more important than formulating public policy and executing laws.

As with their view of the mechanical arts, however, the men of letters were of two minds in their aristocratic aspirations. If they wished to become a predominant class, they at times were respectful of the courtly aristocracy and sought some sort of fusion with it.[161] Toward the end of his "Essai sur la société des gens de lettres et des grands," d'Alembert accepts that the nobles should still govern political life, and occasionally he less aggressively asserts the social value of the men of letters vis-à-vis the nobles. In one concessionary line, he proclaims that "a man of letters, full of probity and talent, is without comparison more worthy than an incapable minister or a dishonored aristocrat."[162] Presumably, the men of letters cannot claim such superiority over the better specimens of noble stock. One reason for d'Alembert's softer stance is that many of the men of letters believed that the upper classes, crowned heads of Europe included, would be much more receptive to the message of the

Enlightenment than the masses.[163] D'Alembert was increasingly frustrated "with the apathy and indifference of the masses who are interested in neither toleration, freedom, nor enlightenment."[164] In this attitude, he follows Voltaire, who believed that 90 percent of humanity did not merit enlightenment.[165] In addition, some *philosophes*, most notably Voltaire, plainly enjoyed the status and luxury that attended life in polite society (though he too could be sharply critical of Paris, as evidenced by chapter 22 of *Candide*). Nevertheless, in the basic narrative of the *philosophes*, the nobles were the bad guys and were supposed to be supplanted. The truce suggested here is offered only as a matter of practicality and *amour de soi-même*.

The most systematic and detailed *philosophe* response to Rousseau is probably Diderot's *Rameau's Nephew*, which was written a few years after the contretemps had run its course. In the dialogue, geniuses are defended as socially beneficial and often virtuous, while the ordinary masses are portrayed as overwhelmed by *amour-propre* and completely vice ridden. The only silver lining for the masses is that they are driven to their behavior by the nobles, who preside over a cruel economy that forces people to behave poorly to meet their needs. Diderot's dialogue, in fact, can be read as a point-by-point rejection of the narrative of intellectual life Rousseau laid out in two discourses and his concerns about the overvaluation of talent. Diderot addresses a number of themes and concepts prominent in Rousseau's early writings, such as the relationship between virtue and talent, *amour-propre* and *amour de soi-même*, economic inequality, the plight of the poor, and the moral depravity in Paris. Given that the dialogue is rarely interpreted as a reply to Rousseau, it is worth analyzing in detail.[166]

The first substantive discussion of the dialogue is about the social value of genius and talent.[167] Although Diderot never mentions his name, several arguments by Rousseau are subjected to careful scrutiny and do not hold up particularly well. They come out of the mouth of the knavish nephew, who ironically represents everything Rousseau hates about Paris, and are decisively refuted. The nephew-*lui* begins the dialogue by trying to make the Rousseauian case that genius is both useless and dangerous—useless because no true social good results from it and dangerous because geniuses are responsible for much of the evil in the world. He admits, however, that he has little knowledge of history and cannot verify his sweeping assertions. He is simply engaging in idle speculation. *Moi*, a philosopher who seems to be a stand-in for Diderot the *philosophe*, has little trouble swatting away his claims and makes several convincing counterarguments.

Geniuses are of tremendous social value, Diderot-*moi* claims, and help the masses understand their prejudices and errors. In direct contradiction to Rousseau's claims in the *First Discourse*, he contends they also promote patriotism. He avers that people only honor nations that produce genius. Interestingly, one of his formulations is Homeric. Referencing the dramatist Jean Racine, he states: "A thousand years from now he will draw tears, will be admired by men all over the earth, will inspire compassion, human kindness, love. People will wonder who he was, from what country, and France will be envied."[168] Like Achilles, Racine will earn cultural immortality through his literary genius. Naturally, Diderot-*moi* defends this fact in democratic terms. After conceding that Racine was by reputation a man of low moral character, he constructs a cost-benefit analysis in which he proves that nonetheless he is responsible for far more good than harm. Frenchmen, and indeed all Europeans, for a millennium will take enjoyment and become better people as a result of his plays. Only a few individuals, by contrast, had to endure him as a person. The same is true of Voltaire and even nephew-*lui*'s uncle. If a few people are hurt by Voltaire's thin-skinned replies to criticism or Uncle Rameau's selfishness, the nation as a whole is likely to benefit for centuries to come. Furthermore, in some instances, the very vices people despise in geniuses are partly responsible for their wonderful achievements. Diderot-*moi* speculates that the talents of the painter Jean-Baptiste Geuze and those of Voltaire cannot be decoupled from their vanity and hypersensitivity to criticism, respectively.

In addition, he quickly disposes of the claim that geniuses are evil and cause much of the misery in the world. While they suffer from vices, they are no more vice ridden than the population at large. Fools are no less likely to be knaves than are geniuses. The only difference is that the vices of the masses do not produce great cultural treasures. Finally, Diderot-*moi* convinces the nephew that critics of genius hypocritically pretend to be geniuses themselves and thus do not make sincere criticisms. It is easy enough to imagine that Diderot had Rousseau in mind when devising this argument.

After adequately defending geniuses against the charges they are useless and dangerous, Diderot proceeds to blame the masses and the wealthy for *amour-propre* and the moral degeneracy in Paris. He develops his case through the nephew, who hypocritically reveals that he would like nothing more than to be a genius almost immediately after suggesting they are evil. The nephew, however, has no hope of attaining the status of genius in the conventional way. His musical talent is middling, and he cannot follow in his uncle's footsteps. Undeterred, he invents a new form of genius that he insists is just as real and admirable as his uncle's. He boasts to Diderot-*moi* that he is a "master scoundrel" who excels in vice. That is, he makes a good living pretending to be a fool so he can live off wealthy and noble patrons. Strangely, wealthy Parisian families like having fools around. They are a source of endless amusement and presumably liven up tedious dinner parties. According to the nephew-*lui*, there is a science to being a parasite. He has to master the art of "pantomime," which requires that he know how to lie, forswear, flatter, gossip, diffuse controversy, perfectly time his comments, and so forth. There is even a physical side to this playacting. The nephew-*lui* claims to have developed a variety of facial expressions and forms of physical posture to help make himself agreeable to his hosts. In general, his genius requires him to have a keen understanding of human nature. He must have an acute sense of what people need to hear, and how and when they need to hear it. Thus, while he appears to be an ignorant, lazy, impudent ne'er-do-well, he in fact is an expert at manipulation.

In making this argument, Diderot relies heavily on Rousseau's psychological concepts and critique of Paris. The nephew-*lui*'s moral psychology is described as a combination of *amour-propre* and *amour de soi-même*. The desire of the nephew to be a genius appears to result from *amour-propre*. He admits he is "full of envy" and resentment when he witnesses genius like his uncle and desperately wants to be praised as a unique member of the species. He also concedes that he likes hearing salacious gossip about geniuses because it lessens his envy and, he says, "brings me closer to them; makes me bear my mediocrity more easily."[169] In general, he wants to expose all great things as mere vanity and pull all decent people to pieces.[170] He likewise takes great pride in playing a fool rather than being one and taking advantage of the rich. He insists to Diderot-*moi* that his patrons are the real fools and knaves, and delights in recounting an anecdote about one of his fellow genius-scoundrels, the Renegade from Avignon, who gets his hands on his Jewish patron's money by turning him over to the Inquisition. The nephew even admits, to foreshadow one of Rousseau's arguments I explain in Chapter 3, that his *amour-propre* results in a new desire—the *libido dominandi*, or the desire to control and dominate people. When he contemplates the possibility of attaining wealth and power, he proudly announces, "I love bossing people and I will boss them."[171]

Yet, the nephew eventually confesses that he chooses vice over virtue and being a fool over being a musician for reasons best explained by *amour de soi-même*. A life of vice, he claims, is more lucrative than one of virtue. As the dialogue progresses, he seems to care less about being a genius and more about money. At one point, he asserts to Diderot-*moi*: "Gold, gold is everything, and everything without gold, is nothing."[172] Rather than defend his chosen occupation on the grounds that it is a form of genius, he suggests it is the surest way to support himself. The nephew explains that the Parisian economy is "hell" for many people. It is unforgiving to everyone but the rich and talented, and a large portion of the city's inhabitants live lives of desperation and poverty. Mediocre musicians like himself cannot hope to make an honest living. Thus, he opts for vice and hypocrisy as the most reliable means with which to avoid poverty and find some enjoyment in life. Best to playact the fool than make an honest living as a music tutor.

Diderot departs from Rousseau's view of *amour-propre* in another important respect as well. He has the nephew reject the idea that *amour-propre* is born of society. Rather, it is a fact of nature that needs no societal catalyst. Referring to his young son as a "little savage," which seems to be a reference to Rousseau's primitive humans in the *Second Discourse*, the nephew asserts that his son "he would of his own accord want to be richly dressed, magnificently fed, liked by men and loved by women, and concentrate on himself all the goods of life."[173] Nature makes us prefer ourselves to and wished to be esteemed by everyone, not civilization.

In any case, much of Diderot's portrait of the nephew is consistent with the account of moral psychology and the characterization of Paris by Rousseau. His narrative is constructed, however, so he can defend the opposite politics. Specifically, he seeks to exonerate geniuses, which presumably includes the *philosophes*, from Rousseau's indictment that they are responsible for the corruptions of the age. Contrary to Rousseau, the intellectuals in *Rameau's Nephew* are not considered to be the best of the species and leaders of French culture. Instead, they are "queer people" who are badly out of step with the predominant values of the day. Although they are not perfect and include numerous bad actors among their ranks, Diderot still believes they tend to be as virtuous as the population at large and have more social value. The villains in his dialogue are the nobles and the wealthy, who hoard all of society's resources and reward knaves and vice rather than virtue and talent.

Finally, it is arguable that Diderot-*moi*'s proposed solution to the nephew's unfortunate predicament is a veiled criticism of Rousseau. At the conclusion of the dialogue, the nephew is encouraged by Diderot-*moi* to take Diogenes as a role model.[174] Rather than slavishly conform to Paris convention and value vice and gold, he could stop being driven by both *amour-propre* and *amour de soi-même* and follow Diogenes by dedicating himself to principles such as moderation and virtue. Notably, Rousseau was viewed by many of his contemporaries as a modern-day Diogenes.[175] Perhaps this reference is a reminder to Rousseau that he has failed to live up to his own philosophy. He still cares too much what people think of him and conforms to the values of the city he claims to ignore and despise.

The Abbé Petit in d'Holbach's Salon

Rousseau had ample reason to distrust the defenses d'Alembert and Diderot give of the mechanical arts and the artisan classes. Their support for the average person is at best uneven and at worse insincere. Even if Rousseau had not read the letters and writings of his former friends (and he could not have read *Rameau's Nephew*), he personally witnessed their contemptuous attitudes toward the masses and working classes. There is one particular experience, in fact, that perfectly sums up Rousseau's criticisms of Paris and his defense of provincial life—one recorded by Baron d'Holbach himself. On Shrove Tuesday in 1754, Rousseau attended a reading on tragedy by the Abbé Petit, a provincial from Normandy, set up by Diderot at d'Holbach's salon. The reading was a disaster from beginning to end, as the abbé began spouting out numerous absurdities on the nature of tragedy and quickly revealed he was utterly lacking in literary talent. Rather than politely allowing the abbé to finish and sending him on his way without any unnecessary encouragement, the attending members of the d'Holbach coterie were determined to humiliate him. They put "up a mock show of admiration for the wretched author's tragedy."[176] Rousseau was horrified by his friends' puerile behavior, and he not so gently informed the author of the humiliating truth of the situation. Rather than thank Rousseau for his candor, however, the clueless abbé turned his anger on him, and the two had to be separated.

Rousseau's Anglo biographers, while intrigued by the story, usually fail to appreciate its significance. Typically, it is read in light of Rousseau's fraying relationship with the *philosophes*.[177] The content of the dispute is far more revealing, however, and ties in with Rousseau's arguments at the end of the *First Discourse*. The poor abbé becomes the object of ridicule for the sole reason that he lacks literary talent. The *philosophes* in the room affirm themselves based on their superior talent. And, worst of all, the value of the abbé's personality would invariably decline in his own eyes if he understood and accepted the truth of the situation. If he would accept the truth, he would be led to erroneously conclude that his contributions to the world as a religious leader are meaningless and that his life has value only if he is a writer. For Rousseau, this must have been a cruel case in which life imitated art, and it probably reminded him of his worry that in a culture enamored of the arts and sciences a great clothier would be shamed into quitting his trade to become "a bad versifier or an inferior Geometer"[178]—or, in this case, an awful literary theorist.

Even if d'Alembert, Diderot, and the other *philosophes* were genuinely ambivalent about the mechanical arts, their occasional praise did nothing to soften the implications of judging people by their intellectual abilities. Rousseau's position is that the *philosophes* could not simultaneously celebrate talent as the true measure of human worth and respect those without it, such as artisans and peasants. Moreover, their confidence that they had unique talents produced in *the philosophes* a subtle arrogance and contempt for the general mass of humanity. How much compassion can one expect, after all, from those who believe that the fate of the species rests on their shoulders? Rousseau asked the *philosophes* to repudiate themselves, and that they would not do. They would become who they were. Any concessions made to Rousseau masked their true intent: to double down on their original claims.

In the years right after the publication of the *First Discourse*, then, Rousseau found himself in a debate not so much about the value of the arts and sciences as about the social value of the artists and scientists themselves. The *philosophes*, he realized, were promoting themselves as a social class as much as they were promoting the knowledge they sought to catalogue and began to adopt the attitudes of classical aristocrats. Included in this aristocratic glorification of the talented was a healthy, if not always publicly expressed, contempt for average people, who according to the new value system were encouraged to view themselves through the eyes of those who looked down on them. The psychological and existential consequences of this project, Rousseau well understood, were devastating to all but a small sliver of the population. As his dispute with the *philosophes* developed, the concept of *amour-propre* would increasingly become one of the most effective arrows in his quiver.

Conclusion

Rousseau's critique of eighteenth-century Europe has much in common with Michael Young's disturbing 1950s science fiction dystopia, *The Rise of the Meritocracy*. Although Young does not mention Rousseau and most likely did not have him in mind, he captures the spirit of Rousseau's linkage between *amour-propre* and the overvaluation of talent. Like Rousseau's two discourses, Young's demi-fictional meritocratic society is really a new aristocracy that holds firm to the belief that the progress of civilization depends solely on the influence of a small cadre of intellectual elites. The historical trajectory of Young's account also follows Rousseau's narrative, as the aristocracy of birth gets replaced by an aristocracy of talent, which is renamed a "meritocracy." Presumably, this neologism makes clear the distinction between a legitimate and an illegitimate aristocracy. Granted, Young's meritocracy is more formal than that of Rousseau's French Enlightenment and is less reliant on hypocrisy and appearances. Whereas the *philosophes* were largely self-proclaimed geniuses who became a class through a process of self-selection or were handpicked by the aristocratic women who ran the salons, Young's meritocracy resembles a Weberian rationalized aristocracy in which the best are carefully chosen through a scientific process designed to identify the best and the brightest.

Nonetheless, the similarities continue. Young's meritocracy is every bit as undemocratic and hierarchical as Rousseau's Paris. The central democratic value, equality, is redefined and narrowed to serve the interests of the talented. It only means that everyone is to have an equal opportunity to become part of the new aristocracy, which for Young is pointless. Since the social scientists in the text are capable of predicting what a person will do for a living and what role he or she will play in society before he or she is born, meritocracy functions in the same way as the old hereditary aristocracy of high birth. In both, people's fates are determined by genetic factors over which they have no control. Young thus agrees with Rousseau's concern from "Preface to *Narcissus*" that "men are rewarded only for qualities which do not depend on them: for we are born with our talents."[179] There is nothing particularly democratic, both men demonstrate, about the equality of opportunity. Even rigidly stratified blood-aristocratic societies have been accepting equality of opportunity in important spheres of life, such as the military. As Augustine demonstrates in *City of God* through his example of Lucius Quinctius Cincinnatus, poor Roman peasants were able to rise to the highest offices in the land through superior military abilities.[180] For Rousseau, the true measure of democracy is whether it can provide a dignified life to the ordinary mass of humans.

In addition, and perhaps at his most Rousseauian, Young claims that the equality of opportunity does nothing to provide dignity to ordinary people. His faux author and sociologist is more than aware of the psychic damage created by meritocracy, acknowledging that "every selection of the one is a rejection of the many."[181] For those forced to confront their natural inferiorities, life is both humiliating and hopeless. This institutional demoralization of the population, Young's fictional sociologist realizes, is a constant threat to political stability.

Finally, in a pièce de résistance that would certainly gratify Rousseau, democracy is openly scorned in Young's text and dismissed as nothing more than a foolishly held aspiration—a position, it bears repeating, popular among several leading *philosophes*.

Young does give his pseudo history a happier ending. Unlike Rousseau's *Second Discourse*, which ends with one aristocrat consolidating power and tyrannizing the population, *The Rise of the Meritocracy* concludes with successful revolution by the masses. Young adds a Marxist twist to his plotline and has ordinary people refusing to suffer the indignities of natural inequality. Despite the confident assurances by the fictional author that the masses are too stupid to foment a successful revolution, they get the last word and murder him during a May Day uprising before his fictional book even makes it into print.

Whatever differences separate the two eclectic writers, both Rousseau and Young primarily understand the problem of natural aristocracy or meritocracy as psychological and conclude that modern democracy is another form of aristocracy—a fact that many people fail to notice because they conceptualize aristocracy as the civilized foppery of the feudal nobility described by Elias and do not appreciate the classical meaning of the term. Furthermore, both believe that for liberalism to deliver on its promises, it must take equality seriously and ensure that it finds substantive expression in political, economic, and cultural institutions and practices. Equality, in short, must do more than provide opportunities for the best and brightest to rise to the top. It must make reasonable efforts to ensure a dignified life for everyone.

Chapter 2

Amor Sui and *Amour-Propre* in Augustine and Neo-Augustinianism

Surrogate Virtue or Gateway to *Libido Dominandi*?

It is probably fair to say that Augustine is the father of *amour-propre*, or in his native Latin, *amor sui*. Although a psychology closely resembling *amour-propre* is present in the Homeric honor culture, Augustine is the first theorist to identity and name it as a distinct concept. All modern theorists who write of this passion are indebted to him. This is especially true of Rousseau, whose aristocratic analysis of the passion closely tracks Augustine's in *City of God* and veers into territory completely foreign to ancient Greek literature. As I argue in Chapter 3, he is as sensitive to its social effects as Augustine and describes its destructive tendencies in remarkably similar terms. In particular, he shares Augustine's belief that the love of glory and honor often leads to domination and cruelty. Rousseau, who once bragged that God broke the mold when he created him, is thus not all that original when it comes to *amour-propre*.

Can Rousseau Be Interpreted as an Augustinian?

The case for an Augustinian interpretation of Rousseau's *amour-propre*, however, is neither obvious nor straightforward. As a result, Rousseau scholars have been somewhat hesitant to trace Rousseau's *amour-propre* back to Augustine's *amor sui*, as evidenced by the fact that few have made such a connection.[1] One obvious reason is that at times Rousseau is highly critical of Augustine, especially his theology. In his "Letter to Beaumont," he forcefully rejects Augustine's story of original sin as incompatible with the natural goodness of humans and argues it makes God responsible for human misery. Augustine's God and religion, he thinks, is both despotic and gloomy. Ironically, he accuses Augustine's God of taking delight in punishing his own creation and hence being driven by a lust for domination, or *libido dominandi*.[2] Despite his call to protect traditional religion from his Parisian associates, Rousseau subscribed to the religion of the Enlightenment, deism.

Of course, there is no reason to interpret Rousseau's rejection of Augustine's theology as a repudiation of the entirety of Augustine's thought. There is plenty of evidence in his writings that Rousseau admired Augustine. He opens *Emile* with a line evocative of Augustine's deficiency theory of evil: "Everything is good as it leaves the hands of the Author of things; everything degenerates in the hands of man."[3] Moreover, he occasionally cites Augustine in favor of his own positions. When confronted with the criticism that he hypocritically employs philosophy to undermine philosophy (and the arts and sciences in general), he cites the example of the early church fathers and Augustine by name in his defense.[4] He also sometimes refers to Augustine as an authority in his dispute with religious leaders, though perhaps this was mostly for rhetorical effect, as Augustine was popular among both Catholics and Protestants.[5] Finally, he wrote a spiritual autobiography in the mold of Augustine's *Confessions* that plagiarizes the title and is similar both structurally and substantively.[6] While he rejects Augustine's religious foundations and attempts to discover his true self through God, both *Confessions* detail a personal conversion and examine inner life.[7] Rousseau starts from the same psychological premises as Augustine and is also interested in interiority, self-consciousness, and questions of identity. In general, he is profoundly ambivalent about the busy bishop of Hippo.

A second and more concerning problem with interpreting his *amour-propre* in light of Augustine's *amor sui* is that there is no evidence Rousseau admired this aspect of his theology. He never mentions Augustine in his many discussions of the passion, and never by name in either the *Second Discourse* or *Emile*. This in itself does not invalidate an Augustinian reading of his conception of *amour-propre*. Rousseau does not cite any philosopher as his source, despite the fact that it has long been established that he neither invented the term nor was unique in making use of it. *Amour-propre* was immensely popular in seventeenth- and eighteenth-century French intellectual life and was employed by a wide variety of philosophers starting from disparate theoretical and religious foundations. It is thus reasonable to conclude that he did not mention possible philosophic sources because of its widespread usage. The term was in the cultural air.

Rousseau's silence about his influences does, however, make it necessary to construct an indirect case linking the two self-love theorists. Thankfully, this is a relatively simple task. There was something of an Augustinian renaissance in seventeenth-century France, which included a revival of Augustine's doctrine of the two loves and *amor sui*. Numerous theorists from a variety of Christian sects who self-identified as Augustinians—Pierre Nicole, Blaise Pascal, Nicolas Malebranche, Jean-François Sénault, Jacques Abbadie, Jacques Esprit, and others—wrote extensively on both concepts, especially *amor sui*.[8] It is reasonable to assume they were making a literal translation of *amor sui* into French. Like Augustine, they believed that, after the Fall, love of God proved impossible, leaving humans dominated by self-love, or *amour-propre*. In addition, the distinction between *amour de soi-même* (originally *amour de nous-mesmes*) and *amour-propre* was first articulated in modernity by another seventeenth-century Augustinian, Jean-Pierre Camus, in his *Défense du pur amour* (1640).[9] There is some textual evidence to support the claim that Rousseau received his Augustinianism indirectly through these seventeenth-century sources. He admits to reading the *Port-Royal* more frequently than any other work in his program of self-education during his time with Mademoiselle Warens, and in *The Confessions* calls himself "a half Jansenist."[10] It is relatively easy to surmise, moreover, which half of Jansenism he does not like. He believed Jansenist theology, like Augustine's, to be intolerant, harsh, sanctimonious, and unpleasant.[11]

Furthermore, François Fénelon, one of his favorite authors, is another possible source of his Augustinianism. He wrote an essay, "On Pure Love," dedicated to Saint Augustine's doctrine of the two loves and the necessity of loving God and repudiating self-love.[12] As Patrick Riley has argued, Rousseau "greatly admired" Fénelon, especially his fable *Telemachus*, and secularizes his "disinterested" love of God to construct his general will. Rather than love God, Rousseau's citizens are supposed to cultivate a "disinterested" love of the state.[13] Notably, the novel, which also defends other republican themes, such as simplicity and the virtues of rural life central to Rousseau's own thought, is the only book mature Emile is encouraged to read.[14] It is probably not a stretch to assume Rousseau was familiar with both Fénelon's Augustinian orientation and "On Pure Love."

In addition, by the end of the seventeenth century and the beginning of the eighteenth, the language of *amour-propre* traveled outside neo-Augustinian circles to secular intellectuals. *Moralistes,* such as La Rochefoucauld and La Bruyère, depicted human nature as if they were dedicated disciples of Augustine, while more systematic political theorists such as Bayle and Mandeville adopted the formula prominent among neo-Augustinians that shame and honor, both born of *amour-propre,* could promote civil obedience and social harmony. Bayle, a self-professed admirer of Nicole,[15] argues that even in a society of atheists the desire for honor and praise compels people to behave in a sociable manner.[16] That is, they calculate that proper behavior will help satisfy their *amour-propre.* Mandeville, following Bayle's lead, made the same argument, ironically enough, to refute Christian criticisms of commercial society. Self-liking, his term for *amour-propre,* is the centerpiece of his political psychology. Even though he does not contrast self-liking with love of God, his conception of it is undeniably similar to the notion of *amour-propre* found among many seventeenth-century neo-Augustinians. Part of his definition of self-liking appears to be practically plagiarized from an English translation of Jacques Abbadie's *L'art de se connoître soi-même.* In the text, Abbadie writes: "Upon this Principle, the utility of Glory should consist in this, that the esteem which other People have of us *confirms the good opinion which we have of our selves.*"[17] The last clause in Mandeville's definition is virtually identical: "It is this that makes us so fond of the Approbation, Liking, and Assent of others; because they strengthen and *confirm in us the good opinion we have of ourselves.*"[18] Given that Rousseau had read Mandeville and makes several mentions of him in the *Second Discourse,* it is plausible to assume he too might be a source of Rousseau's Augustinianism. As I argue in Chapter 3, Mandeville might very well be Rousseau's true target in the *Second Discourse.* It is his theory of *amour-propre,* or self-liking, that he most seeks to discredit.

Finally, from Mandeville and Bayle, neo-Augustinian conceptions of *amour-propre* migrated to the French Enlightenment. Montesquieu, another favorite of Rousseau, was impressed with the psychology, addressing it numerous times in his private journals. In several entries, he ponders its relationship to virtue and talent, and even praises Nicole for observing that "God gave self-love to man, just as he gave flavor to dishes."[19] Moreover, he defines honor similarly to *amour-propre* in *The Spirit of the Laws*[20] and argues, reminiscent of Bayle and Mandeville, that it can be rechanneled to serve the public good.[21]

It is hardly surprising, therefore, that in the period between Rousseau's first and second discourses, *amour-propre* caught the attention of Rousseau and his friends. (He first utters the term in 1753 in his "Preface to *Narcissus*," while d'Alembert references it several times in "Essai sur la société des gens de lettres et des grands" in early 1754.)[22] The term dominated claims about human nature in French thought for the better part of a century. When Voltaire, in his 1764 *Pocket Philosophical Dictionary*, proclaims self-love is so obviously "the basis for all our feelings and all our actions" and that there is no more need to prove the claim than "to prove to anyone that they have a face,"[23] he is doing nothing more than echoing a truth self-evident in French cultural life.

Moreover, Rousseau and his fellow *philosophes* appear to have the same assessment of the Jansenists and neo-Augustinians: they are half right. Like Rousseau, *the philosophes* were suspicious of Jansenist theology and believed Augustine and his ilk represent the superstition from which society had to be liberated to pave the way for science and the Enlightenment. The writings and private correspondences of many of the *philosophes* contain numerous denunciations of neo-Augustinian views, many of which resemble Voltaire's well-publicized swipe at Pascal at the end of the *Philosophical Letters* in which he calls him a "sublime misanthrope"[24] and Diderot's verdict that Jansenism amounts to little more than "a sad and sullen" religion responsible for "fanaticism and intolerance."[25] Nevertheless, *the philosophes* were more than comfortable with the language of *amour-propre* and, like Mandeville, conceived of it in a similar manner even though they did not contrast it with *amour de Dieu*.[26]

It is thus not difficult to draw a genealogical line from Augustine to seventeenth-century Jansenism and neo-Augustinianism to Bayle and Mandeville to the French Enlightenment. Accordingly, it is reasonable to argue that Rousseau appropriates Augustinian moral language, despite the fact he does not mention Augustine once in reference to *amour-propre*. He wrote in an Augustinian age in which the term was used by a wide variety of social and political thinkers.

Democratic Versus Aristocratic *Amour-Propre*

The important question, then, is not whether his usage of *amour-propre* is Augustinian but what exactly Rousseau learned about the passion from the neo-Augustinians and by extension Augustine. This is not a simple question, as Augustine himself uses the term in a variety of ways that are often inconsistent with one another. He wrote nearly 120 works and comes to radically different conclusions about the danger and utility of *amour-propre*. One scholar, in fact, begins his consideration of Augustine's self-love with this exact complaint: "Mutually incompatible assertions about self-love jostle one another and demand to be reconciled. And Augustine himself refuses to undertake this task for us."[27] There are, however, two of Augustine's analyses that dominate the debates about it in modern France. Interestingly, they neatly correspond to both Sophocles' aristocrat-democrat distinction and Rousseau's *amour-propre* and *amour de soi-même*.

The first approach, found in his parable of the Fall of humans, can be characterized as aristocratic. In this account, *amor sui* is intertwined with aristocratic passions such as pride and glory and is discussed in the context of human excellence. It is, arguably, meant as a critique of pagan, aristocratic Rome. As Peter Brown avers, "*The City of God* is a book about glory,"[28] and Augustine aimed to replace classical notions of glory with one based on Christianity. Augustine constructed his *civitas terrena*, or the sinful city of humans, out of Roman attitudes toward the past[29] and in part designed the parable of the Fall so that he could blame aristocratic culture for the fall of Rome. This approach pessimistically views *amor sui* as the source of all human corruption and conceptualizes it as a gateway passion that leads to far more destructive ones, most notably the lust to dominate and control others, or *libido dominandi*.[30]

The second approach is more democratic and stresses the utility of *amor sui*. Augustine's approach here is likewise inconsistent, as he makes three separate arguments. First, he sometimes portrays *amor sui* as benign and suggests it is born of the desire for self-preservation and individual well-being.[31] This version of *amor sui* is similar to, if not the same as, Rousseau's *amour de soi-même*. Second, and more optimistically, he also describes *amor sui* as a source of positive good in the city of humans. In an oft-cited passage from *Ten Homilies on the First Epistle of John to the Parthians*, Augustine encourages fallen humans to mitigate the effects of sin through sin itself—to redirect it toward some socially useful end such as charity. In these instances, *amor sui* does not degenerate into something worse. Rather, it becomes a viable moral psychology with which to manage the consequences of the Fall and promote some semblance of order and justice in the city of humans. Augustine is careful to argue that humans without genuine virtue will not gain salvation and hence will not profit from it: "Divine Scripture calls us off from the display of the face outwardly to that which is within."[32] Still, in this interpretation, *amor sui* is useful in the city of humans and is in line with how Odysseus would most likely view the passion. It is a fact of the world that can be manipulated to help people secure their own self-interest and even the common good. Finally, in *City of God*, Augustine casts doubt on this formula of redirecting vice to serve the common good through his deconstruction of Roman patriotism. In this discussion, he claims that love of glory typically leads to the same place as Adam and Eve's *amor sui*—to *libido dominandi*.

Thus, modern theorists looking to Augustine for guidance have some choices to make. They could follow the more negative narrative threads from *Confessions* and *City of God* and view *amour-propre* as a corruption of the personality born of classical aristocratic attitudes. Or, they could choose the more optimistic and democratic approach from *Ten Homilies* and leave open the possibility that vice can be used to manage vice and promote peace and stability in the city of humans. Most of the major neo-Augustinians—Pascal, Abbadie, Malebranche, Sénault, and Nicole—follow Augustine in holding disparate views of the passion, though they tend to be more impressed with the positive interpretations of it. While they embrace some of the most depressing aspects of Augustine's theology from *City of God* and the *Confessions* and worry that human excellence can be corrupting, they also schizophrenically argue that *amour-propre* is socially and economically beneficial. More so than Augustine, they heartily support the more optimistic, democratic approach in which *amour-propre* promotes charity, social harmony, intellectual achievement, and numerous other goods in the city of humans. Most of the eighteenth-century thinkers were not so conflicted. They eagerly adopted the democratic approach to *amour-propre* in which vices become public virtues and ignored the theological critique of the aristocratic ethos.

It is not always easy to tell where Rousseau fits into these Augustinian confusions. The most obvious conclusion is that he, like Augustine and the neo-Augustinians, is not of one mind about *amour-propre*. As the "positive" *amour-propre* theorists have pointed out, he believes it can be both good and bad. It is also true, however, that Rousseau tends to the more pessimistic and aristocratic expressions of *amour-propre*—much more so than his neo-Augustinian predecessors and Bayle and Mandeville. Like the Augustine of *City of God*, he is especially intrigued by the idea of *amour-propre* as a gateway passion that degenerates into the lust for control and domination. The reason for this is his politics. As I demonstrated in Chapter 1, Rousseau believes modern society retains important elements of classical aristocracy. It thus makes perfect sense for him to fall back on Augustine's more negative approach to *amor sui*—the one designed to deconstruct Rome's pagan aristocracy. While Rousseau makes some concessions to the democratic interpretation of *amour-propre*, his distrust of the *philosophes* and the rising commercial elite draws him nearer to Augustine's darker treatments of the passion. His defense of the positive uses of *amour-propre*, moreover, is limited to exclude Nicole's and Mandeville's economic applications. He is adamant that *amour-propre* should never be used to promote commerce and wealth, even if they are used to help the least fortunate members of society. He only accepts that it can be beneficially employed to promote familial and conjugal love, civic virtue, compassion, and so forth. That is, it can be used to help create a goodness or a virtuous disposition. He never consents to the idea that vice can serve as a surrogate for virtue, as did so many in eighteenth-century Europe.

Aristocratic *Amor Sui*: An Interpretation of Augustine's Parable of the Fall

Augustine's parable of the Fall is not only about aristocratic Rome. Augustine addresses several issues and seems to target at least a few intellectual trends and thinkers that bothered him. It is clear, for example, that he had Stoicism in mind when devising the parable. As Christopher Brooke persuasively argues, he intends to refute several Stoic doctrines, including *apatheia* and *autarkeia*, that is, the ideas that humans can control their emotions and attain happiness through developing a virtuous disposition.[33] Tellingly, Augustine dedicates a full chapter to the Stoic concept of *apatheia* immediately before he addresses Adam and Eve's original sin. A second obvious target is Pelagius and his optimistic belief in the human potential for virtue. Augustine thought this position naïve and by the end of his life little more than a fallacious classical hangover. By the time he pens *City of God*, there is too much Paul in him to take Pelagius seriously. There is also, however, a persuasive case to be made that pagan, aristocratic Rome was on his mind.

To begin, the Fall represents a direct challenge to the central values of classical aristocracy, especially pride in excellences and love of glory. The fundamental distinction in the parable, between *amor Dei*, or love of God, and *amor sui*, seems designed to delegitimize the aristocratic obsession with these twin passions. There is nothing subtle about Augustine's analysis. *Amor Dei* is a strict form of love that demands a radical humility, which is the opposite of glory. It directs humans to love God to the exclusion of loving themselves. In fact, they must love God to the point of holding themselves in contempt. It appears to be a self-nullifying love, though it rests on a higher if indirect form of self-love. The best way to care for oneself is through loving God, as it is necessary for attaining an eternal salvation of blissful paradise.

By contrast, *amor sui*, or love of self, is defined in *City of God* as grounding one's life in one's own individual and distinctly human purposes. It is "living according to his own self that is, according to man."[34] *Amor sui* implies a hatred of God. To live for oneself is to reject God's plans and wisdom in favor of the freedom to follow one's own will. While *amor sui* can express itself in numerous ways and leads to a variety of corruptions, it originates in the aristocratic value of pride.[35] What are Adam and Eve so proud of that earns them expulsion from Eden? In a word, their abilities. It is why they love themselves, just as the root of Ajax's self-love is *aristeia* or Diderot's is his superior intellectual abilities. In Augustine's telling, the first couple become enamored of their cognitive excellences. They experience the thrill of exercising their minds to control their environment (including their emotions and passions à la the Stoics) and revel in their successes and achievements.[36] They become so proud that they soon love their own creations more than God's. They thus contemptuously reject God's guidance and arrogantly demand that they become their own masters. In a revealing passage in the *Confessions*, Augustine refers to curiosity and the desire of gaining knowledge for its own sake as an "itch" and a "disease."[37]

Pride, furthermore, gives rise to another aristocratic passion, love of glory. Like *amour-propre-propre*, glory is a relative and social emotion. If Adam and Eve at first derive satisfaction from the mere exercise of their abilities, they soon demand that others recognize their excellences and superiority as well. They require external validation and hunger after praise; they become insatiably vain. Glory, Augustine claims, invariably "is puffed up and swollen with vanity."[38] In the *City of God*, he asserts that this is the true goal for those suffering from *amor sui*.[39] Their vanity and desire for glory, furthermore, are almost limitless. Like the Homeric heroes, Adam and Eve become drunk with self-esteem and "covet being honored as gods by men."[40] Thus, if *amor Dei* results in humility and self-contempt, *amor sui* leads to arrogance and delusions of divine grandeur. Augustine means to foment a transvaluation of values—he turns the classical aristocratic morality right on its head. "It is a great matter," he proclaims in a letter, "not to rejoice in human praise and honours."[41] Like Rousseau, he holds that excellence and glory can be corrupting. The great, once again, is the enemy of the good.

Augustine's focus on cognitive rather than martial excellences in the Fall is conspicuous. As Augustine was well aware, Roman aristocrats were captivated

by the great warrior heroes of classical aristocracy. It would be logical, therefore, to model Adam on Achilles. From a biographical perspective, however,
Augustine's attention to cognitive excellences also make sense. Like Rousseau,
the young Augustine harbored ambitions of becoming a great philosopher
and teacher of rhetoric. According to Brown, his intellect had currency in
Rome. Important aristocrats valued intellectual life and enjoyed rubbing
shoulders with anyone who could vouch for their sophistication and aid their
intellectual development. Augustine was eager to take advantage of his social
value and hoped to work for these aristocrats as a tutor to their children and
personal administrator in exchange for a life of comfort and privilege.[42] While
he would outgrow these latter ambitions, his connections among members of
the Roman elite nonetheless furthered his career and interest in philosophy.
His true loves, or more aptly lusts, were intellectual ones, right up to his
conversion.

Also reminiscent of Rousseau is that Augustine came to resent the aristocratic pretensions of the intellectual classes, as well as the arrogance of the
well-to-do patrons who supported them. While in Milan, when he began to
doubt Manicheanism, he formed a philosophic clique to help him think
through his increasing spiritual discontent. The members of this coterie
viewed themselves as a special class of humanity superior to others because of
their intellect. Along with the nobles, they saw themselves as the "elite of the
human race."[43] Their outsized egos convinced them that they could perfect
the species and through sheer force of intellectual contemplation create
heaven on earth. As Larry Siedentop comments, "Augustine was no stranger
to the appeal of elitism. When he took up residence in Milan, he found himself surrounded by a refined and congenial company, which for a time impressed him with what cultivated and philosophically inclined minds could
achieve. The imagery of ascent was seductive. It enabled Augustine and his
friends to think of moving towards 'perfection.' "[44] Augustine came to doubt
such optimism and to view the inflated sense he and his associates had of
themselves as corrupting. Thus, arguably, Adam and Eve are modeled in part
on Augustine himself and his fellow Milanese intellectuals.

In any event, the pride Adam and Eve take in their excellence and their
desire for glory are for Augustine dangerous. Although they may appear to be
ordinary vices, he contends that they precipitate a far more troubling passion,
libido dominandi. He considers pride, glory, and vanity antisocial emotions.
They represent a toxic form of self-love that encourages people to benefit
themselves at the expense of their neighbors. Some of this can be attributed to

their independence and responsibility for their own survival. In relying on themselves instead of God to manage their lives, they must prefer themselves to everyone and everything, which become mere means with which to secure their survival and the satisfaction of their desires. Like Odysseus, they work for themselves and see themselves as their own end. It is their thirst for pride and glory, however, that truly makes them enemies to their neighbors. It is the Ajax in them that is most frightening. In believing they are superior to and more special than their peers, fallen humans develop an appetite to rule and even tyrannize others.[45] Augustine opens *City of God* with this very observation: "That earthly city, which, when it seeks mastery . . . has as its own master, that very lust for mastery."[46] Presumably, human attempts to control their environment include the desire to control other human beings. Augustine thus outlines a degenerative process in which merely annoying vices such as pride, glory, and vanity trigger tyrannical ones. *Amor sui* is a gateway passion that leads to a desire to rule and dominate others.

Augustine does not provide the reader with an in-depth psychological portrait *of homo dominandus* comparable to the spiritual angst he writes of in the *Confessions*.[47] He nonetheless leaves a few hints that assist the reader in sketching out his meaning. First, individuals who believe they are innately superior to their peers tend to lack compassion and empathy. *Amor sui* makes them incapable of acknowledging the needs of others or appreciating their hardships. Compassion is in part a product of a shared recognition of all humans' sinful nature—a recognition that increasingly vanishes as Adam and Eve become more convinced of their divine attributes. As with Rousseau (and for that matter Sophocles' Odysseus), it is human vulnerability and weakness that brings out the best in people. To be sure, as Hannah Arendt and Martha Nussbaum argue, Augustine's notion of compassion is limited and may not extend to actual real-world suffering or encourage people to identify with the human misery before their eyes.[48] Still, to love God means to love his creation, which requires that humans treat others with respect and at least try to mitigate their suffering. Second, Adam and Eve's "god complex" may instill in them a desire to mistreat those below them as a way of earning the recognition and admiration of their fellow humans they so crave. Through domination of weaker peers, they can publicize their superiority in front of their whole community.

In some environments, *libido dominandi* is easy to recognize. The term itself is reminiscent of scenes from Homer in which heroes treat average soldiers rudely and violently in order to remind them of their inferior place. In a memorable passage from *The Iliad*, for example, Homer's Odysseus strikes one while lecturing him, "You *fool*—sit still! Obey the commands of others, your superiors—you, you deserter, rank coward, you count for nothing, neither in war nor council."[49] In other societies, especially more democratic ones, domination can appear more benign. For example, bosses can mistreat their employees without laying a finger on them or even insulting them. Rather, they can use their authority to control them and may be cruel in numerous subtle ways that may not seem to live up to the dramatic-sounding term *libido dominandi* but are nonetheless demeaning and destructive of a person's life. Domination can even come in the form of self-effacing morality, such as charity and compassion. As both Augustine and Nicole observe, pride and self-love often motivate great acts of charity and compassion. The distinction between *amor sui* (or *amour-propre*) and charity is so subtle that it is hard to tell the two passions apart. Numerous secular thinkers made much of this insight, especially Nietzsche. Turning Augustine on his head, he contends in his view of "slave revolt of morality" that the weak are able to control and dominate the strong by making them feel ashamed of their excellence and internalizing their *ressentiment*. This dynamic results in high levels of self-loathing and eventually nihilism.

There are, furthermore, two other elements of the aristocratic personality, as defined in Chapter 1, that appear in Augustine's discussions of sin and the Fall. First, talent is intertwined with questions of identity and selfhood. Adam and Eve define themselves by their abilities. Through their abilities they come to know themselves. As Jean-Luc Marion contends, humans before the Fall lack an independent nature. Adam and Eve are at one with God and are defined by him. It is only when they reject God that they come to have their own essence.[50] Once cast out of Eden, they learn to think of themselves almost exclusively in earthly terms. They thus define themselves by their excellences and superiorities and presumably whatever possessions and reputation that result from them.

For Augustine, of course, this is a problem and leads to a dangerous form of false consciousness, if I may borrow a Marxist category. Humans are God's creation—that is who they are. Adam and Eve are utterly confused as to their true nature and are unable to put their abilities in perspective. If it is true that humans in many ways can author their own existence and control their world to a degree not found in nonhuman animals, Augustine is eager to remind them that they are not as special as they think they are. They fail to appreciate the limitations of their creative powers and have vulnerabilities of which they are scarcely aware. Unlike God, as Arendt observes, they "cannot call [themselves] into existence and cannot make anything out of nothing."[51] Their excellences pale in comparison to God's. Moreover, nature invariably gets the best of them, as humans are mortal. Thus, earthly activities and achievements distract Adam and Eve from true self-knowledge. Mesmerized by their own abilities, they lose sight of the fact that to have true excellence is to be in union with God. Their condition, and indeed that of almost all humans, is one of fundamental ignorance.

Second, Augustine's cure for this form of false consciousness touches on the classical aristocratic form of moral reasoning, that is, "reflective reasoning." Augustine encourages people to contemplate or reflect upon the value of their identity and inherent nature. They are to think about life in a manner similar to Ajax. The only difference is that they are supposed to ponder their innate wretchedness instead of their excellence and divine nature. Notably, they do not make use of technical or calculative forms of reasoning. More so than Sophocles, however, Augustine attempts to construct a formal philosophical method of reasoning out of reflection and introspection comparable to the Greek categories of practical and theoretical reason. "Reflective" or "evaluative" reasoning is designed to be a sustained attempt to contemplate inner experiences and emotional life. In practice, it is an inner dialogue in which a person scrutinizes his or her loves, deeds, and emotions to find God.

From a cognitive standpoint, reflective reason is grounded in memory. Augustine was fascinated by memory, and he conceptualized it in a robust and dynamic fashion. While he sometimes writes of memory as merely a repository of past experiences, he ultimately views it as the source of all human thinking and knowledge. He believes its power is "to be amazed at" and an "infinite multiplicity."[52] It involves not merely remembrances of past sensations and deeds but also emotions, imagination, hopes, fears, and even abstract thinking, such as mathematics. It is also the source of self-consciousness and allows humans to gain a sense of self, or in Rousseau's parlance, a "sentiment of identity." Through their memories of their loves and deeds, they come to know themselves as distinct, individual beings.[53] In his *Confessions*, Augustine claims that his mind—that is, the cognitive experience that includes memories of his past—is the thing that defines him: "This thing is the mind, and this thing am I."[54] Thus, contrary to Ajax, who learns his true nature by rationalizing away any temporal experiences that violate his destiny and true nature, Augustine places supreme importance on his experiences.

They teach him who he is—a creature who is inherently sinful rather than innately superior.

His own conversion is largely triggered by contemplation of his past and confrontation with his sinful nature. In his *Confessions*, he recounts youthful indiscretions: his near obsession with sensual pleasures, his overactive libido, and his vain ambitions of becoming a famous rhetorician. All these past loves haunt him and stir in him a profound discontent. Earthly pleasures by their nature are deeply unsatisfying. They cannot make people happy, and all people desire happiness.[55] Throughout his early adult life, Augustine struggles with his discontent and grasps at ways to mitigate his aching consciousness. To that end, he tries numerous philosophies and religions, none of which works. Eventually, his fateful encounter with Ambrose of Milan leads him to God, and he realizes that his miseries are nothing more than a deficiency. He is not evil but rather missing the one thing that could make him good and happy, which of course is God. Before his conversion, he reports that he would do bad things for no identifiable reason. His most famous example is he and his friends stealing pears for the sole purpose of throwing them at pigs. While this may seem like an innocuous sin, Augustine thinks it sheds light on his fallen condition. He contemplates the meaningless of his destructive behavior. His and his friends' actions were without purpose. Augustine was not hungry or trying to save a friend from some homicidal swine; nor was he driven by a hidden incentive to get back at his parents or disobey God himself. Rather, he was simply enchanted by wrongdoing itself: "I loved mine own fault, not that for which I committee the fault, but even the very fault itself."[56] Through reflective reason, then, Augustine realizes the nature of his loves. He was a sinner who loved himself and not God—he had *amor sui* rather than *amor Dei*. Through this insight, he could find his true self in God.

Augustine acknowledges that there are some nettlesome issues with his method of finding God through contemplation of past experiences. Primarily, God is not of this world and thus cannot be understood merely through ordinary memory.[57] Humans do not experience God as they might a warm summer breeze or falling in love with another person, as he cannot be found in the city of humans.[58] To solve this problem, Augustine claims there are parts of a person's memory separate from their temporal experiences. These include *a priori* understanding and willing, which Augustine asserts allows him to transcend his earthly existence and access the infinite truth of God's creation.[59] Through *a priori* understanding, in other words, he grasps that he and the universe are made in God's image. He comprehends the logical order of the world and realizes that God inserted himself into the recess of all human hearts. In short, his God-given ability to understand intelligible things permits him to have a full encounter with his maker.

This part of Augustine finds no counterpart in Rousseau. There is nothing in his notion of memory comparable to these cognitive and metaphysical processes, though he too contends that past remembrances are insufficient for the psychological transformation described in his *Confessions*. Rather than look to the *a priori* structures of the mind, Rousseau believes memories must be supplemented with "creative imagination."[60]

Lastly, Augustine knows that few people are capable of making the arduous journey to finding God through spiritual reflection and *a priori* reasoning. Due to the Fall, the human will is too corrupt and hence too weak and ignorant to compel people back to God of their own volition. Those who manage a conversion like Augustine's do so only because of God's grace. For those not elected by God for salvation, Augustine's narrative is cold and comfortless. In these unfortunate people, the cognitive tools through which to find God, reflective reasoning and abstract thought, only intensify the corruption caused by the Fall. They are dominated by earthly loves and overwhelmed by *amor sui* and *libido dominandi*. For these corrupt people, Augustine's answer to the problem of sin is simple: a coercive state.[61] The hearts and impulses of the wicked cannot be changed, but there are ways to deter the wicked from acting on them. In realist fashion, Augustine argues that coercion is thus an ineradicable feature of human life. Without it, the world would destroy itself. The state exists because humans are fallen, and it is the only possible way for them to maintain life itself. At the same time, Augustine recognizes that the state too is a limited tool to keep the peace. It is populated by humans, which is to say, it is populated by sinners. If sinful people are given authority over other humans, they are sure to abuse it. The state will always lack permanence and stability and always be tumultuous. Even if rulers do not abuse power, humans are limited and cannot know true justice. For this reason, justice in the city of humans will always be an absurdity. If the justice system works, it will never work optimally or reliably. Augustine's conclusion is dark and pessimistic: there are few prospects for moral improvement in humans and the triumph of virtue over vice.

Democratic *Amor Sui* in Augustine: The Deconstruction of Roman Patriotism

Augustine's support for democratic *amor sui*, as I stated earlier in the chapter, is uneven. In some of his letters and shorter works, he makes a few allusions to the utility of vice. The one that caught the attention of the moderns comes from *Ten Homilies on the First Epistle of John to the Parthians*, in which he argues pride is responsible for "great works" and mimics charity and mercy. Specifically, the desire for public applause and honor feeds self-love, inspires feeding and clothing the poor, fasting, martyrdom, and so forth; it "drives at the same end."[62] People assist others through conspicuous displays of compassion in order to earn favorable recognition from their peers. Furthermore, in a letter to Bishop Aurelius, he contends that if someone is honored and cannot distance himself or herself from that honor, it is best "to turn it all to the use and the well-being of those who honour us."[63] Unfortunately, neither his discussion in the letter nor that *in Ten Homilies* is in-depth. The more substantive discussion from *Ten Homilies* is only a few sentences. It is thus impossible to determine how Augustine might reconcile these positions with the Fall of humans and his aristocratic conceptions of *amor sui* as exemplified by the Fall.

He much more carefully lays out his case for how vice might serve as a surrogate for virtue through his deconstruction of Roman civic virtue in *City of God*, though oddly he is much more skeptical of it. In this discussion, he argues that redirecting glory to promote patriotism is likely to end up in the same place as Adam and Eve's *amor sui*. That is, it tends to lead to *libido dominandi*.

Augustine, at least for a time, was a great admirer of Roman patriotism. He could not help but respect the commitment of Roman republicans to their state and their love of country. Among faithful Romans, no one would admit, at least publicly, that her or she would not die for the empire. Augustine seems to jealously wonder why Christians do not show the same devotion to Jesus Christ and God. After some reflection, however, he decides that Roman civic virtue is not what it purports to be and refuses to take it at face value. Whatever the Romans wished to believe about themselves, he thinks that their public virtues were really private vices. More specifically, Roman patriotism was an expression of glory, defined as the desire to be praised and applauded by the public. Thus, it was not Rome but "glory they most ardently loved. For its sake, they chose to live and for its sake they did not hesitate to die."[64]

How did this state of affairs come to pass? Augustine speculates that early Roman history was dominated by monarchy. Many Romans resented such oppressive government and yearned to be free. It became an overriding desire—the object of their love. Eventually, the hated monarchy was toppled, and Rome became a republic. The Romans subsequently fell in love with their republic. As this patriotism established itself and became a centerpiece of Roman morality, however, something interesting happened to it. It transformed from a selfless love to a selfish one. A good person was defined as one who would make sacrifices for the state. To earn public praise a person needed to demonstrate a robust civic virtue. Augustine takes this seriously: it got to the point where Romans "disregarded private wealth for the sake of the commonwealth."[65] This was true even for poor magistrates. Indeed, possession of private wealth was seen as a disgrace—it meant, at least theoretically, that one loved oneself more than Rome. Augustine provides some compelling examples of this extreme patriotism. One individual, twice a consul, was removed from the Senate simply because a silver plate was discovered in his house. In addition, Augustine marvels at the restraint and devotion of Quinctius Cincinnatus, who was born in poverty but climbed the political ladder through his military accomplishments. He eventually became dictator, the most honored office in the empire. When his term expired, he went back to private life and resumed his life of reduced means. Again, the idea that one would privately benefit from public life was unheard of. It would be considered the height of dishonor. For Cincinnatus to retain his honor, he had to serve Rome without materially benefiting from it.

Augustine's analysis here is quite subtle. As with his claim from *Ten Homilies* that pride and charity are indistinguishable, Augustine contends that there is nothing on the surface separating a selfish act of vanity from a pure act of civic virtue. There is no obvious reason not to view Cincinnatus's behavior as genuine, because humans cannot know with any degree of certainty what motivates people to act. Interior motives are not accessible to naked sense perception. So, how does Augustine know Roman patriotism is a sham? Rather than rely on spiritual reasoning, he adopts, at least implicitly, a more deductive approach based on his theory of loves. Romans are pagans and thus cannot not love God. Logically, they must love the city of humans, meaning they must love themselves. Any seemingly selfless act on the part of a Roman must be selfish, which is the essence of all earthly loves. The key to Augustine's analysis is to locate how any behavior serves a person's self-interest. In the case of Roman patriotism, the answer Augustine offers is love of glory. Once the public values something, anyone exhibiting or promoting the value will be honored, while those who violate the value will become shamed. Thus, any public recognition of patriotism touches upon a person's self-interest. So, once the Romans valued patriotism, it ceased to be selfless and became the opposite of what it claimed to be. It first became glory and then the lowly vice of vanity. While it appears as if Rome's great men were suppressing their egoistic desires, they were in fact surreptitiously expressing them through conspicuous displays of patriotism. The paradox here runs deep. In the *Confessions*, Augustine even argues that humility and contempt for vainglory might yet be surreptitious attempts to win public favor: "And with a greater vanity does a man glory often times of his contemning of vain-glory."[66] Vanity, then, is a deceitful emotion. It masquerades as virtue and can quite easily appear to be its opposite.

This is not to say that Augustine believes this formula of vice serving as a surrogate for virtue is completely wrongheaded. He would agree with his seventeenth-century disciples that some vices are better than others and that the better sort can elevate behavior. At least in the case of the Romans, to reiterate, he accepts that love of praise has helped suppress worse vices, such as love of money and encouraged many good ones. At least for a time, the love of glory in Rome sustained attitudes of hard work, just rule over conquered nations, and self-control over passions and appetites.[67] It is a "good" vice that was used to manage "bad" vices. Augustine writes of the Romans: "While these men are not saints, to be sure, they are less vile."[68]

As his discussion progresses, however, Augustine reveals he is much less confident than his acolytes that vice can reliably mimic virtue and be used to manage other vices. His primary argument is that it may interfere with love of God and may drive people away from him. People will love the praise of other men so much that they will favor it above God.[69] Augustine is also not convinced that love of praise typically results in less vile behavior. His overall line of attack is to show that in the short term vice can imitate virtue and function in a similar fashion. In the long run, however, love of praise and glory can turn to something worse. In the Romans, love of glory became so strong that they would do anything to attain it and eventually tried to satisfy it through criminal means.[70] When this happened, love of glory degenerated into *libido dominandi*. In book 5, he avers: "It is an easy step for one who finds excessive delight in human glory to conceive also an ardent eagerness to rule."[71] In blunter terms, although love of glory is not the same thing as love of domination, it often leads to it. Augustine's logic here is simple enough. Glory is a hungry and restless passion. Those seeking it cannot sit still and constantly seek new outlets for its expression. As with all loves, it is a craving that loses its allure upon satisfaction.[72] Thus, once the Romans had reasonably secured their freedom, they had to find new ways to satisfy their growing appetite for public esteem other than through displays of patriotic duty. As love of glory attached itself to new objects, the Romans ceased to be good republicans and reverted to the old aristocratic code that most highly valued military glory and *aristeia*. Like the fabled Homeric heroes, Romans sought to earn glory on the battlefield by subduing and beating down opposing nations. As Herbert Deane notes, Augustine held that the "great heroes of the early period" were so driven by love of glory that they "even longed for wars so that they might have occasions for displaying their valor and winning renown."[73] Moreover, Augustine writes of their motives in Homeric terms: "Since there was no eternal life for them, but merely the passing away of the dying, who were succeeded by others soon to die, what else were they to love apart from glory, whereby they chose to find even after death a sort of life on the lips of those who sang their praises?"[74] As a consequence, the great Roman statesmen disappeared. They were replaced by corrupt and bloodthirsty rulers who sought honor and glory by brutalizing foreign states, terrorizing their own population, and hoarding wealth. Rome's attempt to harness love of glory for noble aims thus proved a failure.

There are few ways to reconcile Augustine's discussions. It might be argued that pride is a less dangerous passion than glory and does not lead to *libido dominandi*. This argument is unavailable to Augustine, however, as he suggests in the parable of the Fall that pride inspires a desire for glory. Adam and Eve, after being drummed out of the Garden of Eden, wish to be viewed as gods among humans. It is also possible to claim that the formula of *amor sui* serving as a surrogate for virtue works well for some ends and not others. Specifically, Augustine is positioned to claim that pride and glory are harmless when they promote charity but dangerous when they operate in formal political activities. He makes no such distinctions, however, nor does he provide analysis to explain his inconsistency with his views from *Ten Homilies*. His readers are stuck with a frustrating contradiction.

The Fall, the Two Loves, and Aristocratic *Amour-Propre* in Seventeenth-Century French Thought

Augustine's doctrine of the two loves and parable of the Fall were highly influential in modernity, and they show up in pristine form in many important seventeenth-century neo-Augustinians representing several sects of Christianity. They were mesmerized by the imagery and metaphors in *City of God* and faithfully adopted them.[75] A quick survey of a few prominent neo-Augustinians confirms this contention. The Huguenot Abbadie, for example, draws upon Augustine's metaphorical distinction between the two cities by identifying what he terms the "man of the world" and the "immortal man." He approves of the doctrine of the two loves and views love of God and love of self as an either-or choice. Predictably, he agrees that the only way to happiness is through love of God. He also accepts that humans are saved only through God's grace. Sénault likewise premises his thought on the Augustinian doctrines of the two loves and the Fall of humans. In *The Use of the Passions*, he contends that human history begins in a state of innocence in which humans love only God. This love is then corrupted by Adam's hubris and results in an excessive love of self, or *amour-propre*. He also agrees with Augustine's contention that to love God requires that humans hold themselves in contempt: "It is why the Son of God wants that we hate ourselves be the foundation of his Doctrine . . . he seems to design to banish self-love from the earth, and to turn this irregular affection into a holy aversion."[76] Moreover, Sénault adopts several of Augustine's other doctrines, including the belief that salvation can only be achieved through God's grace, the deficiency theory of evil, and the rejection of Manichean dualism between mind and body. He even adopts Augustine's insight that good and evil are comingled in the human soul, as humans are a mixture of "Angel and Beast."[77]

Pascal, a Jansenist, fits in here as well. In a letter to his sister and brother-in-law, he contends God created humans with two loves, one for God and one for themselves. The latter love, *amour pour soi-même*, is not originally a bad thing. It is limited and "tends back to God."[78] When humans spurn God, however, *amour pour soi-même* turns into *amour-propre*—an infinite and insatiable form of self-love in which humans love only themselves and like Adam and Eve insist on appropriating and referring everything to themselves. As with Augustine, this self-love is counterproductive and only makes humans miserable and self-loathing. Paul Rahe argues that the central theme of Pascal's *Pensées* is identical to that of Augustine's *Confessions*.[79] Both argue that without God people experience life in a condition of restlessness, boredom, and existential angst. In his theory of *divertissements*, Pascal maintains that humans fruitlessly hunt through *civitas terrena* for answers that can be found only in *civitas Dei*. They resemble the searching Augustine of the *Confessions*— the one who is unable to arrive at a state psychological equilibrium and repeatedly looks for solutions to his malaise in the wrong places. The doctrine of grace is also evident in the theory of *divertissements*. Humans, Pascal claims, can never be sure whether or not they will be saved by God's grace and thus attempt to avoid the question by distracting themselves with math, billiards, and other amusements.

Moreover, several important neo-Augustinians pick up on Augustine's critique of the aristocratic values of pagan Rome, including the glorying in individual excellences and defining self-worth in terms of them that is central to Rousseau's analysis of *amour-propre*. Pascal shares Augustine's concern that human self-love can become so exaggerated it leads to the desire to be divine: it is "an instinct which leads him [a human] to make himself into God."[80] Furthermore, Pascal's theory of *divertissements* arguably is in part a deconstruction of human excellences. Among the examples of diversions from God that Pascal offers, two involve some form of competitive achievement— besting one's peers at billiards and solving algebra problems. People, he thinks, revel in their own abilities at the expense of devotion to God. If it is true that winning a billiards match is trivial, recall that in his *Confessions* Rousseau says he thought becoming best at chess—a game that likewise has little social utility—would be his ticket to joining the new intellectual aristocracy in Paris. Lastly, in *Trois discours sur la condition des grands*, he concedes that while great geometers and others who demonstrate estimable qualities deserve esteem, they should never be rewarded with formal rewards, privileges, and powers (just as nobles should be accorded political preference and respect but not esteem).[81] Any such rewards will inflame *amour-propre* and lead people away from God.

Abbadie similarly contends that people desire worldly excellence in order to flatter their *amour-propre*, which can come at the expense of true perfection in unity with God. They want to be richer, more successful at work, and smarter than their peers in the false belief that they have earned true superiority. Abbadie writes, "The learned men have in vain venerated knowledge, by the interest which they have of making that respected, which distinguishes them from others,"[82] and "everyone boasts of excelling in his profession, however mediocre it maybe, and not because they love the excellence for the sake of excellence, but because they want to be more considered than others."[83]

Of all the neo-Augustinians, Pierre Nicole, another Jansenist, most directly addresses the aristocratic psyche through a concept he terms the "l'idée qu'il se forme de lui-même," which literally means "the idea that he forms of himself" but can be more succinctly translated as "the idea of me."[84] The idea of me has much in common with Ajax's preoccupation with the value of his identity, Augustine's reflective reasoning, and Rousseau's "sentiment of identity." Nicole contends that the idea of me comes from external validation from one's peers, or more specifically, from reflecting upon the opinions others have of me. Presumably, individuals define themselves based on these opinions.

Human excellence looms large in his analysis. Nicole asserts that humans evaluate themselves and others on two criteria: love and glory. Love springs from goodness, glory from the aristocratic value of excellence. Naturally, his primary concern is with the latter, which Nicole contends can only be determined through comparison with others. The desire for glory explains why scientists and philosophers so often boast of their achievements—it is a pure exercise in vanity. According to Nicole, "This idea is the source of all his vain satisfactions."[85] In the essay "Of the Weakness of Man," furthermore, he claims that pride is a problem of excellence, that is, an aristocratic problem. The reason people desire "the approbation of others, is that they affirm and fortify the idea they have of their own excellence."[86]

The idea of me, as expected, begets jealousy and hypocrisy. People come to resent positive attention paid to potential rivals and spend endless amounts of energy to establish and maintain a good reputation, even if it is unwarranted. The desire for a positive self-conception is so strong in some people that they will resort to falsifying their actual achievements and even cheating just to impress their neighbors. They are as hypocritical as Rousseau's Parisians. And, they will go to great lengths to protect their lies and deceptions and challenge the integrity and motives of anyone who has the temerity to question them. In addition, when they are not misrepresenting themselves, they flatter others to elicit positive feedback. Consequently, Nicole realizes that aristocratic pride is a psychic boil that must be lanced—it is a dangerous temptation. And, of course, he follows Augustine in arguing that the pride people have in their excellences is rooted in ignorance of their true nature and insists that humans can only know themselves through God. He too preaches humility and encourages humans to contemplate their weaknesses in the sight of God.

The idea of me is also a political problem, as those deemed excellent typically covet earthly power in proportion to their perceived superiority. They seek, in short, control, or *libido dominandi*. Interestingly, in the process of examining this issue, Nicole addresses the rift between the courtly aristocrats and the new bourgeois elites described in Elias's *Civilizing Process*, though he is more concerned with intellectuals than with administrators. He asserts that political power most appropriately belongs to the nobles and, much like Rousseau, he is highly critical of the claims of the intellectual classes that they are the true aristocracy. While he accepts the claims of the intellectuals as factually true,[87] he then argues that this is why they should be disqualified from ruling. His argument rests upon the distinction between deserved and undeserved praise, or Rousseau's distinction between pride and vanity in *Corsica* that Cooper finds so appealing. Nicole, however, puts a negative spin on it and contends that meritorious inequalities demean those on the bottom of the social-status ladder and corrupt those at the top. For those at the bottom, there can only be demoralization by witnessing deserved superiority.[88] On the other side of the coin, those who know they are truly superior are bound to become corrupted and invariably become arrogant in the same manner as Adam and Eve: "But it is difficult to be humble when one considers that his elevation is the fruit of his labors and his merit."[89]

To dampen *amour-propre* and deflate a person's "idea of me," Nicole suggests that abilities and special talents should neither receive any official validation nor become the basis for the distribution of societal rewards. Political power should thus be distributed on the arbitrary basis of bloodline so no one can reasonably defend his or her elevated social status in terms of just deserts. It is better to endow offices with esteem rather than people. Rulers' only claim to power ought to be that they possess a specific office, not that they have a natural entitlement to rule because they possess the talents to do so successfully.

Nicole's argument is the opposite of Rousseau's; as we will see in Chapter 3, Rousseau proposes that a natural aristocracy ought to be elected to office. He insists it is best to be ruled by the most talented. However, the two men reason from the same place. Rousseau wants to prevent the intellectuals from demoralizing the all-too-ordinary masses by hiding them away in administration, where they will remain mostly invisible to the public at large. He refuses them public recognition for their superiority. Nicole wishes to deny them power altogether and prevent them from physically or materially harming anyone. Presumably, he is willing to sacrifice competency for security. He thus makes the extraordinary claim that average people are better off under a feudal aristocracy than under another governmental arrangement that might allow them a path to power.

To complicate matters, Nicole qualifies his argument by conceding that the honor, esteem, and wealth paid to nobles can be as corrupting as claims to intellectual superiority. Nobles, too, are easily tempted by their earthly superiorities and must be made to recognize that their privileged position results from the grace of God and is in no way earned or merited. Nicole charges the clergy with teaching the ruling nobles to have a uniquely active and enlightened faith so they can comprehend the depths of their vanity. While this is not perfect, he thinks that it is "the best invention Reason could invent to soften the pride of the nobles and to discharge the hatred and envy of inferiors."[90] In addition, what is true of politics is true of intellectual achievement. Nicole urges his readers to admire the use value of science and resist honoring scientists themselves: "When a man is sick, he looks only to his doctor for the science that can cure him, and all the other qualities he may have disappear in his eyes."[91] In other words, it is permissible to celebrate the doctor's deed but not the doctor himself.

Finally, Nicole concludes his argument by returning to Augustine's belief that the only true cure for *amour-propre* is God. The opposite of pride is humility, and humility is learned through a sense of one's own weakness. It is only possible to perceive one's weaknesses through understanding God. Such knowledge pierces through self-deceptions and illuminates the central fact about human existence—everyone is a sinner. Humans thus desperately need to contemplate the spiritual world if they are to appreciate their own insignificance and cultivate a sense of their vulnerability. No matter how smart and wealthy some may be, Nicole wants them to know that they nonetheless are as susceptible to the same diseases, natural disasters, heartbreaks, and tragedies as the poorest and most wretched member of the species. There are a thousand accidents waiting to ensnare people every day. Misfortune lurks around every corner. God alone teaches humans to know themselves and allows them to resist the temptation to see themselves as a higher order of the species. Returning to God, of course, is easier said than done. *Pace* Pascal's theory of diversions, most humans only think of this life and assiduously avoid moral contemplation. They prefer to eat, drink, sleep, work, and even pay their taxes. They are easily drawn into the distractions of the earthly world.[92] Naturally, this only inflames their misery, as they get stuck in a cycle of repose and agitation. They chase after stupid earthly entertainments and petty vanities that fail to amuse them and only make them more anxious for more distractions that cannot relieve their constant boredom.

Not all neo-Augustinians accept this critique of aristocratic excellence. Nicolas Malebranche, a member of the Oratorian order who blends his Augustinianism with Cartesianism, contends that inequality is divinely sanctioned. According to Malebranche, God governs the universe through a set of immutable general laws implanted in humans and learned through reason. These laws represent the proper ordering of the universe and ought to be a person's primary love—that is, *l'amour de l'Ordre*. To love God means to love his order, which is the "mother" of human virtues and the source of all the lesser ones. In God's order, not everyone is equal; some are higher than others. According to Malebranche, "the immutable Order of justice desires that rewards be proportionate to merit, the happiness of virtue, and the perfection of spirit."[93] So, God demands that humans learn to love the hierarchies mandated by divine laws. This inevitably presents challenges and dangers to society, as Malebranche acknowledges that "*amour-propre* does not willingly suffer limits to its honor and glory."[94] People are not inclined to readily submit to the station to which God assigns them. Nonetheless, that is what God requires of them.

Notwithstanding this concern, Malebranche's position on this issue is noticeably at odds with Rousseau's (and Nicole's) view that elevating individuals based on natural talent and merit will surely corrupt them. This disagreement must have been particularly unpleasant for Rousseau, who had a soft spot in his heart for Malebranche. As Riley has also argued, Rousseau's notion of "generality" is constructed out of Malebranche's notion of general providence in his *General Will Before Rousseau*. As I show in Chapter 3, Rousseau tries to accommodate the argument Malebranche presents as much as possible without minimizing his critique of the *philosophes* and the overvaluation of talent.[95]

The Neo-Augustinians and Democratic *Amor Sui*

Despite Augustine's uneven treatment of democratic *amor sui* and his apparent rejection of it in *City of God*, most of the neo-Augustinians are enthusiastic supporters of the more optimistic and democratic strands of *amor sui* found in Augustine's *Ten Homilies on the First Epistle of John to the Parthians* (and other writings), in which it becomes a social good. Their discussions are far more developed than Augustine's and become central to their political thought. By contrast, none of them mentions the possible dangers of the formula of private vices, public benefits expressed in Augustine's deconstruction of Roman civic virtue in *City of God*.

With regard to neo-Augustinians such as Sénault, this is as expected. He was not a Jansenist and did not subscribe to "rigorism," which is the idea that humans were so corrupted by the Fall that they are wholly selfish and incapable of virtuous acts. Rather, he believes that humans maintain a baseline level of reason and that God implanted in them a small amount of virtue to assist them in their passage through the city of humans. In *The Use of the Passions*, he maintains that as long as the passions are under the direction of reason, which he calls the "sovereign of the passions,"[96] they are useful and can ameliorate the human condition. He insists that *all* passions can do this and even trumpets the utility of choler, sadness, despair, and infamy. Repeatedly throughout the text, he makes statements that echo his elemental conclusion: "There is no Passion in our soul, which cannot be usefully managed by Reason and by Grace."[97] Presumably, what is true of despair and choler is true of vanity and *amour-propre*. And, sure enough, he does argue that the desire for glory—or at least fear of its inverse, shame—has important social uses. It inspires sociability itself, as Bayle and Mandeville would later argue. Fear of infamy compels the more powerful members of society to behave more sociably and innocently.[98] As with most Jansenists, Sénault knows that there are dangers that accompany *amour-propre* and worries that attempts to secularize and release it from its religious trappings will lead to disruptive behaviors. Still, he holds that good Christians can keep *amour-propre* from degenerating into something worse.

Interestingly, many of the Jansenists shares Sénault's optimism, despite the fact they hold a more forbidding view of human nature. Having faith in neither the rational capacities nor the virtue of humans, they nonetheless believe *amour-propre* and other vices can be manipulated to establish an orderly and even prosperous society. The only exception here might be Pascal, who traditionally is lumped in with the pessimists. Scholars now reject this assessment, however. For some reason, the Port-Royal editors of the text, which strangely included Nicole, inexplicably omitted fragments in which Pascal contends that the concupiscence born of *amour-propre* could serve as the basis for society. Both passions, Pascal argues, promote "administration, law, morality, and justice," as well as charity, or at least a "false picture of charity."[99] Although Pascal is more ambivalent than his fellow Jansenists on this point, he still leans toward the democratic approach to *amour-propre*. He too believes that faith in God can prevent *amour-propre* from becoming something worse.

There is no such ambiguity casting doubt on the position of the other neo-Augustinians. Abbadie, for example, does not even view *amour-propre* and love of God as necessarily in contradiction. Moving away from Augustine's narrative of the Fall, he argues that the source of *amour-propre* is God himself. To protect his creation, God placed in humans certain vices that would nonetheless benefit them and allow for a modicum of order and peace. God, Abbadie proclaims, "gave it [*amour-propre*] to us for the preservation of our bodies, for the good of Society, and for the exercise of virtue."[100] Abbadie's formula works the same way as Sénault, Bayle, and Mandeville's: human vice is redirected to promote modest and sociable behavior through honor and public recognition. The desire for esteem from others, Abbadie contends, "renders us civil and compliant, obliging and honest, which makes us love the goodness and softness of commerce."[101] It makes the task of governance much simpler. Abbadie also traces advances in fine arts, philosophy, and the sciences to *amour-propre*, thus ignoring the warnings about human cleverness Augustine gives in his parable of the Fall. One of Abbadie's more charming examples comes courtesy of Democritus, who once abandoned society to gain wisdom and knowledge in the solitude of the desert. While Democritus claimed that he wanted to escape the extravagances of human society, Abbadie suspects that he was making a play to boost his reputation and inflate his glory. That is, he may have been "sustained in this design by the desire of having others speak of him."[102] In an apparent homage to Augustine, Abbadie even argues that Roman patriotism is nothing more than disguised vanity: "The love of one's country, which has made the finest character of the ancient Heroes, was but a hidden means by which their self-love took consideration, glory, and dignity."[103] Unlike Augustine, however, he seems to view this dynamic mostly in positive terms.[104] Although he accepts it as a sin and a problem in *civitas Dei*, he has no issues with it in human society.

Like Sénault, Abbadie's principal concern is that people will forget that *amour-propre* is useful only because of God: "Love of esteem is legitimate and natural in faith."[105] When they forget, *amour-propre* becomes excessive and leads to both irreligious and dangerously antisocial behavior. In such a prideful condition, they become unduly competitive, contemptuous of their fellow humans, and rife with envy and jealousy. They wish to win at all costs and demand esteem for things that are not estimable. They come to despise and debase those whom they deem a threat to their social status.[106] Thus, *libido dominandi* does not entirely disappear from Abbadie's narrative. It is always a possibility. In the end, however, Abbadie does not think *amour-propre* necessarily takes antisocial forms, provided that people remain committed to God and religion. It may simply present itself as conspicuous consumption and encourage individuals to try to outshine their neighbors by accumulating more, to borrow Adam Smith's phrase, "trinkets of frivolous utility"[107] (or in Mandeville's, "superfluous Knickknacks and elaborate trifles.")[108] Consequently, it can be of tremendous economic value in the city of humans.

Malebranche belongs in this camp as well, arguing that *amour-propre* is a malleable emotion that can be both a virtue and a vice. If it is guided by love of God, then it is an enlightened self-love and sets a person on the path to virtue. In this form, it represents a healthy self-love. Problems emerge only if it takes direction from sin. In such cases, it leads to vice and becomes a corrupt self-love.[109]

In certain respects, Nicole is the most enthusiastic, and most modern, of the Jansenists. He is fully on board with the maxim of private vices, public benefits and is less skeptical than many of his peers.[110] Nannerl Keohane remarks that he "expresses childlike wonder" at the utility of vice.[111] Nicole writes: "When going to the country, for example, one finds almost everywhere in the country people ready to serve those that pass by." And, "it is cupidity that makes them act, and do so with so much grace."[112] He repeats almost verbatim and directly cites Augustine's argument for conspicuous compassion from *Ten Homilies* that pride and *amour-propre* are so similar to charity in the city of humans that it is almost impossible to differentiate them. In an oft-quoted line, Nicole states that "although there is nothing so opposite to charity, which relates all to God, as self-love, which relates all to itself, yet there is nothing resembling the effects of charity as those of self-love."[113] Furthermore, he argues in favor of the sociability argument found in his fellow neo-Augustinians as well as Bayle and Mandeville that *amour-propre* encourages people to perform acts of civility, esteem equity, and behave in a modest and humble manner.[114]

Nicole also shares with Abbadie the belief that God designed the Fall to make human cooperation possible through such sins as cupidity and selfishness. Helpfully, he clearly explains, at least more so than Abbadie, how *amour-propre* and sin can be prevented from transforming into *libido dominandi* by identifying two passions that serve to contain it. The first, fear of violent death, appears to come from Hobbes: "Fear of death is then the first link of civil society, and the first brake on self-love."[115] When fear proves insufficient,

Nicole proposes the establishment of a powerful government to restrain sin and the passions.[116]

The second containing passion entails a strikingly liberal argument. Material comfort and desire for luxury are stronger than the will to dominate, Nicole claims, and can be trusted to keep it in check. He writes, "But self-love which is the cause of this war, will easily show them the means to live in peace. It loves domination, it loves to subjugate the whole world; but it loves life and commodities and a comfortable life more than domination; and it sees clearly that others are not disposed to let themselves be dominated, and are ready to take away the goods one likes best."[117] Or, in "Of the Means to Conserve Peace Amongst Men," he asserts: "Men are linked together by an infinite number of needs, obliging them out of necessity to live in society; each one in particular cannot subsist without others, and this society is in conformity with God's order."[118] Thus, remarkably, Nicole winds up on the side of Odysseus. Well-being trumps the aristocratic desires of love of glory and *amour-propre*.

There is one obvious reason the neo-Augustinians are so optimistic about redirecting *amor sui* to social goods in the city of humans and ignore Augustine's cautionary tale about Romans civic virtue in *City of God*. Rome is a pagan society of nonbelievers. Recall that Sénault, Pascal, Abbadie, and Malebranche all make the case that faith in God itself can prevent *amor sui* from wreaking havoc in the city of humans. Still, even if the faithlessness of Rome is taken into account, Augustine in *City of God* has much less confidence in the spirituality of the species and believed few could find God through reflective reasoning as he had. Genuine faith, he maintains, is an achievement that requires divine assistance and cannot be expected for the overwhelming portion of the population. His conversion is the exception among humanity, not the rule. The city of humans, Augustine laments, is populated by hopeless sinners; reason and grace are in short supply. He did not look for silver linings in the Fall. It was not designed by God to facilitate peaceful living. This is why Augustine proposes that a coercive state be established. It is the only way to contain the destructive *amor sui* of the population.

Nicole's problems are even worse, as he relies on human institutions such as the state and material necessity to contain and soften *amour-propre*. Augustine rejects both solutions. Although he accepts that a strong coercive government and an influential church are the only means available to contain sin and *amor sui*, he is much less enthusiastic than Nicole that such measures will be effective. For Augustine, life on this earth is characterized by poverty, faction, war, and misery. The state can produce a semblance of order and prevent humans destroying themselves, but not much more can be expected. More-over, political power too can be abused and be directed by the most dangerous passions in human nature. Power is a dangerous temptation and a wonderful instrument for those sick with *libido dominandi* to realize their aims. Taking it out of the hands of the intellectuals and giving it to the nobles, as Nicole sug-gests, is probably meaningless, as is having the clergy teach the nobles to be humble. For Augustine, power, in the hands of sinners, corrupts and does so without fail.

In addition, Augustine has his doubts about human justice, which is ad-ministered by humans and hence also corrupt. Justice in *civitas terrena* is an absurdity, as it requires sinful, ignorant humans to judge and punish other sinful, ignorant humans.[119]

It is even less likely that Augustine would support Nicole's assertion that material desires and needs compel humans to cooperate peacefully with one another rather than try to dominate each other. In *City of God*, love of money is portrayed as one of the most dangerous vices—one that needs to be moder-ated by other vices.[120]

Thus, as with Augustine, the neo-Augustinians make no effort to recon-cile competing views of *amour-propre* in their works. They appear to accept the darker strands of Augustine's thought that pride in excellence is a danger-ous sin. They then minimize these concerns by embracing the most optimistic strands of thinking in Augustine and make them the mainsprings of their political thought, even arguing that pride in excellence and rationality is a net social positive.

Augustine Secularized: From Nicole to Mandeville

The significance of the neo-Augustinians choosing to highlight the optimistic Augustine in their political thought cannot be understated. The formula of rechanneling vice to serve the public good became the most dominant so-cial theory in the eighteenth century, especially among secular theorists. Ni-cole's attempts to control vice through fear and greed served as a model and led some to fully de-Christianize Augustine's political thought. As previously mentioned, Bayle utilizes Augustine's "rigorism"—the idea that humans were totally corrupted by the Fall—to establish a secure and just atheist commu-nity. The most irreligious person, he claims, would behave in a sociable man-ner imaginable if rewarded with public esteem.

Mandeville, a trained physician, followed soon after and more systematically worked out a secular Augustinianism in *The Fable of the Bees*.[121] He describes, almost in the same terms, the cognitive and sociological processes articulated by Abbadie, Sénault, and Nicole. To completely secularize the theory and remove all mention of God, all Mandeville had to do was replace the story of Adam and Eve and original sin with a sociobiological alternative rooted in an anthropological natural history.[122] The Fall is swapped out for evolution; the issues of grace and salvation disappear entirely. Granted, Mandeville does at times shrink from his scientific standpoint. In "The Dialogues Between Horatio and Cleomenes," he adopts a more earnest tone and is careful not to reject the story of original sin outright.[123] Instead, he contends that the Christian story of the Fall, as history, is merely incomplete. His aim, he claims, is to fill in some of the blanks.[124] Of course, this probably is not an accurate description of what Mandeville is doing. He means to deny theology any causal or foundational role in this theory and probably only wants to reassures readers that he is not pushing his argument as far as Bayle did—a "crime" of which he is certainly guilty. Mandeville published the *Fable* over an eighteen-year period and was aware when writing the later parts of the text that he might have crossed a few too many lines. He knew that his reputation as the "man-devil" could cause problems, as early eighteenth-century Europe was not a safe place for atheists. In any event, his general strategy is clear. He makes a naturalistic argument for vice serving the cause of virtue.

Fortunately for Mandeville, he had access to a model of political theorizing that would allow him to sneak in his evolutionary approach to human nature. Many of his immediate predecessors in the natural law and social contract tradition utilized the state of nature concept in their systems. Granted, most, if not all, social contract and natural law theorists did not think of the state nature in terms of actual natural history. Rather, it was a thought experiment designed to legitimize certain political arrangements based on the natural needs of humans as ascertained through some fictionalized portrait of what life would have been like before the advent of government. However popular travel literature was at the time, most theorists were content to define humans as they had always been. They made no distinction between natural humans and the civil ones right before their eyes. Any notion that humans had evolved had not occurred to them. One of Mandeville's contributions to this literature is to challenge this assumption by reviving older Epicurean notions of human and cultural evolution. He speculates, and he is aware that he is only speculating, on what humans were like in a presocial state and contrasts them to socialized humans in a civil state. Or, in his lexicon, he wishes to distinguish "untaught animals" from "taught animals."

Mandeville's untaught humans are analogous to Adam and Eve, though they appear on the surface to have little in common. Untaught humans have a limited emotional economy that includes only self-love and lust—two passions the first couple do not experience until after they are expelled from Eden. These passions, however, are much more benign than the lust and self-love that define fallen humans. Untaught humans are primitive, not sinful. Their self-love is an unoffending passion that refers only to the instinct for preservation. Lust, too, is described as a fact of human nature—one that has the useful purpose of ensuring self-preservation. Its aim, however, is the survival of the species rather than the individual. It is true that untaught humans are wholly selfish and hold a "me first" ethic, which may lead them into conflict. Presumably, individuals who desire the same object may decide to violently engage competitors. Still, their selfishness is mostly limited to survival. They lack the arrogance and ambition of Adam and Eve and are not driven to conflicts because of pride, vanity, and the desire to control others based on arrogant assumptions of superiority. Self-love, for Mandeville, is neither reflective nor comparative. It does not encourage humans to reflect upon their abilities or try to best their peers. Untaught humans thus have much more in common with other animals than with taught humans, as they are little more than a collection of appetites. Mandeville writes, "Raw, ignorant, and untaught Men fix their Eyes on what is immediately before and seldom look further than, as it is vulgarly express'd, the length of their noses."[125]

In addition, Mandeville is eager to make the case that untaught humans are not naturally social.[126] They have little reason to seek out the company of their fellow humans, as self-love is an asocial emotion that involves only material needs. While his untaught early humans might deduce from the desire to survive that cooperation may be in their selfish interests, Mandeville doubts such an epiphany would draw people together, because humans quickly figured out the art of survival. He speculates that humans learned how to control nature and subsequently had less need for one another as time passed. If common challenges for survival at first drew them together, experience and progress pulled them apart. Ultimately, humans in this state had too few needs to make them social.

The degeneration of humanity into a more conflictual and competitive state resulted from the establishment of the first true social living arrangement: the family. According to Mandeville, to boost chances of survival, women and men sought to establish families, preferably large ones. They reasoned having lots of children would translate into more comfort and ease, and more success in the competition for resources. Family life, interestingly enough, forever changed the cognitive makeup of humans. If parents have children to increase odds of survival, they also love them and socialize them. They need to teach them obedience and ensure they do what they are told. Although Mandeville's discussion is thin, he intimates that this need for obedience taught children how to earn their parents' approval. Through this socialization process, children learned how to avoid punishment and obtain the praise of their parents by properly following their parents' directives. Importantly, the ability to earn this approval led to the desire for approval. It awakened the latent instinct of *amour-propre*, which Mandeville terms "self-liking." Children who regularly attained favorable reactions from their parents enjoyed it; it feels good to be praised. Consequently, they tried to gain as much of it as possible and competed with their siblings for it. Thus, neither cognitive development nor the desire for independence corrupts Mandeville's humans. The true culprit is parental discipline.

In keeping with his secular approach, Mandeville focuses exclusively on the social value of self-liking and does not want to evoke moralistic Christian notions of pride.[127] Self-liking has an important evolutionary function. It helps ensure the survival of the species. If self-liking is not original in humans and only first emerges in families and social living, it nonetheless is a biological drive that shares the same purpose as self-love. Presumably, it is a latent capacity in humans that first appears in social settings to help them survive in an increasingly conflictual environment. In "The Third Dialogue Between Horatio and Cleomenes," he argues: "To increase the Care in Creatures to preserve themselves, Nature has given them an Instinct, by which every Individual values itself above its real Worth."[128] So, self-liking may be nothing more than an adaptive form of self-love.

Furthermore, Mandeville follows Nicole and other neo-Augustinians in arguing that self-liking is a useful means to secure political stability, though his approach differs in some respects. He attempts to scale the relational dynamics present in early families—that is, inferiors obeying the will of superiors motivated by the desire for external approval or self-liking. He contends that self-liking is simultaneously an antisocial and a social emotion. It is antisocial because it gives people much more to fight about. It gives rise to the development of a family of comparative emotions—including envy, vanity, and jealousy—that greatly increase the potential for conflict. Mandeville informs his reader: "We have not a more dangerous enemy than our own in-born Pride."[129] At the same time, he contends that self-liking is its own correc-tive, meaning that the conflicts stirred up by pride are also resolved through it. Much like Sénault, Abbadie, and Bayle, he holds that self-liking is easy to manipulate through honor and shame. Like children attempting to please their parents, people who relish the approval of their neighbors to confirm their own self-importance are moved by love of praise and fear of contempt or shame. Self-liking, in other words, induces people to care what others think of them. Consequently, if someone can influence how citizens of a society view and evaluate one another, he or she can use self-liking to promote social harmony—or at least enough cooperation and respect among citizens to allow for economic transactions. In Mandeville's scheme, lawgivers and politicians assume this role by creating norms and eventually laws that honor people for sociable acts and shame them for selfish ones.[130] Just as ancient Rome and Greece honored great warriors through trophies and external rewards, Man-deville's lawgivers and politicians reward individuals who are expert in deco-rum and deem them "Men of Merit."[131] Thus, lawgivers manipulate aristocratic passions to promote democratic ends.

The reason that self-liking is so easily exploited is that it is devoid of con-tent. Its only goal is to attract positive attention and avoid negative attention. Theoretically, such validation could be earned for anything. If a society highly values clean garages, then the person with the cleanest garage will gain the public esteem that all humans crave. Good lawgivers and politicians can de-fine societal values and set the standards of decent and socially acceptable be-havior. They set the moral agenda of society and convince people to behave a certain way.[132]

The heart of Mandeville's paradox is that self-liking is domesticated by forcing it to present itself as humility. Since most human conflict is caused by pride, lawgivers must be sure to honor people who act in the opposite manner—humbly.[133] Norms and laws must be constructed so that the only way to satisfy self-liking and pride is through self-negation. Pride must dis-guise itself. Like Augustine's Roman patriots, Mandeville's humans satisfy their selfish desires for pride and glory by hypocritically pretending to care about others more than themselves. Fortunately, Christianity and the preten-sions of human moralists makes the lawgiver's job much easier. As a species, humans think they occupy the highest links on the great chain of being and refuse to acknowledge the frailty of the species. They believe themselves to be endowed with reason and virtue. They even think they are partially divine, as only they can conquer their passions and appetites. For Mandeville, there is something hypocritical in this Christian formula. Humans are just like any other animals, taught or untaught, in that they seek to satisfy their own desires and inclinations. They are inherently selfish. In fact, they are not even the only species that experiences pride. Although duller animals like cows and sheep do not, or do so imperceptibly, Mandeville assures his reader that horses and certain birds do.[134] In any event, human pretensions are easy to exploit. If humans define their species as rational and virtuous, it is easy to convince them that they ought to behave as such if they wish to receive honor and avoid shame. Lawgivers make these unrealistic standards the basis of all law and manners. Everyone is to be judged by them. So, the lawgiver appeals to human vanity, both that of individuals and that of the species. If a person acts in accord with the high opinion humans have of themselves, he or she will be individually honored. If the person acts like an animal, on the other hand, people will think of him or her as an animal and treat him or her accordingly. The most helpful example in *The Fable of the Bees* involves a refined gentleman seeking sexual relations with a woman. Mandeville invites his reader to imagine how this individual ought to go about satisfying his carnal desires. The first lesson for his gentlemen is to conceal his true intentions. Rather than try to overtly satisfy his sexual urges, he hypocritically pretends not to have them. He asks a woman out, takes her out to eat, kisses her hand, buys her flowers, and declares that he is falling in love with her. He slowly and carefully goes about achieving his goal. If he rushed to have sex with her and immediately announced the purposes of his amorous solicitations, he would have his faced slapped. He knows that if he speaks truthfully and openly about the nature of his desires, he will quickly become a social pariah. So, the only way for him to satisfy his passion is to hypocritically express it as the opposite of his actual desire. The key point here is not that passions are suppressed. Rather, they are disguised and reveal themselves only in certain ways. To gain honor and avoid shame, passions must be hidden, not eliminated.

Society, in other words, requires lots of playacting. People must carefully manage how they present themselves to the outside world. For Mandeville, social life is a careful intersubjective game of, to use the sociologist Erving Goffman's term, "impression management." Goffman's analogy for social life, theater, is revealing of Mandeville's argument. There is a front stage and a back stage. The public is not invited backstage. People only let others see what they want them to see; they carefully present to others exactly what they want them to know. Social life is a performance, and people hide anything that might provoke disapproval. Thus, for both Mandeville and Goffman, what most ethicists call morality is nothing more than an act. According to Goffman, social consensus "is facilitated by each participant concealing his own wants behind statements which assert values to which everyone present feels obliged to give lip service."[135] So, what is called morality is merely lip service. It is nothing more than the language people use to obscure their desires in if they want to satisfy them. Mandeville likewise agrees that good manners are not a reflection of a person's actual virtue. They are simply polite appearances designed to earn honor and avoid shame. Thus, successful navigation of social life requires lots of hypocrisy and lots of lying. Both are necessary for sociability and are evidence that self-liking has been properly redirected. Mandeville reasons that once a system of rewards and punishments is in place and people accept the laws as legitimate, obedience will be a simple affair. Pride and self-liking induce people to imitate their neighbors: "Man . . . naturally loves to imitate what he sees others do."[136]

Self-liking plays an important part in the satirical deconstructions of eighteenth-century European cultural life Mandeville presents, and it allows him to deflate human arrogance and excessive self-liking. He takes great pleasure in puncturing the puffed-up pretensions of the species. In this respect, he copies *moralistes* like La Rochefoucauld and is more interested in the absurdity of the passion than its potential social utility.[137] In volume II, he takes special care to expose the leading professional men in society as cheats, liars, and hypocrites. Self-liking seems to be an urban problem, not a country one, as the "better sort" suffer from certain vices almost unknown among the poor, such as "Envy, Detraction, and the Spirit of Revenge," as well as "Excess of Vanity and hurtful ambition."[138] In the "Grumbling Hive," moreover, the professional classes—the doctors, lawyers, financiers, and priests—receive much of Mandeville's satirical venom. While these so-called honest men all claim to be of great public service and represent the best of society, Mandeville thinks their motives run no higher than money and fame: "Fame, Wealth and Greatness every Body knows are the Things that all the Lawyers and Physicians aim at."[139] He perversely compares them to "pimps" and "players" and goes to great lengths to prove that ambition has a way of making humans look positively ridiculous: "So silly a Creature is Man, as that, intoxicated with the Fumes of Vanity, he can feast on the thoughts of praises that shall be paid his Memory in future Ages with so much ecstasy, as to neglect his present Life, nay, court and covet death."[140] There is almost nothing people will not do to be in the spotlight. Mandeville's most shocking example is that of early eighteenth-century male stage actors who agreed to castration to more realistically portray female characters, all so that they might attain greater fame. In addition, all these professions thrive only because of excess vice. Instead of being portrayed as paragons of virtue, the so-called respectable professionals "are exposed as hypocrites who make their living out of human frailty."[141] Without greed, lust, and traditional Christian vices such as drunkenness, doctors and lawyers would have far fewer patients and clients and less opportunity to innovate.

In volume II, as Istvan Hont demonstrates, Mandeville mostly targets Shaftesbury and the courtly aristocracy.[142] He is utterly contemptuous of the *civilité* that legitimizes their status and goes out of his way to criticize such practices as the custom of dueling that defines the courtly lifestyle. Tellingly, many of his examples seem directed at aristocratic norms: little girls learning how to curtsy, young aristocratic men courting women, and so on. The *Characteristics*, he thinks, is nothing but an ideological glorification of overprivileged parasites.[143] Between the two volumes, of the *Fable of the Bees* there is enough to denigrate anyone who managed to earn distinction in eighteenth-century Europe. Thus, Mandeville is much more of an Augustinian than he appears to be. Arguably, his ridiculing the so-called best and brightest is evidence that one of his primary aims is to promote humility. If self-liking is beneficial in numerous ways, Mandeville still wants to expose those in whom it is strongest. He wants us to know that no human is truly worthy of admiration; there are no heroes among us.

The influence of Nicole, Sénault, and Abbadie is, therefore, easy to detect in the *Fable* and serves as the foundation of its economic, political, and social thought. It colors much of Mandeville's theorizing. First, the importance of hypocrisy, the inability to distinguish virtue and vice, and the use of honor and shame to socialize people are all featured in the text. Moreover, recall that Mandeville's definition of self-liking is remarkably similar to that of an English translation of Abbadie's *Art of Knowing Oneself.* Second, Mandeville is as impressed as the neo-Augustinians that selfish passions spur almost limitless economic growth and cultural flourishing. Third, his humans engage in reflective reasoning, which is presupposed by self-liking and the experiences of honor and shame. They constantly evaluate themselves and ask the fundamental questions begged by such reasoning: "Who am I?" and "What is my worth as a human?" Mandeville contends that this power of self-examination is one of the traits that separates the human species from other animals.[144] His discussion of suicide also touches upon reflective reasoning. Suicide results from self-hatred, which Mandeville describes as a deficiency of self-liking. A person who experiences constant shame and has no hope of attaining favorable recognition from his or her peers will come to experience self-hatred.[145] In such a state, suicide may appear to be a superior alternative to life itself. Mandeville laments that humans often fail to understand the power they have over one another and how nature places them in a dangerous situation of vulnerability. If they need each other to ensure physical survival, they need each other even more for satisfying emotional needs such as self-esteem. Finally, as with many neo-Augustinians, there is little talk of self-liking as a gateway to the lust for power or other noxious passions. Such motives do occasionally appear in the *Fable*. In his "Essay on Charity-Schools," for example, Mandeville claims that individuals who start such schools are drawn to the idea of ruling and governing others.[146] In addition, he accepts that ruling authorities need to be circumscribed by law in "The Grumbling Hive." But this is an afterthought in his works and is not meant to qualify his argument that private vices lead to public benefits. Mandeville's attitude toward domination is mostly playful. It is a concern, but one often amounting to little more than another quirk of the human personality more fit for lampoon than consternation. There can be negative consequences to it, but Mandeville writes of it much less dramatically. It is a problem to be solved, not an inescapable fate everyone must suffer.

The only major difference between Mandeville and the seventeenth-century neo-Augustinians is theology. Mandeville has no theology and includes no discussions of grace and salvation. Furthermore, as E. J. Hundert points out, Mandeville had no notion of human improvement. His neo-Augustinian predecessors believed humans "possessed qualitatively distinct spiritual capacities" and had the capacity to become moral beings.[147]

Conclusion

In formulating his own views of *amour-propre* and the rechanneling of the vice to serve the public good, Rousseau therefore had plenty of modern predecessors with whom to work in addition to Augustine. Many modern theorists began from Augustinian premises that humans are fundamentally driven by vanity and the desire for public approval. They shied away, however, from the more pessimistic sides of their medieval muse and conceived of *amour-propre* or self-liking in more utilitarian or Odyssean terms. If it was tempered by religion or controlled by the state, they were convinced it could improve life in the city of humans. Rousseau recognized the power of the paradox of using sin to contain sin, and he did not entirely reject it. But, as I show in the following chapter, he found it deeply unsatisfying and recovered some of Augustine's patented pessimism from *City of God*. Self-love in his early writings becomes a dangerous passion that, when combined with inequality, can lead to appalling cruelty.

Chapter 3

Amour-Propre in Rousseau

Subverting the Aristocratic Personality

Rousseau does not unequivocally reject Nicole and Mandeville's Odyssean endorsement of *amour-propre* as a source of political, economic, and social well-being. Yet he never expresses "child-like wonder"[1] at its powers to end poverty or promote justice and on balance believed it was more trouble than it's worth. A society that relies on vice for its moral psychology should expect the worst. It is worth repeating the stern qualifications Rousseau gives to his statements that vice is socially beneficial. Recall from the *Second Discourse* that while *amour-propre* is responsible for "what is best and what is worst among men," it yields "a multitude of bad things and a small number of good things."[2] And from *Emile*, *amour-propre* "is a useful but dangerous instrument"; "often it wounds the hand making use of it and rarely does good without evil."[3] Like the pessimistic Augustine, Rousseau attempts to refute the seductive paradox that selfishness and glory make the world go around.

Perhaps most interesting of all is that he seems to take Augustine's deconstruction of Roman patriotism as his model (though there is no textual evidence that he was influenced by the passage or even read it). The narrative trajectory of the *Second Discourse* is remarkably similar to Augustine's own arguments. *Amour-propre* begins with aristocratic desires of glory and being best but transforms into a *libido dominandi* that produces a brutal economic and eventual political tyranny. Accordingly, democratic arguments that *amour-propre* produces higher average utility through economic and intellectual progress cannot justify the potential risk of letting aristocratic personalities run wild.

Furthermore, when Rousseau grants that *amour-propre* can produce some positive benefits, he qualifies his argument by contending that it does so only under specific social and economic conditions. These conditions are not straightforward, as he has several targets and is not entirely upfront about what bothers him most about modern life. Mainly, however, he views *amour-propre* as an aristocratic problem. As I argued in Chapter 1, societies that overvalue individual excellences and create talent-based hierarchies will be home to the worst variants of the passion. Ironically, the modern development that is most likely to produce these aristocratic conditions, Rousseau thinks, is the emerging Enlightenment and commercial society. In other words, the very economic processes that inspired Nicole and Mandeville to argue for the positive benefits of *amour-propre* or self-liking lead to the most virulent forms of it.

Rousseau Contra Mandeville

Rousseau's basic strategy in the *Second Discourse* is to begin from the same Epicurean premises as Mandeville and draw from them downbeat conclusions similar to those we find in Augustine's *City of God*.[4] Consequently, Rousseau begins his discourse in the same manner as Mandeville: namely, by substituting the story of Adam and Eve and original sin as the origin of *amour-propre* with one rooted in natural history and evolution.[5] To be sure, Rousseau is not merely trying to be paradoxical. He is not a self-identified Augustinian and, as I mentioned, has little sympathy for the theology of Augustine. He stridently opposes his story of original sin as contrary to the natural goodness of humans and believes his God exhibits *libido dominandi*.[6] In addition, he has a genuine interest in natural history. He read Buffon and loved the travel literature of his day that described "rude" or "primitive" societies. In *Emile*, he admits to having, in his words, "spent my life reading accounts of travels."[7] His anthropological or natural historical approach to human nature is thus perfectly consistent with his theological and intellectual predilections.

Nonetheless, Rousseau also has a voracious appetite for paradox and may have relished doing to Mandeville what Mandeville did to Christianity, whatever he thought of Augustine. If Mandeville premises his political thought on Augustinian assumptions with designs to undermine religious criticisms of commercial society, Rousseau begins with Mandeville's foundations and attempts to debunk the modern utilitarian democratic ethic of everyone working for himself, representative of commercial democracies. Presumably, this might help reestablish the authority of religion, which, as he notes in the *First Discourse*, was badly damaged by the forces of the Enlightenment.

Scholars have long noticed Mandeville and Rousseau's shared interest in natural history and an evolutionary approach to human nature. Adam Smith, in his "Letter to the Authors of the *Edinburgh Review*," carefully details important points of agreement between Mandeville's narrative in *The Fable of the Bees* and Rousseau's in the *Second Discourse*. Both thinkers assume that humans are naturally antisocial and will not seek out cooperative living arrangements, and they believe that the state of nature is an evolutionary process in which the "talents, habits, and arts" most responsible for the modern condition slowly develop over time.[8] According to Smith, they differ mostly in their appraisal of the state of nature and the importance they attach to pity. Although this is probably unfair to Mandeville, Smith thinks he describes the primitive state "as the most wretched and miserable that can be imagined," while Rousseau "paints it as the happiest and most suitable to his nature."[9] In terms of pity, Rousseau argues that it is the foundation of goodness; Mandeville assumes *pace* the neo-Augustinian "rigorism" that all virtue, pity included, is disguised vice and a form of selfishness.

Smith's observations are hardly exhaustive. Brooke identifies another crucial similarity inexplicably overlooked by Smith: the distinction between self-love and self-liking, or in Rousseau, *amour de soi-même* and *amour-propre*.[10] Brooke contends that there is very little separating the two accounts from a conceptual standpoint. Like Smith, he thinks the only substantial difference between the respective discussions by Rousseau and Mandeville is their valuation of the *amour-propre* or self-liking. Brooke, however, goes into more detail than Smith and demonstrates that their evaluative differences result from some minor conceptual disparities. Mandeville's self-liking shows up earlier in history, as individuals in his state of nature do not live solitary lives as long as they do in Rousseau's state of nature. Human conflict emerges on the scene a lot sooner than it does in the *Second Discourse*. Brooke, however, does not view this difference as "especially significant." If Mandeville went Rousseau's route and put the development of the family later in the state of nature, the two most likely would have agreed that there was no self-liking or *amour-propre* in the earlier part of the state of nature.[11]

Finally, the two thinkers surprisingly share a common politics and enemies list. Both mercilessly assault the "the better sort," or upper classes. Mandeville casts his net wide and plays no favorites. As I argued in Chapter 2, he is contemptuous of both courtly aristocracy and the new intellectual and professional classes with whom he rubbed shoulders while making his living as a doctor in London. He delights in deflating the pomposity of those who deem

themselves superior, be they lawyers or lords, and aims to show they are nothing more than con artists and frauds. While society benefits from them, it is
because of their vices rather than their virtues. To reiterate, in "The Grumbling Hive," Mandeville seeks to deconstruct the so-called respectable professionals such as lawyers, government administrators, and doctors. In volume II
of the *Fable*, his target is the nobles and their commitment to *civilité*. Rousseau goes after the very same people. In the *Dialogues*, he states: "The Nobles,
the Viziers, the Lawyers, the Financiers, the Doctors, the Priests, the philosophers, and all the sectarian people who truly plunder society would never
forgive him [Rousseau] for having seen and shown them who they are."[12]

There is, however, a subtle difference in their politics that is crucial for
understanding Rousseau's critique of Mandeville. If Rousseau had no love for
the courtly aristocrats and their polished manners (and he reveled at playing
the rustic bumpkin in the Parisian salons), he especially has it in for the new
bourgeois urban elite, especially the intellectuals. As I demonstrated in Chapter 1, he was worried that the aristocratic ambitions of the *philosophes* would
spawn the most dangerous forms of *amour-propre* and that their Enlightenment ideologies would undermine the foundations of European morality.
Rousseau is thus more discriminating than Mandeville. He did not want to
impugn soldiers and at least lesser religious authorities, such as abbés. For
him, religion and patriotism are good things that help lessen *amour-propre*. In
this respect, he is a more selective Augustinian. By contrast, Mandeville's
wholesale appropriation of Augustinian rigorism traps him in a hardened cynicism that forces him to deconstruct everything about society. No one is
spared his satire.

The implications of Rousseau's specific emphasis on the intellectuals are
significant and lead him away from Mandeville's Odyssean moral reasoning.
Rousseau is less focused on democratic utilitarianism than on the psychological corruptions caused by inequality. If Mandeville wishes to expose the leading men of society as hypocrites, he nonetheless views them as a net positive
for society. Their private vices lead to public benefits. Rousseau, conversely, is
preoccupied with domination. Thus, Smith's one-off comment that Mandeville and Rousseau differ only in their valuations of primitive society and
Brooke's attempt to diminish the differences between their states of nature are
insufficient. They not only evaluate the state of nature in opposite terms but
also use entirely different moral reasoning despite their similar vocabulary. As
a result, Smith and Brooke do not fully appreciate Rousseau's radical critique
of democratic ethics.

Part I of the *Second Discourse* and the Competition for Esteem

In the first part of the *Second Discourse*, Rousseau appears to reason backward from his concerns about the *philosophes* and their claims to be truly *aristos*, or best. His state of nature is an *amour propre*–free zone precisely because the formula for defining a great person—a public identity based on some socially valuable superiority—could not have existed at the time.

Regarding the first element of the formula, Rousseau's original humans—*les hommes sauvages*—had neither an identity nor the cognitive ability to self-consciously reflect upon themselves as individuals; they lacked the "sentiment of identity" and "reflective reason." According to Rousseau, *les hommes sauvages* were solitary, nomadic creatures who had almost no interaction with their peers. Their entire lives were spent wandering from place to place in search of food, drink, shade, and a safe place to rest. If they encountered other humans, it is unlikely that it registered so much as a blip on their limited consciousness. Such meetings, if they did occur, were rare, brief, and quickly forgotten.

As a result of their solitude, they possessed only a limited emotional economy and were merely a bundle of appetites. They did not think of themselves as individuals so much as they responded to their physical needs or desires and looked out for their self-preservation. They experienced only primal emotions implanted by nature to ensure survival, such as hunger, fear, and lust. None of these passions, Rousseau observes, compelled people to seek the company of others. Resources were plentiful and readily available, which meant that there was no material need for early humans to cooperate or compete with one another to survive. In addition, while sexual appetite temporarily draws early humans together, it did not lead to the establishment of families or societies. Original humans knew only lust and had no notion of the moral side of love. Sex was a purely physical affair that took the form of a one-night stand. Moreover, Rousseau is at pains to argue that these limited encounters did not spurn amorous competitions. Bereft of reason and culture, *les hommes sauvages* had no standards of beauty and merit, and so they did not compare their sexual partners with those of their counterparts.[13] It never occurred to them that more desirable partners might be available. Accessibility was the only criterion they consulted, and it too was not an issue, as there was likely an equal proportion of men and women. Sex was readily available to all in roughly equal measure. To be sure, sexual appetite plays a meaningful part in the drama of *amour-propre* later in the narrative. When humans develop to the point in which they live close to one another, sexual appetite is identified as one cause that induces them to be sociable.[14] Still, as far as Rousseau is concerned, sexual desire is not enough to induce individuals to seek the company of others during the earliest stages of the state of nature.

The only other emotion primitive humans experienced was compassion, which compelled them to empathize with those they witnessed suffering. Rousseau's description of compassion closely resembles Mandeville's. Rousseau even borrows his example of a prisoner watching a sow devour a baby from Mandeville's "Essay on Charity Schools."[15] As with sex, however, compassion did not draw *les hommes sauvages* out of their nomadic lives of solitude. While it is a social emotion and prompts people to think of others, it does not encourage comparison and rivalry. It is a self-regarding emotion that triggers only visceral reactions of revulsion or fear that one could suffer similarly. Individuals experiencing compassion think "That could happen to me," not "I am better than that individual because I am not suffering such misfortune." Accordingly, original humans' love of self, or *amour de soi-même*, had a simple goal: self-preservation and the promotion of physical well-being. Any thoughts beyond that were, for all intents and purposes, inconceivable. Primitive humans had no reason to ask the questions "Who am I?" and "Am I superior to my peers?"

The second element of the aristocratic formula, talent-based superiorities, also could not have existed in the earliest stages of the state of nature. Given the lack of evolutionary development, there were few noticeable differences among early humans in talent and ability. Most of the "natural" inequalities that have social meaning in modern life had yet to develop. There were virtually no intellectual differences, as *les hommes sauvages* had no language. With no language, they had no imagination and no foresight. As a result, they were incapable of reason. No one, therefore, could distinguish himself or herself based on his or her eloquence, cleverness, wit, mathematical ability, and so on. Rousseau concedes that slight physical differences did exist among these early humans. Some were stronger, faster, or more attractive than others. These differences, however, were insignificant because, again, original humans lived in solitude and rarely had the opportunity to compare themselves to others. In the unlikely event that someone witnessed a stronger and faster individual in action, there would be no reason for him or her to care or compare himself or herself to that individual, as it would have no bearing on his or her own survival. Thus, for a creature utterly lacking in self-consciousness with easily satisfied needs who rarely saw the same person twice, inequality was utterly insignificant.

The emergence of physical and cognitive abilities is central to Rousseau's evolutionary narrative. He carefully identifies the specific factors—both natural and environmental—contributing to the development of human talents in the hopes of explaining why humans evolved the way they did. In terms of the natural causes, Rousseau points to the uniquely human trait of perfectibility. For him, humans are self-improving animals and have an almost unlimited capacity to develop their minds and bodies, especially the former. Whereas nonhuman animals stop developing after several months and as a species roughly remain the same for centuries, the human condition is constantly changing. Humans learn to read, pick up a second language, write philosophical treatises, engineer a bridge, play a musical instrument, comprehend other cultures and traditions, interpret others' emotions, try new occupations, and so forth. They have all sorts of latent capacities that emerge only after tens of thousands of years of evolution. Hence, humans live lives much different from those they did a thousand years ago and can be said to be a whole new animal. Rousseau, of course, insists that his readers be skeptical of this human trait: "This distinctive and almost unlimited faculty, is the source of all man's miseries . . . [it] eventually makes him his own and Nature's tyrant."[16] It is what leads humans out of their original Garden of Eden, so to speak, and into a life of domination and control.

Perfectibility itself, however, did not stimulate evolution of the species. Rousseau contends that something else needed to happen to compel humans to develop their latent capacities. They needed some incentive to urge them to try to do new things. He decides material scarcity probably played this role. At some point, nature stopped being so bountiful, and survival became more difficult. Humans, as a result, had to be much more resourceful. To overcome nature's obstacles, they needed to develop their abilities, both physical and intellectual. They did—and learned how to manipulate nature through primitive technologies and to outwit stronger animals in a competition for resources. According to Rousseau, the exercise of ability, not the family, as Mandeville contends, yielded the first stirrings of *amour-propre*. In addition, as survival became more challenging, *les hommes sauvages* eventually apprehended their common interests and learned the value of collective action. At first, such occasions were rare and unreliable. Humans would quit cooperation if it failed to serve their immediate interests. Rousseau's famous example is a man defecting from a stag hunt to pursue a more obtainable rabbit. But as time passed, cooperation became more necessary and more frequent—people became more aware of others and how they more easily able mastered nature through collaborative ventures. As they came to acquire calculative reasoning, they could distinguish between short-term and long-term interests.

These collective activities paved the way for permanent social living arrangements. Progress was slow on this front as well. Rousseau claims it took tens if not hundreds of centuries for humans to abandon their nomadic lifestyles. Progress did occur, however, and the first societies, which took the form of families, at long last appeared. The family introduced an invention that further facilitated survival and ease of living: division of labor. Women were relegated to the domestic sphere, while the men did the hunting, gathering, and fishing. The family arrangement proved to be quite efficient at ensuring survival. With new tools and the division of labor, humans had more conveniences and leisure time than their forefathers.

Furthermore, increased leisure and shared living arrangements created the ideal conditions for the development of speech and language. While Rousseau considers these developments dangerous, as they are "the first source of evils they [*les hommes sauvages*] prepared for their descendants,"[17] he also thinks that these early families represented the happiest age in the life of the species.[18] If they began to experience luxuries and idleness, they did so in small doses and hence were not corrupted by them. And, ever the romantic, Rousseau thinks families experienced "the sweetest sentiments known to man, conjugal love, and Paternal love."[19] In addition, he explains away as harmless the dependencies and hierarchies inherent in family life. They do not lead to domination and tyranny, because they are "natural and temporary."[20]

The next step in Rousseau's evolutionary narrative is the foundation of society itself, which results from the banding together of different families. This is a crucial phase in human development, as it is the first time that humans live in close proximity to many other humans. Invariably, Rousseau speculates, different families developed bonds with other families. Younger members of the opposite sex started to notice one another, which led everyone to start considering their neighbors.[21] As Cooper puts it, "More than just living with others, he [the individual] lives *in* and *through* them."[22] *Amour-propre*, thus, was set in motion. At this stage, Rousseau introduces his parable of the competition for esteem, in which people compete to become the best singers, dancers, orators, and so on.

As I argued in Chapter 1, Rousseau in the competition for esteem identifies the fundamental conditions that give rise to the classical aristocratic ethos: a sense of identity and belief in one's innate superiority. In constant contact and close proximity with one another, these new civil humans became used to seeing others and being seen by them. As a result, they started to develop public identities and became aware of themselves as distinct selves. Social living thus fomented a cognitive revolution. As humans became individuals and developed a sentiment of identity, they learned to think reflectively and self-consciously. Furthermore, it bears repeating, talent and physical attractiveness were the basis of these public identities. In their newly formed communities, people soon realized that these traits did not develop equally in all members of the species. Some individuals were faster, smarter, more eloquent, and more handsome than others. These inequalities proved to be ubiquitous, and civil humans started to obsess about them. They soon became the foundation of all individual identities. People became known by how well they could sing, dance, orate, and so on.

Implied in the competition for esteem, moreover, is that individuals can develop an identity based on their deficiencies. A person, for example, can develop an identity of unusual clumsiness. Others may fail to develop much of an identity at all, if they have no distinguishing traits. These unfortunate individuals have no discernible public identity and are socially invisible.[23] Social classes thus emerged. There was a class of winners who could distinguish themselves based on some attribute and a class of losers who could not. The emotional results, however, are equally corrupting, as everyone comes to suffer from a bad or "inflamed" sort of *amour-propre*. In the winners it is manifested as vanity, arrogance, and contempt for the losers; in the losers, shame, envy, and spite. Natural compassion begins to wane as people use their cognitive abilities of empathy only to manipulate others to obtain the favorable recognition they all come to crave. Thus, Rousseau's natural history of the species boils down to the development of human ability and the eventual ranking of people based on these abilities—a development, it is worth adding, that did not necessarily have to occur.

Granted, this interpretation of Rousseau's state of nature and his passage on the competition for esteem is debatable. Allegories by definition are mysterious and contain hidden meanings. However, Rousseau repeats his argument several times in literal form throughout the text. In four distinct passages, he explicitly states that *amour-propre* originates from the social overvaluation of talent and innate inequalities. First, in the competition for esteem, right after itemizing the various talents that earn an individual public esteem, he states that public recognition of talents "was the first step at once toward *inequality* and vice."[24] Second, he suggests that equality in civil society could have continued only "if talents had been equal."[25] Third, he asserts that "here are all natural qualities put into action, every man's rank and fate is established, not only as to the amount of their goods and the power to help or harm, but also as to mind, beauty, strength or skill, as merit or talent."[26] Finally, he bluntly states: "I would show that of these four sorts of inequality [wealth, nobility, and rank are the others] . . . personal qualities are the origin of all others"[27] and, a little later in the paragraph, "I would show how much this universal desire for reputation, honors, and preferment which consumes us all and exercises and compares talents and strengths, how much it excites and multiplies the passions and, in making all men competitors, rivals, or enemies."[28] It is thus fair to interpret the *Second Discourse* as a generalized version of the polemic against the intellectuals put forth in the *First Discourse*. The target now is anyone who manages to distinguish himself or herself by talent and achievement.

Critics, however, can point to some passages in which Rousseau appears to discount the importance of talent in his narrative. Specifically, in the "Exordium," he makes a distinction between moral and natural inequality that potentially undermines my interpretation. Moral inequality is artificial and depends on convention or agreement of some kind. This includes different privileges or differences in wealth, honor, or power. These inequalities cannot exist in a state of nature and only emerge in civil or political society. By contrast, natural inequality consists in differences in age, health, bodily strength, qualities of mind or sprit, and so forth. They are the attributes with which humans are born. Rousseau thinks it is pointless to speculate where they come from, "because the answer would be given by the simple definition of the word."[29] It is thus plausible to interpret him as arguing there is no point in examining natural inequalities. Furthermore, he concludes the essay by contending that "moral inequality . . . is contrary to Natural Right whenever it is not directly proportional to Physical inequality."[30] Rousseau here appears to be defending natural inequality and insisting only that it be appropriately recognized by conventions and societal institutions. Concerning politics, for example, he argues several times in his works for government by an elected aristocracy.[31] Many important Rousseau scholars, including Dent and Neuhouser, are impressed with these passages and suggest Rousseau's interest is only in the social destruction caused by artificial inequalities.[32] Dent attributes to Rousseau the belief that "Bacon, Descartes and Newton do not diminish us, they enlarge the possibilities of life for each of us."[33] Neuhouser argues that natural inequality is not the source of *amour-propre* but the reverse. *Amour-propre* itself leads to inequality, which can take numerous forms, such as the pursuit of wealth, conspicuous consumption, or anything else to "keep up with the Joneses."[34] That inequality has a natural foundation, Neuhouser claims, is limited at best.

This case, however, is not as strong as it appears on the surface. There are no obvious conclusions to draw from the fact that it is impossible to know the origin of natural inequalities. Rousseau never states natural inequalities are beyond the scope of his inquiry. Moreover, in addition to the allegorical evidence from the competition for esteem, I have cited four distinct passages in which he explicitly states that natural inequalities are the source of conventional inequalities. It would be strange to make an argument four separate times in a seventy-page essay unless the author thought it important.

Also, simply because Rousseau is comfortable with hierarchies and natural inequalities does not mean that he endorses a classic aristocratic worldview or modern meritocracy. He can simultaneously believe that the best and brightest should perform the most challenging and important activities in a society and at the same time reject the ideologies of Ajax and the *philosophes*. What concerns him is not talent itself but how people think about and value talent. Rousseau objects to the celebration of the talented as a special class of humans that are the best the species has to offer. In other words, his aim is to decouple talent from honor—to divorce talent from classical aristocratic trappings in which a person is defined and valued based on his or her abilities.[35] If this does not happen, Rousseau predicts two negative consequences. The first is that it will lead to the bad forms of *amour-propre*. The winners in society will become arrogant and cruel, while the losers will become envious and spiteful. The second is that meritocracy itself will be undermined. When the talented are publicly honored and rewarded, everyone will want to be the best and pretend to possess excellence.[36] Ambitious people will scheme to convince others they are the true aristocrats and through sheer cunning will displace the genuinely talented. Hypocrisy will win the day, and as a result society will be stuck with a fraudulent elite populated by charlatans and phonies lacking in merit and virtue.[37]

Thus, for Rousseau, societies should exploit talent whenever possible but do so in an understated manner in which superior individuals are not publicly recognized as a higher form of the species. If Descartes and Bacon are not to diminish their fellow citizens and encourage dissimulation, in other words, they must not become *aristos* in a new sense. Instead, people's public identities should come from sources people can equally participate in, such as religion or patriotism. All moral inequalities—that is, publicly sanctioned ones— should be rooted in such qualities as virtue, humanity, courage, and moderation.[38] This theme runs throughout all his works and is present even in the passages in which Rousseau argues for the utility of *amour-propre*. Thus, he still agrees with Malebranche's *amour de l'Ordre*.[39] He just wants to honor it in a manner consistent with the development of healthy moral personalities.

From *Amour-Propre* to *"Amour-Propre* Interested" to *Libido Dominandi*

The *Second Discourse*, of course, does not end with the emergence of *amour-propre*, most likely because Rousseau realized that he needed to do more than point out the psychological corruptions caused by it and the societal overvaluation of talent. The variety of theorists who argued for the utility of the passion probably would not be convinced that emotional distress outweighs tangible social benefits such as the reduction of poverty. Thus, Rousseau argues that *amour-propre* has wide-ranging effects that go well beyond its immediate psychological consequences.

As part II of the discourse develops, Rousseau makes his distinctly Augustinian move. He argues that *amour-propre* turns into a *libido dominandi*.[40] Like Augustine, he identifies a degenerative process in which ordinary vices become brutal ones—and he describes it as more than a tendency. For the winners in the competition for esteem, it is not enough to be superior to their neighbors. They become inclined to demean, harm, and even tyrannize them. When "inflamed," therefore, *amour-propre* ceases to be useful and gives rise to innumerable social evils.

The first step in his argument is to show what happens to *amour-propre* when it operates in an integrated and organized economy, which Rousseau claims was set in motion by the application of metallurgy to agriculture.[41] This development radically alters the nature of work. Before society, people worked independently in solitude. Rousseau views this form of labor mostly in positive terms: "So long as they applied themselves only to tasks a single individual could perform, and to arts that did not require collaboration of several hands, they lived free, healthy, good, and happy as far as they could by

their Nature be, and continued to enjoy the gentleness of independent deal-
ings with one another."[42] As humans began to master nature through technological inventions, however, economic production became more sophisticated
and more collaborative. To most effectively utilize new technologies and increase economic output, humans invented a new method for the organization
of production—the division of labor. Or more accurately, they applied the
division of labor from the family to economic production. Each person did
one part of a larger, coordinated task. One consequence of this change was the
integration of labor. Workers became dependent upon each other; one person's job could not be done unless others adequately performed their jobs. As
a result, everyone was far more aware of what his or her neighbors were doing
each day. There was no way to avoid seeing and being seen by others.

In addition, these new production methods led to greater inequalities
and new hierarchies. New technologies and production methods required
more brain power. Those with the strongest intellects assumed the most difficult jobs and became more indispensable. A cognitive hierarchy emerged
(though Rousseau does not discount the importance of physical strength and
chance for success in this new economy), which made it simple to evaluate
and judge everyone in society. People could measure their abilities and talents
simply by comparing the difficulty of different occupations. A person's role in
the division of labor, in other words, broadcast to the whole society a person's
social value and, hence, self-worth. In commercial societies, the labor market
is therefore akin to the battlefield in the classical Greek aristocratic culture. It
is how people become *aristos*.

This transformed *amour-propre* into a new passion, which Rousseau terms
"*amour-propre* interested" (though he uses the phrase only once).[43] *Amour-
propre* interested is a combination of the desire for superiority and the desire
for material gain.[44] *Amour de soi-même* blends with *amour-propre*. As the
aforementioned economic developments became firmly established, everyone
realized they would be ranked and compensated on the basis of his or her
strengths, skills, and talents. Those with more challenging jobs surmised they
could demand financial rewards commensurate with their superior economic
role. In other words, people wanted to be rich and believed they deserved to
be so on the basis of their innate talents. Ability, at least in theory, translated
into socioeconomic rank. Aristocracy thus turned into oligarchy.

According to Rousseau's formulation here, the motivations for wealth are
both democratic and aristocratic. On the democratic side of the ledger, individuals had to seek wealth to satisfy primitive needs for survival and well-

being, or *amour de soi-même*. In an integrated economy, survival becomes a public competition akin to the competition for esteem in the first human societies. To properly take care of oneself and to live a comfortable and luxurious existence, individuals had to worry about being best. With regard to aristocratic motives, wealth accumulation has vital symbolic value. People purchase and show off luxury items in order to publicly reveal their innate superiority—a behavior commonly referred to as conspicuous consumption. External rewards are supposed to reflect internal qualities. Just as Homeric heroes collected *timé*, or honor, after performing well in battle to publicly demonstrate their superiority and secured *kleos*, or glory, productive and talented people in commercial societies come to desire tangible representations of their successes. Thus, merged with economic concerns, Rousseau claims that *amour-propre* "inclines every individual to set a greater store for himself than by anyone else."[45]

Rousseau eagerly informs those theorists who believe such a system is the most just and economically efficient that it will never exist in its pristine theoretical form. In a meritocracy in which the best are entitled to the largest shares of societal honor and material comforts, humans will invariably become deceitful and cunning. Desires for self-preservation and glory, or *amour de soi-même* and *amour-propre*, will prompt people to become the best by any means necessary, even dishonest means. Persons with few abilities will quickly learn to feign otherwise if they wish to eat well and not live demeaning lives on the bottom rungs of society. Rousseau suspects they will often succeed, or at least often enough that hypocrisy will taint all human interaction and ensure that the true best and brightest will not rise to the top.

Worse still, "*amour-propre* interested" will result in dangerous concentrations of wealth that open the door for coercion and abuse. Although Rousseau does not provide a detailed analysis, claiming that almost anyone can figure it out,[46] he does offer a basic outline. Driven by *amour-propre* interested, the wealthy become intent on amassing more riches. They become addicted to "trinkets of frivolous utility" for their symbolic value and develop an endless array of consumptive appetites to ensure a comfortable existence. A race among the wealthy ensues. They all try to get their hands on every last dime in society so they can be the most respected and most comfortable. The poor become pawns in this game, as the wealthy classes discover or invent new ways to get them to serve their needs, be it the fear of starvation or some other contrivance designed to "interest" poor people "in [their] fate and to make them really or apparently find their own profit in working for [them]."[47] Thus, the harmony of interests argued for by the theorists of commerce—"that Society is so constituted that every man gains by serving the rest"[48]—is really a system in which wealthy people exploit the poor for their own vain ends.

As the wealthy successfully accumulated much of society's wealth, *amour-propre* interested transformed itself into something like Augustine's *libido dominandi*. Wealth and power, Rousseau decides, are corrupting. As he bluntly puts it in his "Letter to Beaumont," "Men become wicked."[49] Why? The answer appears to be ennui. The richer people become, the less satisfying they find their wealth. They soon tire of mere consumption and can no longer flatter their *amour-propre* through it.[50] The law of diminishing returns set in; the "trinkets of frivolous utility" cease to have allure. At this point, the pure form of *amour-propre* reasserts itself, and material self-interest becomes less and less of a motive. As their boredom festers, the wealthy classes look for new means with which to enjoy their superiority. The only thing that gives them any pleasure is domination, which can take a few forms. It can be a simple desire to deprive people beneath them and possess things no one else can. As Rousseau puts it, the rich come to enjoy things "only to the extent that others are deprived of them."[51] This desire is not necessarily dangerous. It may be satisfied through the purchase of luxury items or unique experiences, such as a yacht or front row tickets to a sporting event or concert, that do not harm anyone's life prospects. At its worst, however, it can result in depriving the more vulnerable segments of the population of resources necessary for social mobility, such as a high quality education, or even survival itself. Domination can also take much darker forms and drive people to willfully ruin and tyrannize those beneath them. Rousseau's wording here is chilling. People, especially the rich, have "a black inclination to harm one another."[52] They become "ravenous wolves which once they have tasted human flesh scorn all other good, from then on want to devour only men."[53] Ratcheting up the rhetoric even further, Rousseau claims: "My *hero* will end up by cutting every throat until he is the sole master of the universe."[54] *Libido dominandi* indeed. This argument represents the heart of the *Second Discourse*. While the discourse is ostensibly about the origin of inequality, Rousseau seems most interested in its consequences. That is, the masters of the new economic, political, and intellectual universes will enslave the remaining population.

Furthermore, Rousseau subscribed to this view throughout most if not all of his life. In the *Dialogues*, he contends that as *amour-propre* develops, "it no longer seeks satisfaction in our own benefit but solely in the harm of another."[55] Even those who seek wealth to make the world a better place through charity, he warns, cannot help but be corrupted by it. In "On Wealth," he instructs a friend that it is impossible to be "truly human and remain wealthy."[56] The fact is that while "one desires it to make good use of it [wealth] . . . one no longer makes good use of it when one has it."[57] Invariably, it will "harden your soul."[58] Thus, just as Augustine thought *amor sui* and love of glory would eventually lead people to seek control and domination, Rousseau argues that commercial motives, when combined with *amour-propre*, eventually degenerate into tyrannical ones.[59]

To be sure, Rousseau's causal narrative of the transformation of love of glory to love of domination is more complicated than Augustine's. Rousseau adds the step of *amour-propre* interested to Augustine's formula and throws greed into the mix of motives that lead to *libido dominandi*. This makes sense, as Rousseau is writing in the context of emerging commercial capitalism. He knows that in the eighteenth century honor and wealth cannot easily be separated. Some people are honored for the simple reason they are wealthy. Augustine, conversely, is less distrustful of wealth and believes it can be divorced from pride to neutralize its potential dangers. He subscribed to the maxim, "get rid of pride, and riches will do no harm."[60] In addition, Augustine is more skeptical than Rousseau and describes the process of *amour-propre* leading to cruelty and domination as a tendency, not a fait accompli. Nonetheless, the structural similarities between the two narratives are undeniable. Rousseau's story of *amour-propre* is thoroughly Augustinian.

In any event, to finish off Mandeville, Rousseau concludes his argument by highlighting the disutility of all this class warfare and domination. Interestingly, it is the rich, not the poor, who have it worse. Their wealth and property give them a greater stake in security, as they have far more to lose: "The rich, above all, must soon have sensed how disadvantageous to them was a perpetual war of which they alone bore the full cost."[61] The poor, conversely, have nothing to lose but their chains and have every reason to disrupt the existing state of affairs. To secure their wealth and power, the rich commit their greatest act of treachery. They deceive the poor into joining a state designed to protect their ill-gotten gains and maintain the status quo. The means by which they dominate their weaker brethren, of course, is left fully intact by the liberal freedoms and rights they promise to all. Easily fooled by the ideological machinations of their oppressors, Rousseau claims in some of the most memorable language in the discourse, the poor "all ran toward their chains in the belief that they were securing their freedom."[62]

The establishment of an effective government, however, proved difficult.

Rousseau thinks a government never fully succeeds. Like Augustine, he warns the supporters of commerce that the *libido dominandi* of the wealthy was bound to subvert itself, and it does. The final stage of his speculative anthropology is despotism. All wanting to be the best, the wealthy and powerful members of society compete to destroy one another and wipe out all their potential opposition. One by one, masters fall into the slave class until there is only one despot and a population of slaves. According to Rousseau, in such despotism humans return full circle to their original equality—they are but one person away from it. This equality, however, is one of poverty, oppression, and misery. In the *Second Discourse*, *libido dominandi* lives up to its name and expresses itself as a brutal tyranny.

Rousseau's discourse never attracted widespread sympathy, even among later critics of commercial democracy. If they shared the distrust Rousseau had of the wealthy, they would not follow his critique of talent. Those who revolted in his name during the French Revolution took it as an article of faith that occupations and social rewards ought to be distributed to the most talented. Other potential ideological soulmates, such as the leftist Hegelians, including Ludwig Feuerbach and Karl Marx, are far more favorable toward talent and refuse to see it as the cause of class politics, domination, and political tyranny. Both attempt to liberate human talents and productive capacities from God and capitalism, respectively, and to restore them to the center of human nature.

Even philosophers who are skeptical of meritocracy, such as Rawls, cannot be considered close allies of Rousseau.[63] In *A Theory of Justice*, Rawls rejects meritocracy on the grounds people do not deserve their talents and work ethic, as they did nothing other than win the genetic lottery to attain them.[64] Consequently, he argues that successful people are not entitled to fully benefit from their worldly successes and must share their rewards with the least fortunate members of society. Parts of his argument are Rousseauian. Like Rousseau, Rawls worries that unbridled economic opportunities might lead to considerable inequalities that might render formal political freedom and equality as worthless. Also, Rawls includes the social bases of self-respect among his primary goods and fully appreciates the importance of self-esteem.[65] Although he does not use the term *amour-propre*, he plainly understands the importance of passions and emotions such as envy in economic and political life.

Nonetheless, there is still a wide gap separating the two theorists. Aside from the obvious point that Rawls privileges freedom over equality and is far more appreciative of commercial capitalism, Rousseau would probably also contend that Rawls fails to adequately address the personality corruptions caused by inequality and their possible consequences. The central concern of Rawls is justice, and he only makes the case that merit is undeserved. Rousseau's primary worry, by contrast, is domination. Inequality, he thinks, is primarily a psychological problem. It implants in the strong and powerful a desire to be cruel. From Rousseau's perspective, the assumption by Rawls that people are rational and just precludes him from addressing the real reasons his difference principle will never be implemented. The strong and the powerful are corrupted by their strength and power. Hence, they will probably be immune to Rawls's attempts to encourage them to be compassionate and empathetic through such devices as the veil of ignorance and minimax calculations. In his student lectures, Rawls himself acknowledges the gulf that separates his project and Rousseau's, arguing that the *Second Discourse* can be made consistent with *The Social Contract* only if Dent's interpretation of *amour-propre* is correct and the perverse form of *amour-propre* can be neutralized.[66]

It is thus an open question whether Rousseau's argument would attract many takers beyond Ferguson and Young. Rousseau's criticisms of the *philosophes* appear to leave him almost alone on his own island.

The Minimal Self: Solutions to the Problems of *Amour-Propre* and *Libido Dominandi*

Much of Rousseau's career was devoted to resolving the issues of inequality, *amour-propre*, and domination. The general will and education of Emile are undoubtedly his two great solutions, though his oeuvre contains several more that are worked out to varying degrees. Rousseau was constantly looking for ways to at least contain *amour-propre* and keep it from turning into *libido dominandi*. It is difficult to argue that he succeeds. His proposals are not fully developed and often threaten to undermine his commitment to his central value of freedom. Most readers leave his writings with more questions than answers. Furthermore, few of his solutions are entirely consistent with each other and tend to have different, sometimes radically different, points of emphasis. The nationalistic call for civic virtue in *The Social Contract*, for example, is at odds with the cosmopolitanism defended in *Emile*. Scholars, of course, frequently make this complaint against Rousseau's work as a whole, not just his views of *amour-propre*.

Still, all Rousseau's various solutions, even the ones that appear diametrically opposed, share two basic premises. The first is to minimize the importance of individual identity or the self, and the second is to deemphasize the social value of individual excellences.[67] In short, they all disrupt the formula for an aristocratic personality and try to ensure that natural inequalities do not structure social interaction. There is very little disagreement as to how Rousseau solves the first problem—namely, minimizing the self. His most famous solutions to *amour-propre*—the ones from *Emile* and *The Social Contract*—seek to unify people through the establishment of collective identities that become the primary love of all men and women. These include not just civic virtue and the cosmopolitan love of humanity but also attachments to families and neighborhoods. The second element of the aristocratic equation, the public celebration of excellence, has led to much more confusion. Rousseau is not against talent and excellence. As I argued earlier, however, he worries that the elevation of the few will demoralize the many and tries find a way to cultivate and exploit talents to the benefit of the larger community without creating a new class of heroes or making talents the basis of individual identities. He walks a fine line in his attempts to do so and is not always clear about his ambivalence.

Hiding the Aristocracy in Political Administration

His first attempt to blunt the effects of talent-based *amour-propre* can be linked to the distinction Rousseau makes between sovereignty and administration, which holds that the people ought to be sovereign and make the laws but that they require the assistance of an elite class of administrators to manage the day-to-day affairs of the state and execute the directives formulated by the people. As I mentioned, the call for an aristocratic administration shows up throughout his career. In the *First Discourse*, Rousseau instructs the learned and talented to "find honorable asylum in the courts."[68] He echoes this conclusion in later writings, such as *The Social Contract, Letters Written from the Mountain*, and the *Constitutional Project for Corsica*, by advocating for administrative rule by an elected aristocracy.[69] Thus, he is not completely anti-aristocracy. He criticizes only certain forms of it.

The proposal is a perfect example of the ambivalence Rousseau has about talent. He plainly accepts that there are natural inequalities and wishes to exploit them when they are of social value. Nowhere is this truer than in politics. The existence of an administrative aristocracy is appropriate because it is better to be ruled by genius than by imbecility. Intellectuals still have social value. They are necessary for competent government. Thus, in *Emile* Rousseau relays an anecdote in which a Spartan who loses election to a council nonetheless cheerfully returns home pleased with the fact that there were three hundred individuals more qualified than he for the job.[70]

Rousseau is adamant, however, that his elective aristocracy should not behave like Homeric heroes or feudal lords. They are not to be honored as the best that the species has to offer, nor should they even have a cultural presence. They should not represent themselves to the public in any manner. People may not even know who they are. Rather, they are to work behind the scenes so as not to threaten collective identities more consonant with freedom, such as "citizen."

Presumably, this is why Rousseau thinks administration is a safe outlet for the best and brightest. Tucked away in government, they will be less noticeable to the public. Few people, I suspect, are aware who writes a budget or performs any other executive function. Rousseau argues that with the best and brightest less visible, not many people will know of their excellences and feel demeaned by them. As a result, there will be little inclination on the part of the public to compare themselves to superior personalities in society and want to join their ranks. Talent-based identities will not supplant civic ones, and, Rousseau hopes, people will not ask if someone has talent but if he or she has virtue. And, of magistrates, whether or not they possess both.[71] Furthermore, geniuses who manage to attain visibility within a government have no power to dominate and inflict cruelty on the population. The sovereign—that is, the people—will always be at least as powerful as the government and have numerous devices with which to check mischievous government actors.

Rousseau's solution to the problem of honoring excellence is thus more refined than that of Nicole, who supports rule by a feudal aristocracy to prevent a tyranny of the talented. Rousseau finesses the problem and carves out room for the intellectuals to serve their fellow humans through their talents without tempting their *amour-propre*. Accordingly, he does not sacrifice good government to keep the better sorts in check.

Moreover, his administration proposal appears to have been a point of contention with the *philosophes*, particularly d'Alembert. While Rousseau is willing to give the intellectual elite administrative power in exchange for cultural superiority, d'Alembert counsels the opposite. He argues that the excellent men should be sovereign and should assiduously avoid administration and political power.[72] He wants the best and brightest to guide the culture and chart the progress of the species.[73] Far from playing an anonymous role in society, he insists they be celebrated as the finest the species has to offer. As I demonstrated in Chapter 1, they are the true aristocracy and ought to be recognized as such. There is also low-level evidence that Diderot follows d'Alembert on this point. To recall a passage cited earlier from his *Fils naturel*, Constance tells Dorval he must use his talents to serve society in general, not the government specifically.[74] He is to be a leader, not an invisible member of the supporting cast doing the bidding of the people.

As a matter of policy, Rousseau's proposal seems somewhat harsh, as it may not be fair to force geniuses to hole themselves up in the government. Not everyone is cut out for administration. It is possible, however, that Rousseau is not being completely literal and simply means to suggest one possible solution to his aristocrat problem. He only wants to ensure that Bacon and Descartes do not become idols of the population and are not publicly defined by their excellences. If this could be achieved without their retreating to court, then presumably Rousseau would be mollified. It is possible for cultures to support a thriving intellectual culture without deifying the intellectuals themselves. As previously discussed, Rousseau cites the ancients as an example in "My Portrait," as neither Homer nor Virgil (nor any other writer) was considered a great man.[75] In such societies, artists and scientists can, as Dent suggests, "enlarge the possibilities of life" for everyone else without simultaneously demeaning them.

Granted, this may be easier said than done. As Élisabeth Badinter warns in her consideration of the intellectual desire for glory in seventeenth- and eighteenth-century France, where the *libido sciendi* exists, "the *libido dominandi* is never very far."[76] In other words, intellectuals, excited by their achievements, may be overcome with desire for honor and glory. Still, it is a theoretical possibility, even if it is highly unlikely—especially in commercial democracies in Enlightenment Europe.

Civic Virtue and the General Will

It is obvious how the general will solves the problem of *amour-propre* as I have interpreted it. To reiterate, it seeks to promote a collective identity designed to trump individual ones. According to Rousseau, each person has two wills or selves: a private will reflecting narrow self-interest and a general will, or *moi commun*, that adopts the standpoint of the citizen.[77] Throughout *The Social Contract*, Rousseau continuously tries to generalize the will. Consequently, he leaves no room for an aristocratic ethos. Individuality and talent are neither rewarded nor honored. Everyone is defined by his or her dual roles of sovereign and citizen, not by his or her excellences. The "common me" is prior to the individualistic idea of me. The primary issue with this analysis is textual. The ostensible point of establishing dominant collective identities is to protect freedom, not dampen *amour-propre*. Rousseau never mentions the term in *The Social Contract*. In fact, for some unknown reason, he refuses to introduce it even when his analysis opens the door for it. In describing why humans became so corrupt in the state of nature, he does not bring up his narrative from the *Second Discourse*. Instead, he pleads ignorance: "How did this change [human selfishness and conflict] come about? I do not know."[78]

Nonetheless, Rousseau's freedom is distinctly Augustinian in important respects and is easy to connect to *amour-propre*. The goal of the general will is to avert the domination inspired by *amour-propre* described in part II of the *Second Discourse*, in which the wealthy and powerful "ravenous wolves" feast on their fellow citizens. Although Rousseau is most famous for being a proponent of positive liberty, or what he terms "moral freedom," his starting point is negative liberty. His primary concern is to protect individuals from the intrusions of other individuals, or anything that involves one person becoming an extension of another's will. In *Letters Written from the Mountain*, Rousseau explicitly defines freedom in this negative manner: "Liberty consists less in doing one's own will than in not being subject to someone else's; it also consists in not subjecting someone else's will to ours."[79] By contrast, his defense of positive or moral freedom it mostly an afterthought. This freedom is a consequence of his social contract rather than a stated goal and is described as a consolation for losing some of the advantages of the state of nature.[80]

The narrative of book I of *The Social Contract* confirms this analysis. People leave the state of nature to preclude the possibility of domination. Without an effective authority, anyone at any moment could be the victim of coercion. In addition, Rousseau designs his own social contract to prevent both persons (or groups) and the state from injuring individual citizens. With regard to persons, the condition of membership in a state is that everyone is required to forfeit all rights and powers enjoyed in the state of nature and put them in service of the general will. This way, no one has rights and powers with which to harm his or her neighbors. Concerning the state, Rousseau makes it so that every citizen has an equal voice in government and is responsible for any limitations imposed on individual citizens. Since everyone is both sovereign and citizen, he assumes all are adequately protected against state domination. Nobody in their right mind would oppress himself or herself.

Furthermore, Rousseau devotes considerable attention to criticizing popular political theorists whom he thinks fail to address the problems of inequality and domination. In particular, he takes two of the great seventeenth-century architects of social contract theory, Hugo Grotius and Locke, to task for defending all sorts of dangerous inequalities and asymmetries that allow for coercive authorities, as well as chastising Aristotle and Robert Filmer for, respectively, promoting slavery and tyranny within the family.

After the general will has been established, Rousseau takes other precautions to ensure tyranny and domination are kept at bay. Individuals who attempt to manipulate public deliberations to suit their private interests will be "forced to be free." Such individuals are coerced to live up to their agreement because they threaten the freedom of those who remain faithful to the collective by surreptitiously forcing them to serve their interests. In short, they are forced to change and be free because they are harming others. Rousseau also puts in place measures to prevent the forming of factions, such as limiting all political discussion to formal political venues. Finally, he is careful to prevent economic tyrannies. His society of the general will maintains rough economic equality so that no citizen is rich enough to buy others and none so poor that he must sell himself or herself.[81]

Rousseau, however, does not wish to annihilate individuality. Once he is confident that he has blocked the possibility of political and economic domination, he limits the reach of the general will and carves out plenty of room for private wills.[82] In his system, only the public self is subject to the general will.[83] People retain natural rights and freedoms, including private property, as private individuals who are independent of the sovereign. Each citizen, Rousseau claims, has a zone of privacy that cannot be violated by the sovereign and "can fully dispose . . . of his goods and freedom as are left him by these conventions [the general will]."[84] Granted, the sovereign is responsible for determining exactly what counts as a community concern. Still, since everyone is both sovereign and subject, it is unlikely he or she would define the public concern too broadly, as her or she too would suffer from an unduly intrusive state. Rousseau is committed to allowing citizens the right to cultivate their own gardens so long as it does not undermine collective political life and allow for the possibility of domination. He tries to minimize the individual self, not eliminate it.

The same is true for wealth. Rousseau never attempts to create an economically egalitarian society and interferes with individual finance only if it can result in one person coercing another. No one, he thinks, should be rich enough to buy others, and none should be so poor they must sell himself or herself to others. In *Emile*, he provides a model of how a wealthy person might live without arousing the dangerous forms of *amour-propre* and threatening the freedom of his or her neighbors.[85] A rich Rousseau would live close to nature, refuse all ostentation, and have as few servants as possible.[86] He would use his riches to buy leisure and independence rather than to dominate others. A rich Rousseau would also assiduously avoid becoming a slave to his appetites and enslaving others through economic power. Money cannot be a person's primary love for any reason without being corrupted by it.[87] When this happens, "finance" becomes a "slave's word."[88] Last, a rich Rousseau would "never . . . create a feeling of inequality."[89] In other words, Rousseau would never publicize his economic superiority or seek recognition for it. His wealth would be a mere fact about him, like his height or weight, and would have no social meaning. So, economic inequality can and will exist in a society governed by the general will. Wealth, however, will never be permitted to translate into power.

The only place Rousseau aggressively promotes strict equality is in the realm of citizenship. Each citizen is to be completely equal; all contribute equally to public discussions and are equally valued. Likewise, how a person learns to become a citizen is highly egalitarian. Rousseau thinks that responsible citizenship and civic virtue are attainable by anyone. There is no special or aristocratic class of individuals who are superior in terms of the general will. If properly denatured by the lawgiver, everyone has the wherewithal to live according to it, at least for a time. Importantly, the general will cannot be learned through contemplation or study. It is not a question of knowledge or reason.[90] According to Rousseau, everyone begins equally ignorant of the general will and is assumed to be too corrupt to adhere to it. Thus, the individual responsible for teaching it, the lawgiver, does not rely on intellect to persuade future citizens to accept the ethic of the general will. Rather, he or she makes use of religion and superstition, the opposite of enlightenment. People reason from the general will, not to it. Essentially, the lawgiver teaches people to be public spirited and to love the state, which requires no special cognitive abilities.

Arthur Schopenhauer mocks civic virtue or patriotism "as the cheapest sort of pride" for this very reason. He writes, "But every miserable fool who has nothing at all of which he can be proud adopts, as the last resource, pride in the nation to which he belongs."[91] This accessibility, however, is exactly what Rousseau likes about it. Citizenship is perfectly democratic, which means that people's primary public identity is equal and free from the *amour-propre* that characterizes aristocratic societies. People can thus primarily engage one another as equals.

None of this suggests, however, that Augustine would be sympathetic toward Rousseau's general will. Although Riley successfully argues that Rousseau constructs the general will out of the neo-Augustinian Malebranche's notion of general providence,[92] it is easy to imagine several Augustinian criticisms to Rousseau's secular solution to the problem of the Fall. It is doubtful that he would agree lawgivers could socialize people to interpret their sinful self-interest in collective terms or accept that it is possible to remake human consciousness. Despite the fact that Augustine argues in *Ten Homilies* that *amour-propre* can be redirected for positive purposes, his notion of rigorism implies that no human lawgiver could possibly drum out of humans the crude *amor sui* caused by the Fall. The sins of vanity, greed, and lust are too ingrained in the species to be replaced a secular love—that is, love of the state.

Augustine's deconstruction of Roman patriotism in *City of God* likewise casts doubt on Rousseau's lawgiver thesis. The civic virtue and patriotism expressed by the citizens living under the general will, Augustine might argue, most likely reflects little more than the traditional, vicious form of *amour-propre*. Just as Roman civic virtue was in reality love of glory, those claiming dedication to the general will might camouflage their personal ambitions in order to abuse their fellow citizens. It is easy to imagine an individual manipulating patriotic sentiment to further his or her own narrow self-interest. As Samuel Johnson remarks, "Patriotism is the last refuge of a scoundrel."[93] While Johnson qualifies his statement by claiming he is only speaking of a dishonest patriotism that is a "cloak for self-interest" and not an honest love of country, Augustine believes it is impossible to sort out the scoundrels from the patriots. Since vanity presents itself so much like civic virtue, there is no way to tell one from the other. It thus may be impossible to identify the individuals who have to be forced to be free. Augustine makes hypocrisy, in other words, an irresolvable problem. Much as Rousseau might want to direct his readers to the positive dimensions of patriotism, his Augustinianism makes his job harder.

The only part of Rousseau's lawgiver proposal with which Augustine would agree is Rousseau's admission that the existence of such an individual is a remote possibility.[94] After the Fall, no one is virtuous enough to perform the role of the lawgiver. No human soul is capable of acting in such a divine fashion.

Thus, there are limits to Rousseau's Augustinianism. While Rousseau sets up the problem of social living in a manner similar to Augustine, his rejection of Augustine's theology result in his adopting radically different solutions. In his *Confessions*, Rousseau calls himself a "half-Jansenist." At best, he is a half-Augustinian as well.

This should serve as an important lesson for political theorists. Scholars have not been shy about linking Rousseau to the ancient world. He has been interpreted as a Platonist,[95] a cynic,[96] a neo-Epicurean,[97] and a Stoic.[98] There is persuasive evidence to buttress each of these claims. I have tried to show that he should also be considered an Augustinian. I do not, however, want to suggest that he is only an Augustinian. Christopher Brooke rightly argues that it is "silly" and "misleading" to place Rousseau in a philosophical camp. He is simultaneously a Platonist, a Stoic, an Epicurean, and an Augustinian—and one could probably go on. He was well read and borrowed moral vocabulary from different traditions as it suited his purposes. Most of all, he was Rousseau, a highly original thinker who baked marvelous social criticism out of a variety of ancient and modern philosophical ingredients.[99] It is naïve to think that the whole of his thought could be explained by pinpointing one philosophical influence.

The Cosmopolitanism of Emile

Published only a week later, *Emile* follows *The Social Contract* in trying to minimize the importance of both the social estimation of talent and individuality. The overall strategy is roughly similar. Rousseau seeks to create a collective identity superior to any individual identity. The particulars, however, could not be more different. Gone are civic virtue and lawgivers, which are replaced by a cosmopolitan species consciousness and a tutor who exploits biological drives and *amour-propre* itself to lead people away from the worst forms of it.

As with the *Second Discourse*, sexuality plays an important role in the socialization process. When Emile reaches puberty, his sexual desires dictate that he must enter the social world. This can be dangerous, as sexuality encourages people to seek both superiority and celebrity. As with *amour-propre*, however, he contends that sexuality can be sublimated and redirected into healthier outlets, such as friendship and love of humanity itself. Rousseau does not assume this will be a difficult task to achieve, as sexuality first expresses itself as tenderness rather than lust. It seeks emotional connection and affection. The real challenge is to redirect such affection to extend to the whole species, family and strangers alike. In doing so, Emile will never desire to be superior to or dominate his fellow humans. Rather, he will learn to empathize with them and develop a species consciousness. According to Rousseau, empathy is best learned through vulnerability and misery. Most humans experience plenty of both, and Emile is educated to connect his suffering to that of others. Just as Augustine believes shared recognition of sin can draw humans together, Rousseau contends weakness makes people compassionate and sociable. To stay connected to his weakness and vulnerability, Emile thus will be neither rich nor powerful. Elites tend to lack empathy because they cannot imagine themselves in the place of their inferiors: "Why are kings without pity for their subjects? Because they count on never being mere men. Why are the rich so hard on the poor? It is because they have not fear of becoming poor. Why does the nobility have so great a contempt for the people? It is because a noble will never be a commoner."[100]

Emile's motives are still selfish—they come from *amour-propre*. But it is *amour-propre* in an extended sense. Emile privately reasons, "I am interested in him for love of myself."[101] Through self-love, Emile paradoxically develops a collective consciousness and concern for his fellow humans. Again, to reiterate, Rousseau often does not utilize *amour-propre* in the same way as Nicole or Mandeville. With few exceptions (perhaps as a cure for laziness), he believes it is a means through which to create another form of consciousness; it is transformative rather than merely redirected to mimic some noble or moral end. Emile is transformed by his *amour-propre* to become authentically compassionate in ways that Mandeville or Nicole's humans are not. *Amour-propre* is supposed to help create individuals who genuinely take interest in the fate of others, not self-serving hypocrites trying to lessen their own pain or earn the esteem of their peers. Rousseau seeks to create individuals who are truly compassionate, truly patriotic, or truly self-respecting, not ones who only appear to be. Thus, while Cooper is right to argue that Rousseau believes *amour-propre* can be used as a force for good, it is nonetheless helpful to distinguish his manipulations of the passion from the more popular formulations of his predecessors, such as Nicole and Mandeville.

In any event, as with the general will, there is a limit to the collective human identity Rousseau tries to cultivate in Emile. Species consciousness does not require people to stop being individuals. Unlike in *The Social Contract*, Emile the individual is supposed to be superior to Emile the citizen.[102] His first duty is always to himself. Emile even experiences a sort of perverse pleasure in pity when witnessing someone suffer; he "feels the pleasure of not suffering as he does."[103] Moreover, he will not be a crusader for social justice, nor will he to take pride in his moral superiority or try to conceive of himself as the embodiment of justice. His humility does not give rise to pride. Emile is very much a simple man who thinks of his own needs and feelings—that is, his *amour de soi-même*. Also, Emile cares about succeeding in his profession for selfish reasons. He still covets praise from his peers.

At the same time, however, Rousseau identifies maxims and attitudes that will prevent Emile's selfishness from developing into inflamed *amour-propre* and *libido dominandi*. Although Emile will be eager for praise, Rousseau follows Francis Hutcheson and Adam Smith in arguing that he will only accept it for truly praiseworthy acts.[104] He measures himself not against others individuals so much as against an external standard of excellence.[105] While Emile will be pleased at a job well done, Rousseau is clear that he is to value good work, not the individual worker. Talent can be inspirational, but only to motivate good work. If a pupil seems excessively pleased with praise or says, "I made that," Rousseau counsels the tutor to retort, "You or another, it makes no difference; in any event it is work well done."[106] Emile is to work hard and be competent, but his talents or accomplishments do not define his existence. He wants to do a good job, though not for the sake of vanity. He knows he did nothing to earn his talents, whatever they may be. He was born a certain way, and hence is "too sensible to be vain about a gift [he] did not give [himself]."[107]

Emile, moreover, is both fully aware of and indifferent to the distribution of natural inequalities in the population. He even knows and is comfortable with the fact that he is not especially talented. Given that talent has no bearing on honor and shame, there is no reason he should feel otherwise. Consequently, he has no ambition to rise above his station of artisan, craftsman, or farmer. There is not to be a trace of envy or spite in him. In Malebranchean fashion, he should and does accept his role in the natural order of things, for it is ambition that leads to *amour-propre*.[108] As Rousseau writes of himself in the *Dialogues*, "One of the things on which he congratulates himself is that in his old age he finds himself in just about the same rank as the one into which he was born."[109] Thus, Emile will have a minimal self, at least in terms of talent.[110] He will think of his needs and try to improve himself. But, Rousseau makes it impossible for him to define himself by or even take pride in his accomplishments. He is no aristocrat. He knows himself first and foremost as a human.[111]

Finally, given that he occupies a middling to lower rung on the social-status ladder, he lacks the resources to coerce others, even if he had such desires. He is a selfish man but also a humble and modest one. The world has nothing to fear from him.

The Sentiment of Existence in The Reveries

Rousseau presents a fourth means through which to lessen *amour-propre* and the aristocratic *ethos* in *The Reveries of the Solitary Walker*. In the "Fifth Walk," he fondly recalls the almost six weeks he spent on the remote Île de Saint-Pierre. During this time, he claims he could suspend much of his conscious life and experience only a "sentiment of existence." Given that the text describes the period immediately following his forced exile from Môtiers as a result of his controversial writings, it is hardly surprising that he wanted to radically alter his mind-set. He genuinely feared for his life and was hoping to forget that he was Jean-Jacques Rousseau, author.

The sentiment of existence appears to have much in common with the consciousness of *l'homme sauvage* from the *Second Discourse*.[112] In such a state, Rousseau claims that he is able to block out almost every cognitive process other than a sense of being. Time, pleasure or pain, desire or fear, or any other thoughts or passions do not affect him. Most important, he does not feel a trace of *amour-propre* or self-consciousness. He is only aware that he is an existent creature experiencing something. He claims it is a godlike experience rooted in emotional self-sufficiency.[113] Having often entered this conscious state while lying on a boat or sitting on the banks of a lake on the island, he posits that it might be possible to make the sentiment of existence a default mental setting.[114]

His desire to adopt such a consciousness is much more radical than the collective identities Rousseau praises in *The Social Contract* and *Emile*. The goal here is to eradicate the self, not minimize it. The singular concern of Ajax—the value of his personality and identity—is to be expunged from consciousness. Rousseau wants to be of but not in the world. Some scholars have written enthusiastically about Rousseau's notion of the sentiment of existence.

Cooper, for example, believes that Rousseau is arguing for a new cognitive ability that permits him to adopt the consciousness of the early humans from the *Second Discourse* without losing his self-awareness; that he "has added new dimensions or even wholly new capacities to the ordinary complement of mental powers."[115]

Still, there are reasons to be skeptical. Rousseau acknowledges that most people cannot conquer their self-consciousness, and his love of solitude makes him relatively unique. Once people experience the highs of social praise, they seek more and more of it. It is addictive. To not just live in solitude but to extinguish all thoughts related to one's social experiences is thus a genuine achievement. Rousseau prides himself on being able to resist the temptations associated with social living and, as a result, is rewarded by having less *amour-propre*. In one of his fragments, he states that "a proof that I have less amour propre than other men or that mine is made in another manner is the facility that I have at living alone."[116] In "Preface to *Narcissus*," he boasts: "I have learned to do without the esteem of others."[117]

In addition, as he admits, the sentiment of existence is not accessible in most circumstances. He readily concedes it "was done better and more pleasurably on a fertile and solitary Island, naturally closed-off and separated from the rest of the world."[118] If *amour-propre* develops as a result of social living and economic progress, there is no reason to think it is a genie that could be put back in the bottle without undoing the conditions that gave rise to it. For humans to think like *les hommes sauvages*, they need to live like them. His time on the Île de Saint-Pierre, in other words, could not be scaled to apply to the rest of the population or even Rousseau himself once he rejoined civil society. It is not a generalizable solution.

Finally, as Cooper acknowledges, it is at odds with his other proposals to reduce *amour-propre*, especially the ones *Emile* and *The Social Contract* in which Rousseau uses the passion to create empathy and patriotism. By transcending *amour-propre*, all the positive effects of it are lost. Less positive *amour-propre* means less of what is best in humans. The sentiment of existence is thus an outlier inconsistent with much of Rousseau's political and social thought.

Back to the Provinces: Removing the Commercial Catalysts *of* Amour-Propre

It is important to recognize that almost all these solutions to *amour-propre* rest upon an important premise: that minimizing individuality and lessening the social importance of talent can best be achieved in rural life. Recall that in Rousseau's natural history, humans are not corrupted by social living alone. The competition for esteem and resulting emergence of *amour-propre* portend badly for the future but do not turn people into "ravenous wolves" overcome by a "frenzy to achieve distinction." Rousseau still refers to the historical period in which humans start living in communities as a golden era. As a species, it is "our most happiest epoch"[119] and is "a just mean between the indolence of the primitive state and the petulant activity of our amour propre"[120] As Keohane, Hont, Neuhouser, and others argue, it is only when *amour-propre* is combined with commercial society that it truly becomes dangerous. So, one way to lessen *amour-propre* is to avoid the new commerce and the cities that housed it. In several of his texts, Rousseau repeatedly encourages people to do this very thing. In *Emile*, he praises country simplicity and disparages city life as corrupt. He writes of "the black morals of cities"[121] and claims they "are the abyss of the human species."[122] They are places of vice, crime, and inflamed *amour-propre*. "One must go to the remote provinces," he argues, "in order to study the genius and the morals of a nation."[123] In the provinces, the right things are honored—patriotism and religion trump genius and money. By contrast, he contends that "it is big cities which exhaust a state and cause its weakness."[124] Rousseau begins *Julie*, his love letter to small-town life, by proclaiming that "great cities must have theaters; and corrupt peoples."[125] Furthermore, in both *Corsica* and *Julie*, he warns agrarian people not to "look covetously at residence in cities and envy the fate of the sluggards who live there"[126] and laments that provincials slavishly consume the novels and plays of Paris despite the fact they "all heap derision on the simplicity of rustic morality."[127] This is why Rousseau insists Emile be raised in the country and contends that peasants are the most suitable citizens for a society governed by the general will, writing approvingly of "when, among the happiest people in the world, troops of peasants are seen attending the affairs of State under an oak tree and always acting wisely."[128] It also why he wants to protect his hometown of Geneva from Voltaire's theater.

His early critics recognized the rejection by Rousseau of modern progress. Voltaire takes his primitivism at face value, wryly accusing him of suggesting in the *Second Discourse* that he wants humanity to return to walking around on all fours. Benjamin Constant charges him with naïvely trying to recreate ancient Sparta. Both criticisms are wide of the mark. It is not difficult to locate textual evidence with which to defend Rousseau against these indictments. Two passages should suffice: "human nature does not go backward"[129] and "ancient peoples are no longer a model for modern ones; they are too alien to them in every respect."[130] Nonetheless, Voltaire and Constant do touch upon something true about Rousseau. He is nostalgic for a simpler age. If it is impossible to literally go back in time, he realizes that the past still lives in much of modern life, especially in the provinces. By being behind the times, the provincials manage to escape modern corruptions.

To repeat some earlier points, the economic conditions in commercial society that "inflame" *amour-propre* do not exist in the provinces.[131] Provincial economic production calls for less cognitive ability and less division of labor. Most people either work in agriculture or as skilled craftsmen. Such professions require some specialized technical knowledge, but none so sophisticated that it would distinguish practitioners as a distinct superior social class. Moreover, if bankers, administrators, and educators exist in the provinces, there are too few of them to incite envy and jealousy. In addition, economic life in the provinces is less integrated. People mostly work out of view of their neighbors and are less dependent upon them in their day-to-day tasks. Farmers, for example, have few professional relationships and often work alone. Few have the opportunity to judge people employed in other occupations. Accordingly, Rousseau assumes that few think of climbing the social ladder and most, like Emile (and himself in the *Dialogues*), are content with their lot in life. When people do engage socially, they thus tend to be drawn together by their collective identities, which are far stronger in the country than in the city. Provincial men and women are more likely to define themselves through their religion and nationality rather than their achievements.[132] Finally, the generally modest standard of living and lack of wealth compels provincials to focus more on *amour de soi-même* than on superiority. They do not have the luxury to think about their social status and worth as humans. They are too busy trying to put food on the table. So their *amour-propre* probably will not transform into "*amour-propre* interested." With precious little money to be had, even people who suffer from inflamed *amour-propre* will probably not think to demand financial compensation commiserate with their perceived superiorities. There is not enough money in the community to make it worthwhile.

Amour-propre, then, takes a qualitatively different form in the provinces.

The importance of individuality and the overvaluation of talent—the two fundamental elements that constitute the consciousness of a Homeric hero—do not have much opportunity to develop. The rural political economy tends not to expose natural inequalities, and the solitary nature of most occupations means people will not become publicly defined by such inequalities. And, without inflamed *amour-propre*, there will no *amour-propre* interested and no *libido dominandi*. Freedom will have a chance to reign, and no one will be so rich that he or she can buy others. Rousseau thus advises the people of Corsica that "commerce produces wealth but agriculture assures freedom."[133]

Non-Rousseauian Solutions

There are other possible solutions to the conundrum of *amour-propre* that do not explicitly appear in Rousseau's works. Axel Honneth turns to George Herbert Mead for a solution. Mead argues that the division of labor ought to be expanded to allow everyone a socially valuable and productive role and hence create more opportunities for people to earn recognition from their peers and build up their self-esteem.[134] The idea is simple: the more socially valuable economic roles that exist, the more people will perform those roles and have their emotional needs met. Mead's model is lawyers and surgeons: "One is a good surgeon, a good lawyer, and he can pride himself on his superiority."[135] If such occupations are multiplied, then large swaths of the population can become the equivalent of a surgeon.

It is doubtful, however, that Rousseau would look favorably upon Mead's plan. It is hard to imagine an economy producing large spate of jobs that are equally challenging and respected by the population. Aside from the unlikelihood of creating challenging enough white-collar jobs, humans driven by *amour-propre* are especially good at establishing hierarchies even when there is little reason to do so. The drive to be superior is so strong that engineers or surgeons in Mead's utopia may begin to look down on lawyers or teachers. Furthermore, most economies require some people to do simple and unpleasant tasks. So it is unlikely Mead's expanded division of labor will eliminate the hierarchy of occupations. Also, even if it were possible to create a world in which there are enough challenging white-collar jobs for each member of society, it is far from obvious whether everyone would be able to perform such jobs equally well. As Rousseau acknowledges, there are wide disparities in human talents, and advanced economies both develop those talents and make them more visible. Finally, Mead does nothing to squelch competition within professions. Individuals might constantly compete to be the best lawyer, doctor, and so forth.

Neuhouser makes a more promising suggestion. He thinks Rousseau should follow Hegel and encourage individuals to find esteem in noneconomic spheres of life, such as the family or civil society.[136] A good parent might not compare himself or herself to a surgeon. Or, someone with low socioeconomic status might find respect in a noneconomic activity, such as singing in the church choir or playing in a pickup basketball league. Rousseau would probably argue, however, that Neuhouser's solution presupposes the cultural overhaul he already proscribes. Thus, his argument is redundant. People would need to reject the aristocratic values of talent and achievement to make room for identities from other institutions and activities. This is easier said than done, as entrenched cultural beliefs and practices do not die easily. Rousseau himself thought a lawgiver or an all-encompassing education is needed to exorcise the commercial spirit from the populace.[137] Merely pointing out that people should value things other than intellectual or productive talent may not be enough. In aristocratic or meritocratic societies, the political and economic is personal. People become defined so much by their occupational roles that other parts of the personality almost cease to matter. Commercial society thus may not allow for the sort of pluralism and social fragmentation that Neuhouser thinks will take the sting out of class-based inequalities. It overvalues certain forms of achievement and has trouble appreciating any activity outside its purview.

Furthermore, Neuhouser, like Mead, does not pay enough attention to Rousseau's warning that those on the top of the economic and social ladders will actively work to deprive people of self-respect and the resources to make a good life. Led by a *libido dominandi*, the "ravenous wolves" at the top enjoy their wealth and superiority only to the extent others are deprived of them, and they seek to control and dominate those beneath them. For everyone to be afforded recognition, Rousseau thinks the aristocracy must be dismantled. Mead and Neuhouser seem to think that the psychological corruptions of inequality occur mostly at the bottom; the poor and mediocre must find some way to attain respect and self-esteem. Rousseau, by contrast, is equally if not more concerned with those at the top. The truly awful stuff that happens in the world is more likely to be committed by people who think too well of themselves than by those who think too little.

Conclusion: Public Recognition, Private Honor

Rousseau's approach to limiting *amour-propre* might be summed up as "public recognition, private honor." When in public, everyone is equally deserving of recognition—that is, to have his or her needs and rights respected and to be appreciated as a valuable member of society. Public life ought to be a place of equality. Citizens should concern themselves only with the well-being of the community and/or humanity itself. Honor, on the other hand, ought to be private and should be distributed out of public view unless it is to further one of the collective identities that Rousseau believed would deflate excessive *amour-propre*. If democratic societies would be foolish to ignore differences in ability, they nonetheless ought to recognize the dangers of classical aristocracy—of honoring the best and brightest. Few humans can handle such designations. Those who believe themselves to be truly superior cannot be expected to honor values of freedom and equality or to recognize the dignity of their "lesser" neighbors.

Chapter 4

Tocqueville's Liberal Reply

It requires little effort to uncover Rousseau's influence on Alexis de Tocqueville.[1] Tocqueville was well versed in Rousseau's writings and occasionally
admits to being profoundly affected by them. As a teenager, he claims he
gave up his Catholicism upon reading Rousseau and Voltaire. Later in life, in
an 1852 speech delivered at the Academy of Moral and Political Sciences, he
praised Rousseau as one of the most significant political thinkers of all time.
In addition, in a much-cited letter, he states that he communes with Pascal,
Montesquieu, and Rousseau a little each day. Granted, the letter only states
that his interest in the philosophers refers to writing style, not ideas. Since,
however, he rarely mentions any philosopher by name in his published works
and private correspondence, this admission has encouraged scholars to seek
out substantive connections.

These attempts have largely been successful, as numerous conceptual
and theoretical similarities between Rousseau and Tocqueville have been un-
covered. Tocqueville's portrait of Native Americans in the first chapter of
Democracy in America closely resembles Rousseau's natural humans from the
Second Discourse.[2] Likewise, Tocqueville's genealogy of capitalism in the
Memoir on Pauperism also borrows liberally from the discourse.[3] In addition,
it is tempting to interpret Tocqueville's New England in Rousseauian terms.
As Sheldon Wolin observes, "With its town meeting democracy, civil religion, covenantal myths, and heavy sense of community," it is "more Genevan
than Rousseau's Geneva."[4] Tocqueville is even sympathetic to Rousseau's critique of democratic materialism. As one scholar remarks, in this sense "Tocqueville was not an apostle of the bourgeoisie."[5] It has also been argued that
the views Tocqueville offers on women are constructed out of Sophie,[6] his
description of American compassion "is based on the discussion of compassion in the *Emile*,"[7] and his notebooks detailing fifteen days he spent in the

wilderness near Saginaw, Michigan, are reminiscent of Rousseau's notion of the sentiment of existence.[8]

Tocqueville's Rousseauism, furthermore, extends to moral psychology. While he does not use the locution *amour-propre*, Tocqueville was thoroughly familiar with and sympathetic to the neo-Augustinian and Jansenist traditions responsible for its popularity in modernity and describes human nature in identical terms.[9] His admiration for Pascal is well documented, and his primary tutor as a child, Abbé Lesueur, was a committed Jansenist.[10] Also, one of his biographers, André Jardin, reports that Tocqueville reread Rousseau's *Second Discourse* immediately before writing volume II of *Democracy*.[11] It is thus hardly a stretch to read him as a student of Rousseau. His analysis of bourgeois democracy is psychological in the same way as Rousseau's.

At the same time, the political disagreements dividing the two men are just as obvious. Rousseau refuses to make peace with the emerging commercial democratic order and its social contract and *doux*-commerce foundations, largely because he believes it erodes the freedoms of the average person. He thinks the so-called progress of modern life, as I have argued, amounts to little more than ideological cover for new forms of elite tyranny.

Tocqueville, by contrast, defends the new democratic order as flawed but workable. His greatest fears about democracy, in fact, overlap with Rousseau's cores values. Tocqueville has few kind words for common people, whom Rousseau was dedicated to protecting against the forces of modernity and held up as paragons of virtue. He belittles them as mediocre and contends they, not the elite, are most likely to be the source of tyranny in the modern world.[12] Similarly, the element of liberalism that appeals most to Rousseau, equality, is one Tocqueville views with a high degree of suspicion.[13] If Rousseau believes freedom cannot exist without equality, Tocqueville contends the foremost threat to freedom stems from the intellectual habits and social mores engendered by equality. To save and preserve democracy, he asserts that it must be less democratic, not more so. He is also less troubled by commerce than is Rousseau. Although sensitive to Rousseau's criticism of the crass materialism in commercial societies, as previously mentioned, he could not help but admire the New England Yankee traders he believed represented the soul of America. Like many European visitors, he was awestruck by their work ethic and ingenuity. For him, the word "finance" is not necessarily a "slave's word." At the very least, he does not think wealth in and of itself can eradicate freedom.

Even the agreements between Rousseau and Tocqueville are sustained by a radically different politics. While both men are skeptical of the *philosophes* and piqued by their attempts to undermine patriotism and religion,[14] they are so for contrary reasons. Rousseau seeks to protect the dignity of the provincials; Tocqueville tries to salvage at least remnants of the ancien régime and carve out some social space in the new democratic world for the nobility of which he was part.

Not all scholars characterize Tocqueville's relationship with Rousseau as one of simultaneous embrace and rejection. Some downplay their political differences and interpret Tocqueville as a full-fledged Rousseauian. Wilhelm Hennis, for example, asserts that "Tocqueville's actual teacher, if there is to be one associated with him, is Rousseau" and that "in all of Tocqueville, I find not one sentence which would contradict Rousseau's teachings when these are correctly understood."[15] Others do not go as far as Hennis but still stress Tocqueville's deep debts to Rousseau. John Koritansky aims "to show that Tocqueville is a thinker in the modern tradition inaugurated by Rousseau" and that compared to Pascal and Montesquieu, his "debt to Rousseau was his greatest among the three."[16] Most interpreters, however, are more cautious and mindful of their specific political and intellectual disagreements.[17] It is only argued that Rousseau is source material for Tocqueville.

This is the more sensible position, as it is probably impossible to disentangle Tocqueville's philosophy and politics.[18] It is not just that Tocqueville applies Rousseau's values and insights in ways that contradict the political lessons of the discourses and *The Social Contract*. Rather, Tocqueville alters the substance of Rousseau's philosophical concepts in his applications of them. For example, theoretically, Tocqueville defines freedom in almost the exact same manner as Rousseau. Both agree that it involves self-rule and rationally setting one's limitations. In *Democracy in America*, Tocqueville defines it as the people governing and ruling so as "to remain their own masters"[19] There is, however, very little resembling Rousseau's moral freedom in Tocqueville's Americans. They never stop being materialistic and selfish, and their moral reasoning does not ask them to sacrifice their own good for the common good. Self-determination means something different for Tocqueville from what it does for Rousseau. If Tocqueville had insisted that democrats develop a political consciousness akin to the general will, he never would have written about America. Ultimately, he chooses his philosophical vocabulary and employs it in the manner he does in part because it can forward his political agenda.

This extends to moral psychology and *amour-propre* as well. His liberal politics lead Tocqueville to reject almost everything about Rousseau's political analysis of this passion. He thinks *amour-propre* results not from aristocratic attitudes but from the democratic value of equality. He also believes that in democracies it is the people themselves, not the rich and powerful, who are most likely to behave tyrannically. They are the ones who are prone to exhibit *libido dominandi*. Yet, Tocqueville's spurning of Rousseau does not translate into enthusiastic support for the democratic interpretation of *amour-propre* found in Augustine's *Ten Homilies* as well as numerous neo-Augustinians and Mandeville. While Tocqueville ultimately accepts that vices and passions can and do promote social well-being, he does so only reluctantly. The formula is unreliable. Vices and passions are just as often disadvantageous and threaten the health of the polis. In short, Tocqueville adopts a middling position that stands between the neo-Augustinian optimistic enthusiasm for it and Rousseau's mostly pessimistic fear of it.

Democratic and Aristocratic Moral Psychology in Tocqueville

Tocqueville anchors his discussion of American moral psychology on Sophocles' insight that aristocrats and democrats not only hold opposing values and moral reasoning patterns but also develop different personalities as a result (though there is no evidence Sophocles is his direct source). He too realizes that to commit oneself to democracy has profound cognitive and emotional consequences. He follows Rousseau, however, in rejecting Sophocles' strict dichotomy between democratic and aristocratic consciousness. His democrats are a composite of Odysseus's democratic prudence and the aristocratic concern Ajax has for the social value of his identity. Tocqueville is forthright about this in his writings. In the *Souvenirs*, for example, he describes the spirit of the members of the rising middle class as predominantly shaped by both vanity and the desire for well-being, or *amour-propre* and *amour de soi-même*. They are "active and industrious, often dishonest, generally orderly, but sometimes rash because of *vanity* and selfishness, timid by temperament, moderate in all things except a taste for *well-being*."[20] Like Augustine's Romans with their love of glory, they are not saints but at the same time less vile.

This composite structures Tocqueville's portrayal of Americans in *Democracy* as well. The democratic side of the American personality is easy to identify. Americans pride themselves on their pragmatism and are obsessed with their personal well-being. They care little for virtue and believe the only sound moral reasoning emanates from self-interest. Tocqueville sums up American moral psychology with an epigram from Montaigne's *Essays*: "Should I not follow a straight path for its straightness, yet would I do it because experience hath taught me that in the end it is the happiest and most profitable."[21] At their best, Americans are motivated by "self-interest properly understood," which is an enlightened form of selfishness that encourages them to act in their long-term self-interest by delaying gratification and behaving in a cooperative and sociable manner.[22] It is the self-interest of Odysseus. Through "self-interest properly understood," they come to understand that their interests are inextricably intertwined with the good of the larger community and that short-term sacrifice can produce long-term gain. At times, Tocqueville is genuinely impressed with his subjects, claiming that he "cannot find words adequate to express how much I admired their experience and common sense."[23] They have a practical knowledge that allows them concrete understanding of abstract terms such as rights and freedom—a knowledge he finds lacking in Europe.

This prudent common sense, however, is but one strand in a much richer psychological tapestry. Tocqueville does not take proclamations Americans make of their moral motivations at face value. He thinks it is an affect. While Americans celebrate self-interest and defend every action they take as individually beneficial, he assures his readers that his hosts can be charitable and self-sacrificing. Like all other humans, he argues in Rousseauian fashion, they are moved by natural compassion. In *Democracy*, he reports witnessing "citizens of the United states . . . yielding to the disinterested, spontaneous impulses that are part of man's nature."[24]

In addition, Tocqueville's Americans frequently do not exhibit "self-interest properly understood" and are hardly exemplars of Odysseus's reasoned pragmatism. Often they act out of emotion and inclination. They "feel far more than they reason"[25] and sometimes make important decisions "far more by instinct than by reasoning."[26] Similarly, they can be more ideological than rational. Rather than weigh competing values, as does Odysseus, they become moral absolutists. Tocqueville describes Americans as stubborn and dogmatic: "When an idea, whether just or unreasonable, takes possession of the American mind, nothing is more difficult to than to get it out."[27] This often makes political debate contentious and unproductive, as Americans dispute rather than discuss. Their ideological temperament also makes them prone to holding absurd beliefs, such as the idea that everyone is of equal intellect and that truth can be had by majority vote. Furthermore, Tocqueville

exposes the fanatical materialism of Americans and details how it is sometimes contrary to their rational interests. Their near obsession with their property makes them anxious and unreasonable and at times encourages them to
assume great risks for a slight increase in profit. Such behavior, Tocqueville
thinks, has more in common with the Homeric honor culture than with democratic rational acquisition: "There is something heroic about the way American do business."[28] Indeed, he claims that Americans define honor as *audacious*
economic behavior.[29] Tocqueville's Americans thus are not model democrats—
they are a more neurotic version of Sophocles' Odysseus. Their passions sometimes work against their interests.

Despite Americans' Odyssean moral language, the aristocratic strand of
the democratic personality is hard to miss. In addition to defining honor in
classical terms of manliness and audacity, Tocqueville's democrats are as obsessed with pride and honor as Ajax. They see the world in relational terms
and have a persistent desire "to be strong and esteemed."[30] Commerce, Tocqueville claims in contrast to Rousseau, "makes men independent of one another" and hence "gives them an exalted idea of their individual worth."[31]
Even a poor person has a "high idea of his personal worth . . . and willingly
believes that others are looking at him."[32]

Democrats are, moreover, are among the most envious humans on the
planet: "We must not blind ourselves to the fact that that democratic institutions develop the sentiment of envy in the human heart to a very high degree."[33] They hate to be outdone and insist on favorable public recognition. At
one point, Tocqueville asserts that American materialism is ultimately an expression of *amour-propre*. When Americans lose out in market competition
and see people around them becoming richer, "their feelings and passions suffer more than their interests."[34] Moreover, Tocqueville claims Americans have
no taste for electing men of merit to political office, as it reflects poorly on
their own quality.[35] If they are consulting their reason, it is the reason of Ajax,
not Odysseus. Only in times of crisis does *amour de soi-même* overpower this
expression of *amour-propre*. In ordinary times, American democrats train
themselves to ignore talent. Not being the best dancer, singer, or orator is too
painful to bear, so they engage in magical thinking and erase any such observations from their consciousness. Also, Americans demand from their politicians a constant stream of flattery about their superiority as a people, which
results in an irritating, jealous patriotism that demands everything and gives
nothing.[36] Politicians themselves are not immune to this vanity. A politician is
"constantly spurred by the need to play an important role . . . and feels an ir-

repressible desire to keep his ideas perpetually in the public eye."[37] Even Tocqueville's celebrated civic associations are motivated by disguised pride.[38] To repurpose one of Mandeville's quips, pride and vanity build more than hospitals in America. They give shape to social, political, and economic life—for better and for worse.

Granted, as previously mentioned, Tocqueville never uses the term *amour-propre* in his writings, *Democracy in America* included. His concept of "egoïsme," or "egoism," however, is defined much like many seventeenth- and eighteenth-century neo-Augustinian definitions of *amour-propre*. Egoism, Tocqueville claims, is the "passionate and exaggerated love of self that impels man to relate everything solely to himself and to prefer himself everything else."[39] For him, it expresses itself in terms of both well-being and pride, covering both *amour de soi-même* and *amour-propre*. Tocqueville's language finds close parallels in Pascal and Nicole as well as Mandeville and Rousseau. Allan Bloom speculates that Tocqueville does not use the term *amour-propre* because he was trying to convince the rich and the nobility to accept modern democracy and knew such an obvious reference to Rousseau would scare them off.[40] When Tocqueville decided to write about America's experiment with democracy, 1789 still loomed large in France's collective psyche.

Democratic Sources of *Amour-Propre*

Tocqueville separates himself from his predecessors, however, by arguing that egoism is as much a democratic passion as an aristocratic one and is as likely to result from the value of equality as the aristocratic value of being best. Although it is "a vice as old as the world" and "is not to any great extent more characteristic of one form of society than of another,"[41] he asserts that in the United States it originates from the commitment to equality: "The restless and insatiable vanity of democratic peoples is a product of equality and the fragility of conditions."[42]

To support this claim, Tocqueville makes a two-pronged argument. The first, also made by Rousseau, is that commercial societies inflame *amour-propre*. As I demonstrated in Chapter 1, *amour-propre* results from societal competitions in which people compare themselves on the basis of socially relevant ability. In these competitions, people are encouraged to interpret their social rank as indicative of their inherent worth as humans. So they develop a strong sense of self and become unduly concerned with their social status. Tocqueville adds to this narrative by contending that such evaluations depend on at least some measure of political, legal, and economic equality. Without rough equality of opportunity, people will have less reason to interpret their social ranking as an accurate reflection of their intrinsic value and may attribute their lot in life to arbitrary social forces that have nothing to do with anything specific about them.

Tocqueville clarifies this point through his favorite heuristic device: comparing feudal aristocracies to democracies. In feudal aristocracies, individual traits matter much less than social class. People are born into their stations. There is almost nothing the lower and middle ranks can do to enter the upper echelons of social and political life. Their abilities, while not meaningless, are far less determinative of their fate and have little social value. As a result, there is no reason for them to ponder their individual self-worth and compare themselves with their peers. Social life is so stratified and unchanging that nothing compels self-examination and reflection. People do not have to care much about who they are. This is true of the nobles as well. They defend their superiority on the basis of bloodline rather than individual attributes and define themselves mostly by their family name and estate.[43] They have less reason to think about, to return to Nicole's term, the "idea of me" and thus do not suffer much from *amour-propre*. Despite labeling themselves as aristocrats, their moral psychology has little in common with Ajax's.

In commercial democracies, by contrast, people are free to rise and fall. No one inherits privileges, and everyone depends upon his or her talents and wits to make a living. Individual traits matter greatly. People must constantly evaluate who they are and compete with their fellow citizens for societal honors and rewards. Hence, they are every bit as concerned with talent and achievement as the participants in the competition for esteem from Rousseau's *Second Discourse*. Emotionally, they share much in common with Rousseau's civil humans. They are insecure, envious, spiteful, and self-conscious. As Mark Reinhardt concludes, for this reason and several others, "modern individuality . . . [is] the source of Tocqueville's most anguished fears."[44]

The most helpful example Tocqueville gives of this argument is found in his contrast between aristocratic and democratic domestic servants. Aristocratic servants, he claims, fully buy into the social class structure and their inferior station within it. They do not revolt against their demeaning condition and serve their masters with a sense of honor and pride. They are so devoted to their masters' estates that they have almost no sense of their selves or self-interest and can be inspired to commit extraordinary acts of sacrifice.

Tocqueville aptly describes their attitude as "servile honor."[45] Aristocratic servants accept their lowly position and self-nullifying lot in life without question. Life hands them a set of duties, and they set about fulfilling them. It never occurs to them that they should be more than an appendage of their master's desires or that they are better than the fate to which they have been assigned. They adopt the perspective of the social system. They are submissive yet are not dominated by ill-tempered masters. Quite the contrary, their masters paternalistically govern them and look after their needs.

Tocqueville's own manservant Eugène, whom he describes in his *Souvenirs*, provides a perfect illustration of "servile honor." During the 1848 uprisings, Eugène fought against the insurgent socialists on behalf of the established order. Astonishingly, in the middle of a battle, he returned to Tocqueville's residence to perform his chores. Upon completion of them, he asked for permission to return to battle, which Tocqueville promptly granted. He not only protected his master's unearned and privileged lifestyle, he insisted on making him as comfortable as possible in the midst of doing so. Tocqueville finds nothing strange about Eugène's behavior. He makes no attempt to peer beneath the servant's words and actions and locate some trace of discontent or wounded *amour-propre*. He takes them at face value and interprets them as an unquestioned acceptance of the social system. Tocqueville assumes that, like Rousseau's savage humans from the *Second Discourse*, Eugène was "contented with his lot" and "enjoyed as a gift of nature that happy balance between powers and wants."[46] There is not a trace of envy, jealousy, and vanity in him, nor does he have an "idea of me." He is simply Eugène, a manservant concerned only with his duties.

Democratic servants, by contrast, are much less accepting of their position. They refuse to grant that their masters are naturally superior and feel ashamed of their predicament. Unlike their aristocratic counterparts, they have an emotional response to their condition. As individuals responsible for their fates, they interpret taking orders from another human as a disgrace. It triggers in them an existential crisis; being a servant says something about their self-worth. Tocqueville thinks American servants only tolerate their status because it is temporary. Given the fluidity of American social classes, there is always the hope they can supplant their master and perhaps someday give him orders (and in nineteenth-century America, it is always a he). Democratic masters do not exhibit *libido dominandi* for this reason. Their authority is too tenuous to lead to an authoritarian mind-set.

Tocqueville's second argument, his primary one, is much bolder than the first and takes him well past Rousseau. According to Tocqueville, equality engenders *amour-propre* because it defines self-worth in democracies. The institutional definitions of equality—political equality based on rights and economic equality based on roughly equal opportunities to earn societal rewards—give rise to a third and more fundamental idea of equality. Tocqueville terms this form of equality "complete equality." Complete equality is what it sounds like; Tocqueville's democrats believe they are as good and socially valuable as anyone else. In his notebooks, Tocqueville makes the point that Americans believe they can marry anyone—no one is too good for them.[47] He is immediately impressed by this attitude upon his arrival in the United States, observing that "at bottom, they [Americans] feel themselves to be, and they are, equal."[48] Tocqueville's American democrats are thus identical to Aristotle's democrats in the *Politics*. Both think that because they are equal in terms of free birth they are equal in every respect.[49] More so than Aristotle, however, Tocqueville stresses the existential aspect of equality. It is a means by which humans understand and value their existence. It defines their nature. For this reason, equality is also the source of morality and right and wrong. To be superior to one's neighbor is to do violence to his or her humanity. As Claude Lefort states, equality is "not simply a social fact, but a *moral* and political fact."[50]

This moral equality is analogous to the notion Ajax has of his destiny. Just as he believes he is by nature a hero and irretrievably superior, Americans cling to their inherent equality as an essential fact about them that can never be disproven by events on this earth. It is, to return to Pindar, who they are. The equality of conditions, then, is quite powerful and goes beyond rules of distributive justice. It is an underlying ethos that structures consciousness and is a way of apprehending the world: "Its influence . . . extends well beyond political mores and laws . . . it creates opinions, engenders feelings, suggests customs, and modifies everything it does not produce."[51]

How does complete equality contribute to feelings of vanity and envy—of *amour-propre*? Tocqueville argues that it is naïve and unrealistic, and hence bound to be frustrated. While democrats imagine themselves inferior to no one, the cold reality is that humans are unequal in many respects. Nature does not distribute talents equally. Invariably, some people are smarter, stronger, more physically attractive than others. To quote Samuel Johnson, "No two people can be half an hour together, but one shall acquire superiority over the other."[52] Or, from Diderot's *Rameau's Nephew*, the nephew-*lui* claims that equality can only be realized in death and bowel movements.[53] Around every corner and in every encounter some inequality is waiting to reveal itself. When people compare themselves with one another, they will not see equality.

Moreover, these natural inequalities are of immense social value. Given that complete equality entails both economic and political equality, wealth and public honors can only be distributed along the lines of competition.[54] Superiorities should be earned and ought not to be distributed by family name or monarchical proclamation.[55] Presumably, those with more natural ability could amass more wealth and honors. So, while equality implies competition, the logic of competition is to annihilate equality. Competitions are designed to create winners and losers. Once everyone is free to utilize his or her talents and has the opportunity to climb the social ladder, natural variability will be set in motion and be visible for all to see. Accordingly, equality will be frustrated, and a person's public identity and self-worth will always be in play as individuals are free to rise and fall. This is one of Tocqueville's most seductive paradoxes. Democrats are socialized to think they are as good as everyone else and thus deserve the same political and economic rights. The exercise of those rights, however, both draws attention to and rewards existing natural inequalities that undermine any idea that everyone is equally good, deserving, and valuable. Tocqueville thus concludes "democratic institutions awaken and flatter the passion for equality without ever being able to satisfy it to the full."[56] The equality they crave taunts them; they see it right before their eyes but cannot fully attain it. Not surprisingly, Tocqueville's Americans are suspicious of talent, wealth, or any other phenomenon that inherently leads to inequality. They become resentful and bitter, and "no form of superiority is so legitimate that the sight of it is not wearisome to their eyes."[57]

This problem, in fact, is more complicated than it first appears and cannot be resolved through efforts to limit real-world inequality. When most people have roughly the same social standing, even minor differences take on tremendous importance. Democratic "sameness" results in the magnification of all variations.[58] The democratic consciousness thus has a heightened sensitivity to inequality and can spot it with little effort. Comparisons become more and more fine-tuned, and even the most mundane activities can touch upon powerful and frightening questions of a person's value. They can quickly alter one's social standing and force democrats to constantly take stock of the evaluations others make of them. This is why democrats are so agitated, demoralized, and envious. Democrats thus have a bruising relationship with equality. They love and celebrate it, but it often disappoints them and fails to live up to its promise. It is the source of dignity and indignity alike.

Ultimately, Tocqueville contends that complete equality is a perverse interpretation of the "equality of conditions." Equality is only meant to refer to institutional equality, such as equal political and legal rights and the opportunity to earn wealth and power. It was never meant to imply a general equality of humanity. As Jean-Claude Lamberti remarks, Tocqueville was genuinely astonished that "under certain conditions men in America lived unequally in unequal situations nevertheless considered themselves to be equals."[59] Thus, many of the psychic wounds democrats suffer are self-inflicted. Like Bernard Williams's Ajax, they are done in by their expectations of life. If they were better political theorists, they would have more accurate self-knowledge and not demand something from the world that it cannot deliver.

In any event, Tocqueville rejects Rousseau's claim that roughly equal public identities and equal civic identities are a cure for *amour-propre*. Rather, he thinks they are a condition of it.[60] He also would be skeptical of Rousseau's critique of modern life as a classical aristocracy in democratic clothing. The adverse psychological reaction to inequality, *amour-propre*, only makes sense in a society committed to a variety of forms of equality, particularly complete equality. Of course, this argument may not run in both directions. Rousseau would most certainly predict that *amour-propre* would be a problem in Tocqueville's America.

Tocqueville and the Redirection of Vice

His pragmatism also makes Tocqueville more accepting than Rousseau of the "Roman formula" of manipulating vice to serve as a surrogate for virtue that so impressed Abbadie, Nicole, Mandeville, and numerous other neo-Augustinians. In fact, he makes the exact same assertion about Americans that Augustine does about Romans. American patriotism and public-spirited behavior, he claims, is often driven by vanity. The argument shows up in a few different forms in *Democracy*.[61]

First, in the religious and virtuous New England township democracies he so admired, Tocqueville concedes that the "desire for esteem" and the "taste for attention" in part inspire political participation.[62] Second, as previously mentioned, American politicians seek office to garner public esteem. Unable to achieve distinction in other activities, they crave the social importance that public office confers upon them. Third, also previously mentioned, pride and vanity are central motives to participate in civic associations. Once they are prompted to join the public sphere by some annoyance or dispute, Tocqueville thinks something very interesting happens to democrats. Their dormant vanity reawakens, and they become eager to attract favorable attention from their peers. In the public sphere, this occurs only by serving the general interest. "When the public governs," Tocqueville asserts, "no one is unaware of the value of the public's good will, and everyone tries to court it by winning the esteem and affection of the people among whom he is obliged to live."[63] Elsewhere, he describes it as resulting from disguised pride.[64] Granted, Tocqueville at one point suggests that civic associations are transformative and elevate the democratic condition. Through them, he asserts, "feelings and ideas are renewed, the heart expands, and the human spirit develops only through the reciprocal action of human beings on one another."[65] This passage is probably the most optimistic claim in the text. Tocqueville's language, in fact, is reminiscent of Rousseau's definition of moral freedom from book I of *The Social Contract*. Rousseau writes, "His [a person's] faculties are so exercised and developed, his ideas enlarged, his sentiments ennobled, and his whole soul is elevated."[66] If read apart from the rest of the text, it would appear as if democrats can transcend their vanity and develop a virtuous disposition. Naturally, however, one should not read too much into one rhetorical outburst. As Reinhardt observes, "*Democracy* is a work of many moods by turns, dire, somber, hopeful, celebratory."[67] And what is true of the book is also true of Tocqueville's discussion of associations. If American hearts and minds are sometimes elevated through civic associations, they never stop being driven by pride and vanity. These Augustinian passions are an indelible part of democratic moral psychology.

Finally, "self-interest properly understood" serves as evidence of Tocqueville's at least partial acceptance of the idea that private vices can be redirected to serve the public good. Although his ideal is always virtue, Tocqueville happily reports that Americans can simultaneously work for themselves and the larger community. As previously discussed, "self-interest properly understood" is an educated and more refined form of self-interest that helps them see the value of cooperation and delayed gratification. According to Tocqueville, it allows democrats to remain free. It produces "a multitude of citizens who are disciplined, temperate, moderate, prudent, and self-controlled."[68] It creates, in other words, a population who are masters of themselves. So, freedom results from selfishness, not virtue.

At the same time, despite his obvious adoption of the "social utility of vice" argument, Tocqueville is less enthusiastic than his neo-Augustinian predecessors, such as Pascal and Nicole. While he accepts that the formula works, to reiterate, it is not as seamless as these earlier theorists imply. Tocqueville tells a complicated story. He knows vices are often just vices. His Americans can just as easily be undone by their flaws as saved by them. For example, Tocqueville understands that pride often turns into envy and can lead to self-defeating political behavior. As I argued earlier, envy induces democrats to elect mediocre political leaders who are more likely to institute foolish policies, to the detriment of almost everyone. Pride can also result in stubbornness and dogmatism. In *Democracy*, American political life is typically described as a contentious, low-minded affair conducted by pigheaded, insecure, and thoughtless men. One early commentator credits Tocqueville with being "the first person who said that Democracy lowers the intellectual level of governing bodies."[69]

Tocqueville also knows that his central value of freedom cannot be assured by letting self-interest and impulse run amok. The notion "self-interest properly understood" is as much a repudiation of attempts to redirect vice to serve the common good as an endorsement of it. It recognizes that democratic self-interest needs to be enlightened and constantly reinforced through a variety of institutions and practices. Life is not as simple as Mandeville's epigram "private vices, public benefits." While Mandeville holds that human impulses and passions give shape to political, economic, and social institutions, Tocqueville thinks the influence runs both ways. Institutions can and do alter the nature and expression of the passions, which for him is a good thing. For example, although an agnostic, Tocqueville is fond of religion because it educates self-interest so people can resist their most dangerous impulses and understand the need to behave sociably. Specifically, he argues that while the circumstances of America make American people audacious, bold, and spirited, religion compels them to follow laws and social duties: "The law permits the American people to do everything, religion prevents them from conceiving everything and forbids them to dare everything."[70] Similarly, legal institutions help smooth over the rougher edges of the democratic personality. Tocqueville views lawyers as a faux aristocracy—power brokers who conservatively defend the status quo against dangerously impulsive behavior and provide society with much-needed stability. Tocqueville is similarly impressed by juries, which he claims provide an essential political education. They teach participants the principles of justice, equity, and right and show Americans how such ideas can work in practice. Moreover, jury service promotes sociability by prompting empathy in Americans. While sitting in a jury box, they are forced to think of problems that they personally will never encounter and place themselves in the shoes of those on the wrong side of the law. As they judge their neighbors, they cannot but help contemplate themselves as the ones being judged. This exercise in empathy induces them to think more generally about how their actions affect others.[71] In this sense, jury duty is similar to Rousseau's theory of extended compassion from *Emile*. It pushes Americans to more broadly define their self-interest in terms of their collective identities.

Nonetheless, Tocqueville does not go as far as Rousseau. The idea of self-interest properly understood should not be confused with the general will. If self-interest can and must be refined and broadened, it will never be transformed to the point in which people define their self-interest solely in terms of the interest of the state. American democrats are still selfish individualists who work for themselves. Tocqueville accepts Benjamin Constant's argument that there is no going back to Sparta. In a letter, he concedes that self-interest properly understood is "a far cry from the ancient republics."[72] Likewise, Rousseau's moral freedom, the ability of rational self-determination, has no equivalent in *Democracy*. Tocqueville's Americans never stop acting on prejudice, impulse, and instinct. Thus, as Jason Neidleman claims, Tocqueville "stands somewhere in between Rousseau and the liberals; he thinks of politics as more than an instrument but stops short of elevating citizenship to the heights it reaches in Rousseau."[73]

Finally, Tocqueville is adamant that there is a cost to vice and self-interest. They do not lead, as Mandeville supposes, to happy and flourishing societies. Democracies can succeed insofar as they allow people to be "masters of themselves," but they do not represent the high point of humanity. Tocqueville admires certain aspects of American democracy and claims to be a friendly critic.[74] Yet, however friendly, he is still a critic and does not paint a flattering portrait of the American and democratic character. It is difficult to leave the text thinking his angst-ridden and insecure Americans are happy. They seem almost emotionally tortured by their freedom. And, although they desire a "manly" freedom, they are often bogged down in vice and seem to muddle their way to self-rule. The central tension in *Democracy* between freedom and equality at times verges on the tragic—both values will ultimately destroy each other. In the end, Tocqueville believes the United States can avoid tragedy. But his optimism is somber. The logic of equality and lots of lucky historical happenstances allow Americans to be both equal and free. The journey to this happy balance, however, is perilous and at times undignified. The romantic view of rational self-determining agents choosing enlightenment is missing from *Democracy*. His America survives; it does not flourish.

Tocqueville Contra Elias: The Aristocratic Foundations of Modern Freedom

In his heart, Tocqueville is an aristocrat, at least in the modern sense of the term. He was able to trace his ancestry back to William the Conqueror and reveled in the grandeur of his aristocratic lineage.[75] As one biographer put it, "First and foremost he was a noble, to the end of his days, and cannot be understood unless this is recognized."[76] He never identified with the new democratic age he supported and thought inevitable. It is thus hard to imagine him sympathizing with Elias's argument in *The Civilizing Process*. If aristocrats are polite and exemplify *civilité*, Tocqueville thinks that there is much more to them than mere manners. They are not frauds propped up by scheming monarchs trying to counterbalance the rising middle-rank administrators and lawyers. Rather, they have more in common with classical aristocrats than Elias suggests. Tocqueville's aristocrats are dedicated to the eternal and unchanging and eagerly sacrifice themselves for the good of the state. Arguably, whether his portrayal is accurate or not, Native Americans in *Democracy in America* represent the noble classes and exemplify all the virtues that Tocqueville cherished. Like his own social set in France, he claims, they possess *civilité*, noblesse oblige, and warrior manliness. Despite living in "rude" conditions, they have a "habitual reserve and a kind of aristocratic politeness" and exhibit all the compassion, self-sacrifice, hospitality, and courtesy of a European lord.[77] A Native American man would "brave starvation to assist the stranger who knocked on his door of his hut at night."[78] As far as Tocqueville is concerned, no society can have enough of these sorts of people.

His praise for European nobility seems to know no limits. Ironically, Tocqueville claims that the French aristocrats are the architects of modern freedom and progenitors of democracy. In *The Old Regime and the Revolution*, he romantically describes the small towns and villages of medieval France as bastions of freedom in which the nobles cared for and schooled the lower classes in the art of self-government and sustained liberty through a "manly" spirit of independence.[79] If such freedom was "irregular and intermittent," he still insists that "there was much more freedom then than in our day."[80]

He likewise begins *Democracy in America* with an encomium to feudal

Europe. Its people valued excellence and protected their superiority but did not show a trace of *libido dominandi* or contempt for those beneath them. They lived and breathed civic virtue and would gladly sacrifice themselves for the good of the state. Tocqueville does not consider for a moment that their virtue is reducible to mere vanity. Believing that they were invested by God with political power, the nobles took special care not to abuse their authority and were duty bound to care for the people as a shepherd for his flock: "Without regarding the poor as equals, they watched over the destiny of those whose welfare had been entrusted to them by Providence."[81] For their part, the people had full trust in and love for their rulers. They did not demand God-given rights and submitted to the rigors of their lives without complaint, provided their rulers were behaving leniently and justly. Like Tocqueville's manservant Eugène, they accepted what they took to be the natural order of things à la Malebranche. Despite such inequality, Tocqueville assures his reader that in such a hierarchical system "souls were not degraded."[82] The elite segments of society—the monarchs and the nobles—also sustained productive relationships. Feudal Europe maintained perhaps the central feature of modern liberal democracy: checks and balances. In practice, this meant the nobles checked princely power. As a result, Tocqueville reports, nobles and the crowned princes peacefully governed Europe for centuries. In his mind, at least theoretically, there is no downside to the feudal era. It represented all that was admirable in both aristocracies and democracies. It combined beauty and excellence with freedom and compassion.

Furthermore, as previously discussed, one of the main arguments in *Democracy* is that aristocratic mores are crucial for a well-functioning democracy and serve as a useful corrective to democratic vices. Although at times Tocqueville contends that America needs to push its democracy to its logical end—that is, John Dewey's oft-cited dictum that the cure for the ills of democracy is more democracy[83]—much of his advice counsels moderating democracy through the establishment of institutions that promote an aristocratic worldview. In *Democracy*, he desperately tries to convince democrats that they have much to learn from aristocracy. To be sure, his plea can appear understated. Tocqueville recognizes that democrats are too dedicated to equality to take calls for aristocracy seriously. So, he does not confront democrats head on and never suggests recreating actual aristocratic institutions and practices or persuade Americans to moderate their commitment to equality. He does not ask democrats to alter their ideologies or forms. Rather, he seeks to identify existing institutions in democracies that function as he imagined aristocratic ones would. Specifically, he hoped to find institutions that would mitigate against democratic restlessness, materialism, and shortsightedness—ones that would prevent democrats from choking on their excesses. Law and religion, to reiterate, are the best examples of such institutions.

Rhetorically, Tocqueville carefully presents his case to his democratic readers. He almost seems to anticipate a book like Elias's, which is why he treads lightly in his criticisms of American life. On the surface, this may not seem to be the case. Tocqueville does not appear to like Americans much. He depicts them as egotistical, mediocre, materialistic, crass, pigheaded, insecure, and angst ridden. Yet, he is far more even-handed, as James Kloppenberg attests, than many authors of the European travel literature of his age.[84] His Americans are also industrious, possess good sense, have an admirable founding generation, maintain decentralized political institutions such as civic associations, and are on the forefront of the democratic future. *Democracy in America*, in short, is not an exercise in character assassination written from the perspective of a bitter aristocrat. From the American standpoint, Tocqueville was the first European commentator not to run down the New World. As John Bigelow avers in the 1899 introduction, "It was the first book written about the United States by any European of repute that was not conceived in a spirit of disparagement and detraction."[85] Other aristocratic European travel writers were far harsher than Tocqueville and made no attempt to conceal their disgust for Americans. Quite the contrary: they furiously tried to outdo one another in describing the depths of American vulgarity and depravity. One of the more colorful examples cited by Kloppenberg comes courtesy of Frances Trollope, who compares Americans to swine in her *Domestic Manners of the Americans*: "Let no one who wishes to receive agreeable impressions of American manners, commence their travels in a Mississippi steam boat; for myself, it is with all sincerity I declare, that I would infinitely prefer sharing the apartment of a party of well conditioned pigs to being confined to its cabin."[86] And, of course, she cannot resist commenting on the apparently unique American habit of spitting: "I hardly know any annoyance so deeply repugnant to English feelings, as the incessant, remorseless spitting of Americans."[87] There is no equivalent of such venom in *Democracy in America*, and the bulk of the criticisms Tocqueville levels are no worse than his attacks on the French bourgeoisie in *The Old Regime*. He aims to be, it is worth repeating, a "friendly critic."

Tocqueville, therefore, would undoubtedly claim that Elias misunderstands the true social value of the feudal nobility. They do much more than protect monarchical power by counterbalancing the lawyers and administrators. And their *civilité* is not some made-up criterion for being *aristos* that serves no purpose. The success of democracy depends on some form of it. *Democracy in America*, then, is in part an appeal—an appeal to democrats to retain at least shards of the splintered ancien régime. And it makes its appeal on democratic terms. Aristocratic attitudes are useful.

Finally, by way of qualification, Tocqueville's explanation for the decline of the aristocrats does somewhat overlap with Elias's. He agrees with Elias that the problems of the nobles started well before the eighteenth century and first emerged centuries earlier, during the Middle Ages. In his narrative, however, religion is the driver of modern history. The idea of equality first begins with the emergence of the church as a political power in the twelfth century. Unlike the aristocratic power, church power was premised on equality. Anyone could join the clergy. Its "ranks were open to all, to the poor as well as the rich, the commoner and to the lord."[88] For seven hundred years, the value of equality slowly became a principle of government and an uncontested maxim of moral philosophy. As it seeped into the collective consciousness, it would eventually translate into the belief that everyone is as good as everyone else, the belief in complete equality. Later developments would hasten this process. One of the more important ones is the rise of the lawyers and administrators— the heart of Elias's narrative. Tocqueville's argument is similar. To effectively rule their lands, princes developed a complex set of civil laws. In turn, this required the establishment of a special class of men—lawyers—to draft and administer these laws.[89] Princes recognized their value, and lawyers became an important part of court politics. Furthermore, Tocqueville recognizes that economic power could also be wielded by the commoners against the feudal powers. Commercial activities are open to all, and while kings financially ruin themselves in great public undertakings and nobles waste their money in private wars, "the commoners enrich themselves in commerce."[90] Nonetheless, these later processes—the ones that make up Elias's argument—were only accelerants. The source of modern representative democracy and the equality of conditions is the church.

Tocqueville's genealogy thus raises interesting causal issues. If *amour-propre* is a modern version of the medieval Christian concept of *amor sui*, it originates in another Christian idea, equality. Again, the problem is not classical aristocracy and the overvaluation of talent. It can be explained exclusively by Christian categories.

Liberalism and *Libido Dominandi*

Perhaps the most intriguing similarity between Rousseau and Tocqueville is their fixation with the Augustinian concern of domination and tyranny, which shows up throughout *Democracy in America* in a few distinct forms. The great threats to individual freedom in the text are almost all described as tyranny or despotism. Unlike Rousseau, however, Tocqueville does not focus on the wealthy and talented. He thinks democratic societies have little to fear from them. They do not turn into the "ravenous wolves" bent on depriving or abusing their weaker neighbors. While Tocqueville accepts that in America there are people rich enough to buy their neighbors and poor enough to have to sell themselves, he thinks such power is harmless because of the fluidity of wealth and the precariousness of social status. Individuals are always rising and falling, and no one is so secure in his or her superiority that he or she can tyrannize neighbors without future repercussions. Importantly, the rich and poor do not develop different personalities akin to Rousseau's competition for esteem. The poor do not simmer with resentment, and the rich have no appetite for cruelty. In fact, in Tocqueville's telling, the upper classes are the vulnerable ones. It is they who have to fear the masses! The people are the almighty demos and are in firm control of the polity: "The people reign over the American political world as God reigns over the universe."[91]

To protect themselves, the elite retreat into private life and stay "almost entirely out of politics."[92] They fully understand their compromised position in democracies and do not dare to fight for their own interests. Tocqueville claims they "submitted without a murmur or a fight to an evil that was now inevitable."[93] This is not to say that wealthy classes are fully resigned to their public banishment. According to Tocqueville, they silently seethe at their vulnerability and are filled with contempt for the masses. Behind closed doors, they bitterly complain about democracy. Underneath their seeming acquiescence and even "obsequious politeness toward the dominant power, it is easy to see that the rich feel a deep disgust with their country's democratic institutions."[94] If they could dismantle their government and revolutionize their culture, they surely would. Tocqueville thinks that if monarchy were ever to come to the United States, it would be because of the wealthy. Still, he considers this possibility remote.

Even if the economic elite had the courage to seek political power, there is little chance they would win elections. Ordinary citizens badly outnumber them and, as previously argued, refuse to vote for men of merit, partially because talented individuals offend their notion of complete equality.[95] While Tocqueville reports there is no strong hatred against the talented and upper classes and no desire to inflict cruelty on them, there is a low-level jealousy that prevents them from attaining public office. Tocqueville thinks democrats have little taste for them and are careful to keep them from power. Excellence is a liability. In his notebooks, he makes special mention of a conversation he had soon after his arrival. He was informed by one American that "here, one finds a permanent and active jealousy on democracy's part, not against the upper classes for they do not exist, but against all those who rise from its ranks by their wealth, their talents and their services."[96] If a person of merit did manage to win an election, moreover, Tocqueville claims he is almost sure to be accused of corruption and drummed out of office. Interestingly, such charges, while often true, are inspired as much by vanity as by ethical outrage: "To attribute his rise to talent or virtue is inconvenient, because it requires them[Americans] to admit to themselves that they are less virtuous or clever than he."[97]

Intellectuals do not fare much better. There are not many of them, and they attract little respect. While most Americans receive a baseline primary education, few are sent off to college and have the leisure to contemplate truth and beauty. Only a sliver of the population attains enlightenment. Tocqueville remarks, "I do not think that there is any other country in the world where, as a population, the ignorant are so few and the learned still fewer."[98] In America, everybody works, including the wealthy, and just about everyone is so preoccupied with amassing fortune that he or she ignores the pleasures of imagination and the intellect. Even the most educated Americans view the arts and sciences in terms of their practical value. They do not contemplate the eternal verities. In the United States, there is certainly nothing comparable to the Parisian salon culture, nor are there intellectuals vying to become the preeminent social class à la the *philosophes*. They could not be less of a danger.

Moreover, Tocqueville argues that Americans hold so firmly to equality that they refuse to acknowledge intellectual superiorities of any sort. Despite their low-level education, they have full confidence in their ability to understand almost any problem, no matter how complicated. They dismiss any claim or argument beyond their comprehension as silly. If an American d'Alembert could dazzle them with logic, they would immediately deny his brilliance and laugh him off as a charlatan. For Tocqueville, this is a problem of pride and leads to an absurdity: "It is the theory of equality applied to intelligence."[99]

Tocqueville does qualify his claims. First, there is a sectional element to his analysis. Tocqueville exempts New Englanders from his charges. In New England, "people have become accustomed to respecting intellectual and moral superiority and submitting to them without discomfort."[100] Outside New England, however, particularly in the South and the Southwest, morality and religion mitigate against such attitudes. Second, Tocqueville argues that American anti-intellectualism is distinctly American and may not be a true reflection of democratic cultural life in general. Seemingly contradicting his sectional claims, one reason America is exceptional regarding intellectual development is its Puritan roots. Puritanism, or English Calvinism, is one of the stricter Christian sects and "naturally offers little encouragement to the fine arts and is only reluctantly tolerant of literary pleasures."[101] In addition, America's close cultural ties with Europe obviate the need for a productive intellectual class. As a European people, Americans inherited a robust intellectual tradition and could claim the masters of Europe as their own. Other democracies, however, might be capable of establishing an active and vigorous intellectual community. Tocqueville's argument here is neo-Augustinian and especially Rousseauian. The emergence of a democratic intellectual elite would result from the successes of the natural aristocracy (though not the sort of formalized meritocracy proposed by Henri de Saint-Simon). The most talented individuals, Tocqueville surmises, will assume a disproportionate share of the social and economic rewards. Invariably, some will attain so much wealth that they no longer have to work and hence have the leisure to dedicate themselves to intellectual pleasures. As leading members of their communities, their successes will attract the attention of their fellow citizens. At first, people will envy them only for their wealth. Once they witness their intellectual cultivation, however, they will begin to desire such abilities as well. Their envy, in other words, will lead to emulation. As a result, the arts and sciences might very well become fashionable. Everyone will attempt to gain "fame, power, or wealth" by excelling at such activities.[102] So, there is a formula for democratic intellectual elitism, though Tocqueville is only speculating and cannot provide a historical example to back up his claim.

Notwithstanding these qualifications, Tocqueville would almost certainly argue that Rousseau looks for tyranny in the wrong places. There is little reason to assume the rich will become ravenous wolves and inflict cruelty on the poor. Likewise, his concerns that the intellectuals will demean the working classes and convince them they have social value only if they contribute to the arts and sciences has yet to occur and is by no means inevitable. The wealthy have no political power, and the intellectuals receive much less respect in American democracy than religion and patriotism, which Rousseau assumed would never survive the Enlightenment. Excellence has much less currency in the new democratic age.

The true source of tyranny in the democratic age, as previously argued, is the demos itself. Everything changes due to the equality of conditions, and tyranny is no exception. Democratic tyranny assumes two basic forms: the tyranny of the majority and a paternalistic welfare state elected by "we the people." Tyranny of the majority, Tocqueville avers, is a cultural tyranny that insists upon absolute conformity. Tocqueville thinks the masses completely control the zeitgeist in America: "It is clear that there can be no durable obstacles capable of preventing the opinions, prejudices, interests, and even passions of the people from making their influence felt on the daily direction of society."[103] The tyranny results from the logic of equality. Americans, to recall, think they are as good as everyone in everything. This means that everyone is equally intelligent. Accordingly, finding truth is simply a matter of counting heads. So, if 80 percent of the people agree on a policy, it must be right. The typical Americans reasons, "Who are these 20 percent to think they are smarter than everyone else?" More brains equals more intelligence. Americans treat the majority like the French did some of their kings: it can do no wrong.

For Tocqueville, tyranny of the majority is an especially insidious form of domination, as it goes for the soul and not the body. It seeks to ostracize those who think differently or step out of the crowd. There is a formal veneer of freedom—people are officially allowed to think, say, and do as they please. But the consequence is virtual banishment from social and political life, which amounts to the undoing of the substance of democracy. The majority communicates to those who reject its maxims, "You are free not to think as I do. You may keep your life, your property, everything else. But from this day forth you shall be a stranger among us."[104] Émile Faguet captures the spirit of this tyranny even better than Tocqueville himself: "Democratic despotism is subtly diffused through all the air which the nation breathes. It does not fall from above, it does not exactly rise from below, it surrounds us, encircles us, and creeps around us on all sides. One is tied down by all one's neighbours."[105] The majority is smothering—it "surrounds" and "ties" people down. There is no escape from it. What is so troubling about the tyranny of the majority is that few people, among the majority and the victims alike, consider it to be tyranny. They do not call it by its right name and mistakenly believe it is democracy in action. From the standpoint of democratic theory, the consequences are devastating. Individuals lose the ability to think for themselves and surrender to majority opinion. Public discussions go nowhere, and free speech does not result in truth or progress. It is merely a reflection of the lowest common denominator.[106]

Tocqueville worries there is no force in America that is even willing to stand up to the majority. Political leaders rarely serve as a defense against it, as most come from the same mediocre masses and ride the tyranny of the majority to power. American government is thus populated by yes-men and spineless toadies who follow the public rather than lead it. Only a truly great, charismatic leader might be able to thwart the majority—one who possesses "virile candor" and "manly independence of thought."[107] Unfortunately, such statesmen are not frequently found in democratic government. American moralists are not much better. They are just as obsequious as politicians. Indeed, they are just as obsequious as aristocratic courtiers, even if they do not address the people as "sire" and "Your Majesty." As evidence, Tocqueville cites one example he finds particularly galling: "We know that the people to whom we speak are too far above human weaknesses ever to lose control of themselves. We would not speak thus were we not addressing men whose virtues and intelligence so far outshine all others as to render them alone worthy to remain free." Tocqueville is astounded by this fawning. He rhetorically asks, "How could the flatterers of Louis XIV do better?"[108] Finally, minorities themselves tend to defer to the majority, though only for the most self-interested reasons. They expect one day to be that majority and drive it.

Nonetheless, Tocqueville refuses to despair. He is adamant that the majority is not invincible and is confident it can be managed. There are a variety of institutions and mores that slow it down and prevent it from reaching its more virulent forms. The founders, upon whom Tocqueville repeatedly lavishes praise, were aware of the dangers of the people and put in numerous obstacles to slow down the deliberative and legislative process so the temporary passions of the masses would have time to cool down. Tocqueville is especially impressed by American decentralization and the Humean federalism that characterizes its constitutional structures.[109] The diffusing of power makes it much more difficult for majorities to quickly translate their dominance into legislative action.

Also, to return to an earlier point, Tocqueville believes that lawyers themselves function as a break against the passions of the masses. Lawyers in democracies, he observes, tend to be conservative and antidemocratic. They "have an instinctive preference for order," "natural love of formalities," "and secret contempt for popular government."[110] In particular, Tocqueville thinks that precedent is of crucial importance. Anglo lawyers—English and American ones—are educated to respect precedent, which gives them a "taste and respect for what is old."[111] Lawyers are unusual in American life for this very reason. They are among the few classes of citizen who lack the desire to innovate. Any alteration of the legal code must be explained as a development or a completion of work that started with previous generations of lawyers. This puts lawyers directly at odds with democratic instincts for novelty, innovation, and the new, new thing. For Tocqueville, this makes them of inestimable social value.

The second great tyranny in American life is the government, which Tocqueville argues can surreptitiously create an "administrative" or "schoolmaster" despotism. Essentially, he is concerned that the people, so weakened by their condition of equality, will rely on the government to fulfill all their needs and ensure their survival. Dependent upon this paternalistic nanny state, Americans will lose their inclination to remain their own masters and become infantilized by their lack of efficacy. This tyranny is also insidious, as it, too, is difficult to perceive. Americans barely notice the invisible violence being done to them because it works for the happiness of its subjects and appears to be an instrument of self-interest. Although technically sovereign, citizens become slaves to the comforts provided by the state, which in time extends to the minutiae of life. It is thus a "more extensive and more mild" form of tyranny and tends to "degrade men without tormenting them."[112] To prevent this potentiality, citizens must collectively take responsibility for their lives and look to one another to survive the vicissitudes of life through civic and political associations rather than the government.

Lastly, Tocqueville does not fully ignore the sort of economic tyranny of the wealthy that so bothered Rousseau. But it is a distant third behind the other two types of tyrannies and, as far as he is concerned, has yet to become a true threat in America's commercial democracy. At least in Jacksonian America, he thinks, there is little chance the moneyed classes could buy government and set up a shadow oligarchy in which their economic power controls political power. For a variety of reasons, he thinks American politicians are too difficult to buy. Even if they put themselves up for sale, there are probably too many to bribe, and most Americans do not trust them anyway.

Tocqueville does, however, fear the rise of an industrial aristocracy—a new oligarchy for the commercial age. He knows this threatens to undo his thesis and only reluctantly addresses it: "Tocqueville had great difficulty in squaring his theory that modern society was becoming more democratic and equal with the fact that modern industry was expanding and producing its own type of stark inequality."[113] Still, he does dedicate a full chapter to the rise of an industrial aristocracy and offers a sketch of his concerns. Interestingly, he pays careful attention to the cognitive consequences of the division of labor, which he fears could create not simply a moneyed elite but an intellectual one. He begins his argument with the assumption, common among some leading lights of the Scottish Enlightenment, that the division of labor causes great harm to the average worker. While it is remarkably productive and efficient, it turns the average person into a dullard. Obviously referencing Adam Smith, Tocqueville rhetorically asks, "What should we expect from a man who has spent twenty years of his life making pinheads?"[114] Division of labor has the opposite effect on the managerial classes. Their minds expand as the scale of their enterprises increases. The larger the economic operation, the greater the cognitive demands that are placed on the managers and owners. The managers and workers thus represent opposite ends of an intellectual caste system and almost appear to be two difference species: "One comes more and more to resemble the administrator of a vast empire, and the other to resemble a brute."[115] Thus, an economic aristocracy eventually transforms into a cognitive one.

Tocqueville grudgingly admits that this new caste system resembles the old feudal aristocracy in a few important ways. First, as with the lord-serf relationship, there is a rigid, unbreakable dependency in the relationship. The worker needs the job, as he or she is unprepared to do anything else. His or her choice is stark: either do mindless toil or starve to death. The factory owner is also in a position of dependence, as factory production requires a sizable labor force. Thus, "each one occupies a place that is made for him, which he does not leave."[116] Second, it leads to permanent social classes. The master commands, the worker obeys, and there is almost no chance for the relationship to reverse itself: "The poor have few ways of escaping their condition and of becoming rich."[117] Third, repeating himself, Tocqueville points out that the owners and workers come to have dissimilar personalities. Finally, industrial capitalism results in a disturbing concentration of wealth. A few people accrue almost all the societal wealth, while the overwhelming mass of people live in squalor. Tocqueville's conclusions echo those of Smith, who also remarks that successful capitalist societies sustain immense inequality: "Wherever there is great wealth, there is great inequality."[118]

In other ways, however, Tocqueville thinks these new industrial aristocrats are much worse than their feudal counterparts. They possess all the vices
of the nobility but none of their virtues. They are the worst of both worlds.
Unlike the old aristocrats, who subscribed to an ethical code that stressed republican values and duty to responsibly govern society and take care of those
beneath them, the new industrial elite feel no obligation to their workers and
treat them callously if not cruelly. In the industrial economy, workers are not
tied to any one master and may work for several different employers during
their lifetime. Even if they remain in the same job, the employer-employee
relationship is far less substantial. Owners and workers see each other only at
work and are very distant from each other. Consequently, owners view their
relationship with their workers instrumentally, not paternalistically. They are
united only by "callous cash payment." The owner wants labor, while the
worker desires wages. As a result, the owners have no interest in governing or
taking care of their workers. In times of crisis, they leave them to be "nour-
ished by public charity."[119] Tocqueville does show real concern here and warns
democrats that they should watch for such developments. If he does not go as
far as Rousseau in condemning the bourgeois elite as being primarily driven
by *libido dominandi*, he nonetheless does not trust them and believes them ill
fit for sustaining a healthy democratic society.

His sensitivities, however, may be disingenuous. Writing more than a
half century before Tocqueville, Smith believes the emergence of an industrial aristocracy is a fait accompli, not a possible threat looming on the hori-
zon. He fully accepts that under capitalism there is a financial and cognitive
divide separating the owners from the workers. In his *Lecture on Jurisprudence* and *The Wealth of Nations*, which I cited in Chapter 1, he states as a
matter of fact that the working classes are "stupid." Given that Tocqueville
uses Smith's analogy of the pin factory in *Democracy*, he must have at least
been familiar with Smith's views. Moreover, in 1835, he visited the industrial
capital of England, Manchester, and witnessed firsthand the degrading lifestyles of the working classes. He did not turn a blind eye to its horrors. As
Hugh Brogan reports, he "was appalled by Manchester."[120] In his notebooks,
he writes that there are "a few great capitalists, thousands of poor workmen
and little middle class."[121] Some of the poor "live in damp cellars, hot, stink-
ing and unhealthy; thirteen to fifteen to one," and in one of the larger factories he visits, "three-quarters of the workers . . . are women or children."[122]
After witnessing both the prodigious output and abject inhumanity of industrial capitalism, he concludes that while "civilization works its miracles . . .

civilized man is turned back almost into a savage."[123] So, it is not as if Tocqueville were ignorant of the extreme poverty caused by industrial capitalism
in his day. Five years before he published volume II of *Democracy*, he had seen
it in action, warts and all.

There is, moreover, no reason to suppose that American capitalism would
work any differently. If English factory workers endure humiliating poverty
and children in England perform the same work as their fathers, presumably
the same thing will occur in America. Tocqueville never makes a case for
American exceptionalism in this regard and never bothers to explain why
American factories would provide a spate of cognitively challenging working-
class jobs and produce an enlightened workforce. Tocqueville also cannot
argue that America might not join the Industrial Revolution. It was quickly
establishing itself by the 1830s, and Tocqueville himself argued the future of
America lay with the industrial North rather than the faux-patrician South.
Indeed, there is every reason to think that industrial tyranny is every bit as
dangerous as the tyranny of the majority or the tyranny of the nanny state. It
is hard to maintain, as he does, that it is "the most limited and least dangerous" of all tyrannies."[124] He should have taken it more seriously.

Perfectibility

There are two other concepts that are part of Rousseau's narrative of *amour-
propre* that make an appearance in Tocqueville. The first is perfectibility. Unlike Rousseau, Tocqueville sees it as only a minor problem. He begins from
Rousseau's starting point that humans differ from other animals in that they
alone can improve themselves. This idea, like egoism, is "as old as the world"
and was not invented in democracies.[125] As is the case with almost every other
idea, however, it is modified and transformed by the ideology of equality.
According to Tocqueville, democrats take the idea of perfectibility too seriously and are convinced everything can be improved all the time. They fail to
respect how difficult it is to achieve true progress and falsely assume that they
can achieve anything. Nothing is beyond their grasp, they tell themselves, and
absolute good can be attained through continuous hard work. Failure only
teaches them to keep trying.

While Americans tend to view such optimism as one of their virtues, Tocqueville is less impressed. Unfortunately, he does not take the time to identify
all the negative consequences that flow from this naïveté. He lists only one—

bad faith. Recounting a conversation he had with an American sailor about the poor quality of American ships, the sailor indicated that since the art of navigation is continuously progressing, there is no point in building high-quality boats. Even the best of boats become obsolete in short order. Absurdly, American sailors do not demand improved working conditions, because constant improvement renders such requests pointless.

Notably, Tocqueville does not consider the Rousseauian argument that perfectibility will develop the species and reveal wide-ranging natural inequalities. To recall Rousseau's contention, human development makes apparent the wide gulf in talent that exists between humans and paves the way for the emergence of a superior class of individuals. Tocqueville's discussion of perfectibility, conversely, assumes American democrats talk more about improvement than make it. It is yet another example of democratic pomposity. Still, it is strange that Tocqueville's democrats are not wary of perfectibility, as it leads to all sorts of change that will most likely inflame American envy and egoism. If perfectibility does not produce permanent inequalities, it certainly leads to temporary ones that threaten to upset complete equality. Assuming Tocqueville's reporting is accurate, these concerns never cross the mind of American democrats. Instead, they focus exclusively on the positive short-term benefit of change inspired by perfectibility. If it improves their lot, they view it with rose-colored glasses.

Compassion, Weakness, and Sociability

Finally, Tocqueville presents a mild challenge to Rousseau's notion that weakness leads to compassion and sociability. He sets himself up perfectly to adopt Rousseau's argument. By definition, he thinks democrats are weak and vulnerable. Everyone is rising and falling, and most people lack the financial resources to shield themselves from unexpected misfortune. Tocqueville conjectures that democrats are so weak that "they can do almost nothing by themselves."[126] He also partially accepts Rousseau's conclusions. Such vulnerability *can* make people compassionate and sociable. Due to social fluidity, Tocqueville's democrats tend to identify with one another. They see themselves reflected in their fellow citizens and can easily imagine themselves in the place of both superiors and inferiors alike. Even the rich empathize with the poor, as they often come from humble origins and are more than aware that today's fortunes may be gone tomorrow. Thus, Tocqueville happily notes,

Americans can be counted on to help a stranger in need, rich or poor: "When there is an accident on a public way, people will rush to the victim's aid from every direction."[127]

This, however, is only one response to equality and weakness. Americans also can be indifferent to their neighbors and do not necessarily form strong social attachments. Instead, their sympathy is weak and transitory. Even after helping a stranger, Tocqueville reports, they quickly move on and do not give victims a second thought. The reason for this is surprising given the Pascalian portrait of the vain and envious Americans that shows up repeatedly in *Democracy*. In much of the text, Americans cannot stop thinking about their peers and what their peers think of them. Tocqueville claims, however, that there is another side to the American personality—one that reflects confidence and self-assuredness. He terms this disposition "individualism," which he contrasts with "egoism." Under the sway of individualism, people evaluate their lives through the abstract category of equality, or more accurately, complete equality. Equality becomes an *a priori* logical truth and cannot be disproved by empirical experiences. Just as Ajax knows he is naturally superior, to reiterate, Americans know they are equal to their neighbors. No earthly experience can alter this fundamental fact about their existence. Tocqueville thinks individualism is the Cartesian element in Americans. Ideology overpowers observation and allows Americans to interpret away any threats to their self-conception.

Individualism also makes democrats asocial and isolated. When in this frame of mind, they deduce from "complete equality" that there is nothing to be gained from interacting with their peers. If a person's neighbors are in no way superior, they reason, what useful advice or aid could they possibly offer? Everything a neighbor could do could easily be done by oneself. They interpret their equality, in other words, as a call for self-sufficiency. The problem is, however, that self-sufficiency is not realistic for democrats. If it is a fact that Americans are equal, then it is also a fact that they are weak and cannot survive without some form of external help. It is crucial that this help does not come from the government, as it results in the paternalistic tyranny of the welfare state that infantilizes the population. To remain "masters of themselves," democrats need to join forces through civic associations and collectively overcome their challenges. They need to reach out and rely on each other.

Tocqueville, therefore, would probably not support Rousseau's attempt in *Emile* to create compassion out of a sense of weakness and vulnerability. If combined with the ideology of equality, weakness just as easily leads to social isolation as it does to cooperation and assistance. As a result, it produces a watered-down compassion that only occasionally inspires people to reach out to their neighbors, usually in times of crisis. If democrats become too Cartesian in their thinking, in other words, they may stop thinking about their fellow citizens altogether, no matter how much they suffer from the blows of fate. Ultimately, his concept of individualism would probably lead Tocqueville to condemn Rousseau's praise of self-sufficiency and solitude in texts like *The Reveries*. Progress, for him, is inevitable. There is no going back to feudal agrarian lifestyles and undoing the economic dependencies created by commercial capitalism. Social integration is a fact of life. The trick is getting people to appreciate it.

Conclusion

Tocqueville is a reluctant liberal. He endorses the commercial democratic order out of pragmatism; he does so grudgingly, for Odyssean reasons. Its supremacy is inevitable, and hence it is the only available option furnished by history. The only choice, Tocqueville thinks, is to make it work. If history were contingent, he most certainly would work for the restoration of the old regime.

Accordingly, his portrayal of democracy is not exactly flattering. In many respects, Tocqueville turns Rousseau right on his head and attributes the vices of aristocracy to democracy. *Amour-propre* and *libido dominandi* are democratic problems, not aristocratic ones. The masses suffer most from the former and are most likely to act out of the latter. It is the Voltaires and d'Alemberts of the world who need to be afraid, for they will be the ones most likely to be dominated and controlled. Even if Rousseau is right about the motives inspiring the elite, Tocqueville would remind him that he fails to acknowledge that they lack the power to realize their goals. The poor and the middle class themselves serve as effective constraints. Power comes in many forms; not all of it is economic.

Likewise, Tocqueville is much less appreciative of the paradox of vice serving as a surrogate for virtue that mesmerized so many neo-Augustinians as well as generations of liberal theorists. It is less reliable and less elegant than its supporters imagine. Democracies can succeed because of it, but not thrive.

Conclusion

Despite widespread concerns about inequality these days, there has been surprisingly little soul-searching among liberal theorists and intellectuals. Few believe it to be a systemic problem inherent in liberalism or connect it to popular ideologies such as meritocracy. Distressingly, Nietzsche's narrative of inequality as a problem of the *ressentiment* of the weak and the poor appears to be far more popular than Rousseau's concerns about the *libido dominandi* of the rich and powerful. Criticisms of the elite are too often set aside as nothing more than the jealousy of those at the bottom, as if only poor people can be corrupted by inequality. For example, consider Harry Frankfurt's admonition to average Americans not to envy their more distinguished neighbors or Pankaj Mishra's ridiculing of contemporary right-wing populism as an expression of Rousseauian resentment.[1] That Rousseau, the most ardent defender of equality in the West, is singled out as a troublemaker by Mishra in an age of inequality is revealing. He is still not taken seriously. He is not even given credit for providing an evenhanded treatment of *amour-propre* with regard to class. Unlike Frankfurt and Mishra, he contends it affects rich and poor alike.

Rousseau is a populist in the best sense of the word. He is dedicated to the freedom and dignity of the average person, and carefully tries to balance this populism with the needs of superior people to develop and exercise their talents. This balance, it goes without saying, does not require turning a blind eye to puerile, narcissistic, and destructive behavior by those at the top.

What is most remarkable about Mishra's slight, however, is that the diagnosis Rousseau offers of the ills of modern society is hardly radical. Indeed, his most important insights have been validated by recent research in social psychology and economics. One recent study purports to show that wealthy people define themselves aristocratically through their achievements rather than through their relationships.[2] In addition, several studies demonstrate the upper classes tend to have less compassion and are more willing to cheat than the general population.[3] That is, they are more inclined to be cruel. Other studies prove that conspicuous displays of inequality, such as first-class airplane tickets, may make rich and poor alike less cooperative and more likely to behave in an antisocial manner.[4] And according to some economists, people conceptualize economic life in terms of *amour-propre* rather than *amour de soi-même*. They view their wealth in relative terms and would rather have less wealth if it means having more than their neighbors.[5] Finally, other studies prove that being a have-not results in higher levels of depression.[6]

Social science aside, Rousseau's thesis is grounded in common sense. It is scarcely surprising that powerful elites have trouble identifying with the struggles of the poor and are prone to abusing them. Most people accept that power corrupts, even if they do not apply the maxim as readily to economic and intellectual elites as to political ones. Rousseau's position can even find support among his avowed enemies. For example, Isaiah Berlin, one of those World War II–era theorists who puts Rousseau in league with Hitler, fully appreciates the dangers the rich pose to the poor and even analogizes the wealthy to ravenous wolves: "Both liberty and equality are among the primary goals pursued by human beings through many centuries, but total liberty for wolves is death for the lambs, total liberty of the powerful, the gifted, is not compatible with the rights to a decent existence of the weak and the less gifted."[7]

This does not suggest Rousseau's detractors, Mishra included, are without reply. Several possible criticisms of Rousseau are easy to imagine. First, Rousseau perhaps wrongly downplays the psychological defenses that allow people to cope with disappointment and failure. In many cultures, learning how to live with failure and not being the best is part of growing up and becoming a well-adjusted adult. Even in meritocratic societies, ordinary people need not obsess about achievement and can lead unambitious yet satisfying lives. Second, future social science research may show that the talented and wealthy are not a class of ravenous wolves who wish to devour the weaker parts of the population and deprive them of the means of living a dignified life. If libertarians such as William Graham Sumner write nonsense when they assert that the wealthy "rejoice to see any man succeed in improving his position,"[8] it is more than plausible to assume there is still compassion in the world, and some members of the upper class genuinely try to relieve the emotional and economic suffering of less fortunate citizens. Finally, the wealthy do not have a monopoly on cruelty and the desire to dominate. The humiliation caused by poverty has inspired racism, anti-Semitism, and some of the most destructive and barbarous acts in human history. Rousseau's analysis of cruelty is thus limited and partial. If he rightly observes that both rich and poor suffer from *amour-propre*, he fails to acknowledge, as do Tocqueville and other theorists, the libido *dominandi* of the weak and the poor.

None of these objections, however, decisively refute or even are more tenable than Rousseau's fundamental insight that modern commercial democracy is classically aristocratic and home to dangerous forms of inequality. While they are well worth considering, at present they cannot begin to justify either ignoring Rousseau's concerns or our stubborn refusal to consider moral language other than Odyssean democratic reasoning and utilitarianism in political discussion. Rousseau deserves better, and so do we.

Notes

INTRODUCTION

1. Jacob Talmon accuses Rousseau of authoring a totalitarian democracy and links him with Robespierre, Saint-Just, and Babeuf. See J. L. Talmon, *The Origins of Totalitarian Democracy* (New York: W. W. Norton, 1970), 38–49. World War II–era intellectuals did not hesitate to interpret him as the founding father of Nazism. See Bertrand Russell, *A History of Western Philosophy* (New York: Simon and Schuster, 1972), 685; Isaiah Berlin, *Freedom and Its Betrayal: Six Enemies of Human Liberty*, ed. Henry Hardy (Princeton: Princeton University Press, 2002), 41.

2. Russell, *A History of Western Philosophy*, 685.

3. The most famous work in this tradition is Irving Babbitt's *Rousseau and Romanticism*. Although the text is not based on Rousseau's writings, Babbitt calls Rousseau "the great modern romancer" and believes he exemplifies modern romanticism. His Rousseau privileges emotion and spontaneity over rationality and is animated by faith in nature and the natural goodness in humans. Babbitt also characterizes Rousseau as a frustrated "beautiful soul" who refuses to acknowledge moral ambiguity, and he compares his "imaginative activity" to "the delights of daydreaming." See Irving Babbitt, *Rousseau and Romanticism* (New York: Houghton Mifflin, 1919), 5 and 72. As expected, Babbitt also blames Rousseau for the French Revolution: "If we wish to see the psychology of Rousseau writ large we should turn to the French Revolution." Babbitt, *Rousseau and Romanticism*, 135.

4. See Ernst Cassirer, *The Question of Jean-Jacques Rousseau* (Bloomington: Indiana University Press, 1963).

5. Manfred Kuehn, *Kant: A Biography* (Cambridge: Cambridge University Press, 2001), 131.

6. See H. J. Paton, *The Categorical Imperative: A Study in Kant's Moral Philosophy* (Philadelphia: University of Pennsylvania Press, 1948), 171.

7. See Arthur O. Lovejoy, *Reflections on Human Nature* (Baltimore: Johns Hopkins University Press, 1968), lectures I, III, IV, and V.

8. See Thomas Hobbes, *Leviathan*, ed. Edwin Curley (Indianapolis: Hackett, 1994), 96–97; Samuel Pufendorf, *On the Duty of Man and Citizen*, trans. Michael Silverthorne (Cambridge: Cambridge University Press, 1991), 164–65; John Locke, *An Essay Concerning Human Understanding*, ed. P. H. Nidditch (Oxford: Clarendon Press, 1975), 231–32.

9. In an earlier book by Smith, *The Theory of Moral Sentiments*, his moral psychology is heavily influenced by the language of *amour-propre*.

10. See Albert O. Hirschman, *The Passions and the Interests: Political Arguments for Capitalism Before Its Triumph* (Princeton: Princeton University Press, 2013), 112. See also Pierre Manent, *The City of Man*, trans. Marc A. Lepain (Princeton: Princeton University Press, 1998), 86–92.

11. Granted, modern democracies contain moral vocabularies other than utilitarianism. The language of natural rights and republicanism remains influential. Those vocabularies, however,

did not originate in democracies. Rights talk emerged as a response to absolute monarchies, and republicanism from ancient aristocracies.

12. See Jeremy Bentham, *An Introduction to the Principles of Morals and Legislation* (New York: Hafner Press, 1948), V, 33.

13. Against this view, Robert C. Solomon argued for much of his career that emotions ought not to be considered temporary bouts of insanity or purposeless disruptions of our rational nature. See Robert C. Solomon, *The Passions: Emotions and the Meaning of Life* (Indianapolis: Hackett, 1993), and Robert C. Solomon, *True to Our Feelings: What Our Emotions Are Really Telling Us* (Oxford: Oxford University Press, 2001). Martha Nussbaum similarly characterizes Western views of emotions and passions as "unthinking energies that simply push the person around." Martha Nussbaum, *Upheavals of Thought: The Intelligence of the Emotions* (Cambridge: Cambridge University Press, 2003), 24.

14. John Rawls, *A Theory of Justice* (Cambridge: Belknap Press of Harvard University Press, 1971), 143.

15. Harry Frankfurt, *On Inequality* (Princeton: Princeton University Press, 2015), 11–12.

16. As Raymond Geuss contends, "Politics allows itself to be cut up for study in any one of a number of different ways, and which cuts will be most illuminating will depend very much on the context, and what one is interested in finding out." Raymond Geuss, *Philosophy and Real Politics* (Princeton: Princeton University Press, 2008), 17.

17. Adam Smith, *The Theory of Moral Sentiments*, ed. D. D. Rafael and A. L. Mackie (Indianapolis: Liberty Fund, 1982), 50.

18. See Bohan Zawadski and Paul Lazarsfeld, "The Psychological Consequences of Unemployment," *Journal of Social Psychology* 6, no. 2 (1935): 224–51. More recently, see Erica Solove, Gwenith G. Fisher, and Kurt Kraiger, "Coping with Job Loss and Reemployment: A Two-Wave Study," *Journal of Business and Psychology* 30, no. 3 (2015): 529–41.

19. Michael Harrington, *The Other America: Poverty in the United States* (New York: Pelican Books, 1981), 2.

20. For example, see S. Beilock. R. Rydell, and A. R. McConnell, "Stereotype Threat and Working Memory: Mechanisms, Alleviation, and Spill Over," *Journal of Experimental Psychology* 136, no. 2 (2007): 256–76.

21. See my Conclusion for a brief discussion and citations.

22. Rousseau, *Discourse on the Origins and Foundations of Inequality Among Men*, in *The Discourses and Other Early Writings*, trans. Victor Gourevitch (Cambridge: Cambridge University Press, 1997), hereafter referred to as the *Second Discourse*, n. XV, 218 and 166/ *Oeuvres complètes*, ed. Bernard Gagnebin and Marcel Raymond (Paris: NRF Edition de la Pléiade, 1959–1969), hereafter referred to as *OC*, III, 219 and 169–70. All Rousseau citations are followed by their French equivalents from the Pléiade editions of the *Oeuvres complètes*, edited by Bernard Gagnebin and Marcel Raymond, abbreviated as *OC*, followed by the volume number and page number.

23. N. J. H. Dent, *Rousseau: An Introduction to His Psychological, Social and Political Theory* (Oxford: Basil Blackwell, 1988). See also N. J. H. Dent and Timothy O'Hagan, "Rousseau on Amour-Propre," *Aristotelian Society* suppl. 72, no. 1 (1998): 57–73; Timothy O'Hagan, *Rousseau* (London: Routledge, 1999), 171–73. Dent specifically seeks to discredit John Charvet, whom he names as his target. Charvet claims that Rousseau's thought is incoherent because he is unable to fully eradicate *amour-propre*, which he thinks Rousseau argues is wholly negative. Dent rightly argues that Rousseau's understanding of *amour-propre* is more nuanced and allows for positive expressions. See John Charvet, *The Social Problem in the Philosophy of Rousseau* (Cambridge: Cambridge University Press, 1974).

24. See also Laurence D. Cooper, *Rousseau, Nature, and the Problem of the Good Life* (University Park: Penn State University Press, 1999), 123–30; see also Laurence D. Cooper, "Rousseau on Self-Love: What We've Learned, What We Might Have Learned," *Review of Politics* 60, no. 4 (1998): 664–671.

25. As evidence, Cooper cites the passage in which Rousseau states that "the habit of living together gave rise to the sweetest sentiments known to man, conjugal, and Paternal love" as well as some passages from *Emile*. While Rousseau does not explicitly credit *amour-propre* as the source of these sentiments, Cooper rightly claims that it would be impossible to experience them without it. See Rousseau, *Second Discourse*, 164/ *OC* III, 168.

26. David Lay Williams, *Rousseau's Platonic Enlightenment* (University Park: Penn State University Press, 2007), 166–67. See Jean-Jacques Rousseau, *Rousseau, Judge of Jean-Jacques: Dialogues*, in *The Collected Writings of Jean-Jacques Rousseau*, vol. 1, trans. Christopher Kelly (Hanover: Dartmouth College Press, 1990), 122 and 144/ *OC* I, 817 and 846.

27. Frederick Neuhouser, *Rousseau's Theodicy of Self-Love: Evil, Rationality, and the Drive for Recognition* (Oxford: Oxford University, 2008), 2. Joshua Cohen also is a proponent of this view. See Joshua Cohen, *Rousseau: A Free Community of Equals* (Oxford: Oxford University Press, 2010), 115–16. Neuhouser is rather skeptical in *Rousseau's Theodicy of Self-Love* that Rousseau is a Kantian. In his second book, *Rousseau's Critique of Inequality*, he is much closer to Dent. See Frederick Neuhouser, *Rousseau's Critique of Inequality: Reconstructing the Second Discourse* (Cambridge: Cambridge University Press, 2014). I address this point in Chapter 1.

28. Rousseau, *Second Discourse*, 184/ *OC* III, 189.

29. Jean-Jacques Rousseau, *Emile: Or On Education*, in *The Collected Writings of Rousseau*, vol. 13, trans. Christopher Kelly and Allan Bloom (Hanover: Dartmouth College Press, 2010), 400/ *OC* IV, 536.

30. For example, see Charles Hendel, *Jean-Jacques Rousseau: Moralist*, vol. II, 2nd edition (Indianapolis: Bobbs-Merrill, 1934), 114; Judith N. Shklar, *Men and Citizens: A Study of Rousseau's Social Theory* (Cambridge: Cambridge University Press, 1969), 19, 21, 28.

31. Dent, *Rousseau*, 21 and 114.

32. Cooper, *Rousseau, Nature, and the Problem of the Good Life*, 118.

33. Neuhouser, *Rousseau's Theodicy of Self-Love*, 5. See also p. 157 and Neuhouser, *Rousseau's Critique of Inequality*, 66 and 72.

34. Neuhouser, *Rousseau's Critique of Inequality*, 115.

35. Ibid., chapter 2.

36. David Lay Williams has drawn attention to Neuhouser's analytic reading in a review essay and argues it comes at the expense of the historical dimensions of Rousseau's critique of inequality. See David Lay Williams, "Review Essay: Rousseau on Inequality and Free Will," *Political Theory* 45, no. 4 (2017): 556–57.

37. Neuhouser argues in *Rousseau's Critique of Inequality* that Rousseau concerns himself only with social inequality, not natural inequality. See Neuhouser, *Rousseau's Critique of Inequality*, 16–17. In Chapter 1, I contest this interpretation both through textual analysis and through historical context.

CHAPTER I

1. Rousseau, *Second Discourse*, 166/ *OC* III, 169–70. Italics mine.

2. See Victor Goldschmidt, *Anthropologie et politique: Les principes du système de Rousseau*

(Paris: Vrin, 1974), 452. See also Pierre Force, *Self-Interest Before Adam Smith: A Genealogy of Economic Science* (Cambridge: Cambridge University Press, 2003), 38.

3. Jean Starobinksi, *Jean-Jacques Rousseau: Transparency and Obstruction*, trans. Arthur Goldhammer (Chicago: University of Chicago Press, 1971), 27.

4. Rousseau, *Second Discourse*, 162/*OC* III, 165–66. Similarly, Emile's self-love becomes a problem when he compares himself to others and comes to have a "desire to be in the first position." See Rousseau, *Emile*, 389/*OC* IV, 523.

5. Dent, *Rousseau*, 81–82. This comment, I should add, results from his unduly analytic approach to Rousseau. If Dent were willing to look at historical context, his query could be easily answered.

6. Cooper, *Rousseau, Nature, and the Problem of the Good Life*, 152–53.

7. Ibid., 160–72. For Rousseau's distinction, see Jean-Jacques Rousseau, *Plan for a Constitution for Corsica*, in *The Collected Writings of Jean-Jacques Rousseau*, vol. 11, trans. Christopher Kelly (Hanover: Dartmouth College Press, 2005), 154/*OC* III, 937–38.

8. For an excellent critique of Neuhouser on this point, see Robin Douglass, "What's Wrong with Inequality? Some Rousseauian Perspectives," *European Journal of Political Theory* 14, no. 3 (2015): 368–77.

9. See Neuhouser, *Rousseau's Theodicy of Self-Love*, 61–70.

10. Neuhouser, *Rousseau's Critique of Inequality*, 68.

11. Ibid., 81.

12. See Cohen, *Rousseau*, 101–4.

13. Rousseau, *Second Discourse*, 166/*OC* III, 170.

14. It is more likely that Rousseau is referencing the *doux-commerce* argument that civility and politeness can mitigate the potential damage self-love can cause to social harmony. If pride and vanity can be socially disruptive, the argument runs, they must be neutralized with "duties of civility" to ensure everyone can get along well enough to engage in commercial transactions. Hume, for example, contends in his *Enquiry* that "the eternal contrarieties, in company, of men's pride and self-conceit, have introduced the rules of GOOD-MANNERS, or POLITENESS." Rousseau, of course, rejects the *doux-commerce* formula as mere hypocrisy and thinks societal politeness masks a hate-filled civil war. The *Second Discourse* is designed to pierce through the civility that blinds people to the nature of the societies they inhabit. So, it is probably more appropriate to interpret this passage as a political criticism rather than as a philosophical precursor to German Idealism. For the Hume quote, see David Hume, *Enquiry Concerning the Principles of Morals*, ed. J. B. Schneewind (Indianapolis: Hackett, 1983), 68.

15. For the former claim, see Nannerl O. Keohane, *Philosophy and the State in France: The Renaissance to the Enlightenment* (Princeton: Princeton University Press, 1980), 431. For the latter, see Ruth W. Grant, *Hypocrisy and Integrity: Machiavelli, Rousseau, and the Ethics of Politics* (Chicago: University of Chicago Press, 1997), 157.

16. See Helena Rosenblatt, *Rousseau and Geneva: From the First Discourse to The Social Contract, 1749–1762* (Cambridge: Cambridge University Press, 1997), chapters 3–4. Specifically, she argues that Rousseau's aim is to discredit "the main tenets of modern natural law theory" in order to subvert "the theoretical justification for Geneva's patrician regime." See Rosenblatt, *Rousseau and Geneva*, 164.

17. Istvan Hont, *Politics in Commercial Society: Jean-Jacques Rousseau and Adam Smith*, ed. Béla Kapossy and Michael Sonenscher (Cambridge: Harvard University Press, 2015), 64 and 71; Neuhouser, *Rousseau's Critique of Inequality*, 88–108. See also Force, *Self-Interest Before Adam Smith*, 34–42.

18. Moran argues, correctly I think, that Rousseau plainly had an interest in accurately summarizing the most up-to-date knowledge in the natural sciences. He read Buffon and the current travel literature of the day. Nonetheless, he was acutely aware of the limits of eighteenth-century science and knew that he was only speculating. He admits this several times in the essay. See Francis Moran III, "Between Primates and Primitives: Natural Man as the Missing Link in Rousseau's Second Discourse," *Journal of the History of Ideas* 54, no. 1 (January 1993): 37–58. Kelly also has a compelling discussion of Rousseau's state of nature. See Christopher Kelly, "Rousseau's 'Peut-Etre': Reflections on the Status of the State of Nature," *Modern Intellectual History* 3, no. 1 (2006): 75–83.

19. Rousseau, *Second Discourse,* 125/*OC* III, 123.

20. See Force, *Self-Interest Before Adam Smith,* 38; Hont, *Politics in Commercial Society: Jean-Jacques Rousseau and Adam Smith,* 44. Force uses the terms "praise" and "consideration," while Hont employs the Kantian term "recognition."

21. In the "Preface to *Narcissus,*" Rousseau claims: "All our Writers regard the crowning achievement of our century's politics to be the sciences, the arts, luxury, commerce, laws." Although he does not suggest that there is a bourgeois class made up of men of commerce, administrators, and intellectuals, this list of achievements implies that the three professions represent the new power brokers in society. See Rousseau, "Preface to *Narcissus,*" in *The Discourses and Other Early Writings,* 100/*OC* III, 968.

22. Jennifer R. March, "Sophocles' Ajax: The Death and Burial of a Hero," *Bulletin of the Institute of Classical Studies* 38, no. 1 (1991–93): 9.

23. See Bernard Knox, *Word and Action: Essays on Ancient Theater* (Baltimore: Johns Hopkins University Press, 1979), 144.

24. If Homer's world can be described as an honor culture, it is also by definition a shame culture. Some people are celebrated for displaying excellence, while others earn shame by acts of exceptional incompetence, malevolence, or embarrassment. See Bernard Williams, *Shame and Necessity* (Berkeley: University of California Press, 1993).

25. Sophocles, *Aias,* trans. Herbert Golder and Richard Pevear (Oxford: Oxford University Press, 1999), 520–30.

26. Knox notes that he views the world "as a pattern of change and concession." See Knox, *Word and Action,* 147.

27. Paul Woodruff, *The Ajax Dilemma: Justice, Fairness, and Rewards* (Oxford: Oxford University Press, 2011), ix.

28. Sophocles, *Aias,* 150.

29. Ibid., 1550–60.

30. Woodruff, *The Ajax Dilemma,* 61 and 75. See also March, "Sophocles' Ajax: The Death and Burial of a Hero," 9.

31. He reasons that "the same fate could be mine." See Sophocles, *Aias,* 150.

32. Sophocles, *Aias,* 1510–20.

33. Notably, he does not do the same with Ajax. His selfish desire for glory might overlap with some principle of justice. His vices, in other words, can serve as surrogates for virtue, just as Odysseus's selfishness can compel compassion. In the play, however, Sophocles makes Ajax's quest for glory entirely self-regarding and at odds with the common good.

34. It might also be compared to Cephalus's maxims of truth telling and paying off debts from book I of Plato's *Republic.* Both Odysseus and Cephalus define self-interest as avoiding conflict and the wrath of others.

35. See Herbert Golder, "Sophocles' 'Ajax': Beyond the Shadow of Time," *Arion: A Journal of the Humanities and Classics*, third series, 1, no. 1 (1990): 10.

36. Ibid., 12. Thucydides famously remarks that the aristocratic values were viewed as ridiculous in democratic Athens. See Thucydides, *The Peloponnesian War*, trans. Walter Banco (New York: W. W. Norton, 1996), 3.83, p. 131.

37. See Williams, *Shame and Necessity*, 72–73, 84–85.

38. Dent, *Rousseau*, 20.

39. Ibid., 93–96.

40. Jean-Jacques Rousseau, *Moral Letters*, in *The Collected Writings of Jean-Jacques Rousseau*, vol. 12, trans. and ed. Christopher Kelly (Hanover: Dartmouth College Press, 2007), 182/*OC* IV, 1090.

41. Rousseau, *Emile*, 372/*OC* IV, 503

42. This view finds some contemporary support. Simon Blackburn similarly argues that self-esteem is "at best an aggregate of a whole different raft of specific valuations of one's own abilities, achievements, talents, or capacities." Presumably, possessing the world's largest collection of snow globes will not confer aristocratic status. See Simon Blackburn, *Mirror, Mirror: The Uses and Abuses of Self-Love* (Princeton: Princeton University Press, 2014), 80–82.

43. For the connection between honor and identity, see Alexander Welsh, *What Is Honor? A Question of Moral Imperatives* (New Haven: Yale University Press, 2008), 15–16.

44. Viroli rightly contends that inequality for Rousseau is a problem of personal identity. See Maurizio Viroli, *Jean-Jacques Rousseau and the "Well-Ordered Society,"* trans. Derek Hanson (Cambridge: Cambridge University Press, 1988), 4.

45. Rousseau, *Second Discourse*, 187/*OC* III, 193.

46. Rousseau, *Emile*, 209/*OC* IV, 301.

47. Ibid., *OC* IV, 300.

48. Ibid., 398/*OC* IV, 534.

49. Rousseau, "Preface to *Narcissus*," 98 /*OC* II, 966.

50. Rousseau, *Second Discourse*, 187/*OC* III, 192. Italics mine.

51. That Rousseau discusses the intersection of death and *amour-propre* in classical terms is evidence he is not easily categorized as a German Idealist. Hegel, in the "Master/Slave" allegory, argues that death undermines the human need for recognition. Through death and then slavery, Hegel claims, humans eventually realize that they can only gain the recognition they crave by respecting others as free and equal autonomous beings. For Rousseau, the promise of immortality strips death of its power to alter human consciousness in this way. People can always hope to gain recognition for being best by future generations, who presumably will admire them irrespective of how they treat their fellow humans.

52. Perhaps his most substantial treatment outside *Considerations on the Government of Poland* comes from the *Essay on the Origin of Languages*, in which Rousseau argues that Homer sang but could not have written the *Iliad*. See Rousseau, *Essay on the Origin of Languages*, in *The Discourses and Other Early Writings*, chapter 6/*OC* III, 389–90. He does mention Ajax in "Discourse on Heroic Virtue" but does not discuss Sophocles' version. See Rousseau, "Discourse on Heroic Virtue," in *The Discourses and Other Early Writings*, 309–10/*OC* II, 1267.

53. As Waldock observes, "It would have been a very dull spectator who, called away from the theatre at the point where the hero dies, had failed to take with him a strong impression that Ajax was noble." See A. J. A. Waldock, *Sophocles the Dramatist* (Cambridge: Cambridge University Press, 1966), 61.

54. Jean-Jacques Rousseau, *Considerations on the Government of Poland and on Its Planned*

Reformation, in *The Collected Writings of Jean-Jacques Rousseau*, vol. II, 177. In general, see pp. 172–79/*OC* III, 963.

55. Ibid., II, p. 173/*OC* III, 958–59. See also Rousseau, "Discourse on Heroic Virtue," *in The Discourses and Other Early Writings*, 309–310/*OC* II, 1267; Rousseau, "Discourse on Political Economy," in *The Discourses and Other Later Political Writings*, 16/*OC* III, 255. In this essay, Rousseau contends patriotism is a blend of *amour-propre* and virtue, which results from sublimated self-love. Finally, he makes a similar proposal in *Emile*. He enters young boys into running races in which the winner is to receive cake and be lavished with praise. He thinks there is no danger in arousing the bad forms of *amour-propre* through such races, as the great vice of children is gluttony, not vanity. See Rousseau, *Emile*, 283–84, 295/*OC* IV, 393–95, 409–10.

56. Rousseau, "Discourse on Heroic Virtue," 307/*OC* II, 1265.

57. Ibid., 308/*OC* II, 1265.

58. Ibid., 305/*OC* II, 1262.

59. Judith N. Shklar, "Jean-Jacques Rousseau and Equality," *Dædalus* 107, no. 3 (1978): 24.

60. Friedrich Nietzsche, *The Will to Power*, trans. Walter Kaufmann and R. J. Hollingdale (New York: Vintage Books, 1968), #1021, p. 529.

61. See Keith Ansell-Pearson, *Nietzsche Contra Rousseau: A Study of Nietzsche's Moral and Political Thought* (Cambridge: Cambridge University Press, 1991), 50.

62. Woodruff, *The Ajax Dilemma*, 19.

63. Lilti applies this to the *philosophes* themselves. They wanted to be great heroes who wield pens and paintbrushes rather than swords. See Antoine Lilti, *Figures publiques: L'invention de la célébrité, 1750–1850* (Paris: Fayard, 2014), 125–27.

64. As I argue later in the chapter, the *philosophes* were more trusting of the ancien régime than of the masses.

65. Saint-Lambert, for example, argues that inequality in itself is not a problem. Rather, it is inequality attained "without work or by means of abuses," which results in "idleness and the need for frivolous dissipations." By contrast, those who earn their wealth through industriousness provide the social benefits of luxury without the moral corruptions that bothered Rousseau. Thus, if economic inequalities are earned, there is no need for moral censure. As will be made clear in the next few chapters, Rousseau would probably denounce this position as ideological flimflam. It is earned superiority that might bother him most. See Jean-François de Saint-Lambert, "Luxury," in *Encyclopedia Selections*, trans. Nelly S. Hoyt and Thomas Cassirer (Indianapolis: Bobbs-Merrill, 1965), 219. Saint-Lambert arrived in Paris in 1750 and became friends with Rousseau, Grimm, Diderot, and d'Holbach. See Alan Charles Kors, *D'Holbach's Coterie: An Enlightenment in Paris* (Princeton: Princeton University Press, 1976), 23. It is thus reasonable to assume that he was well aware of Rousseau's criticisms of the Enlightenment and the emerging liberal order.

66. Thomas N. Bisson, *The Crisis of the Twelfth Century: Power, Lordship, and the Origins of European Government* (Princeton: Princeton University Press, 2009), 2.

67. For the tensions and problems with this ideological marriage, see Richard W. Kaeuper, *Holy Warriors: The Religious Ideology of Chivalry* (Philadelphia: University of Pennsylvania Press, 2014).

68. Johan Huizinga, *The Autumn of the Middle Ages*, trans. Rodney J. Patton and Ulrich Mammitzsch (Chicago: University of Chicago Press, 1996), 69.

69. Keith Thomas, *The Ends of Life: Road to Fulfillment in Early Modern England* (Oxford: Oxford University Press, 2009), 239.

70. Huizinga, *The Autumn of the Middle Ages*, 120.

71. See Norbert Elias, *The Civilizing Process: The History of Manners and State Formation and Civilization*, trans. Edmund Jephcott (Cambridge: Blackwell, 1994), 412–14.

72. Jonathan Dewald, *The European Nobility, 1400–1800* (Cambridge: Cambridge University Press, 1996), 47.

73. Elias, *The Civilizing Process*, 476.

74. See C. Stephen Jaeger, *The Origins of Courtliness: Civilizing Trends and the Formation of Courtly Ideals, 939–1210* (Philadelphia: University of Pennsylvania Press, 1985), and *Ennobling Love: In Search of a Lost Sensibility* (Philadelphia: University of Pennsylvania Press, 1999).

75. See Dewald, *The European Nobility, 1400–1800*, chapter 4.

76. Antoine Lilti, *The World of the Salons: Sociability and Worldliness in Eighteenth-Century Paris*, trans. Lydia G. Cochrane (Oxford: Oxford University Press, 2005), 20.

77. Quoted from Isaac Kramnick, *The Rage of Edmund Burke* (New York: Basic Books, 1977), 7.

78. The best version of the economic argument comes from Rosenblatt. She persuasively argues Rousseau had a less direct view of the *amour-propre* of the commercial elite by following the takeover of Genevan politics from afar. I contend that while his notion of *amour-propre* can apply to Geneva, it was mostly likely constructed to challenge the aristocratic attitudes he found in the salon culture. If Rosenblatt is correct that he is attacking "the whole value system of contemporary civilization" through the arts and sciences, it is notable that he begins by focusing on the intellectuals. See Rosenblatt, *Rousseau and Geneva*, 44.

79. Maurice Cranston, *Philosophers and Pamphleteers: Political Theorists of the Enlightenment* (Oxford: Oxford University Press, 1986), 38.

80. Rousseau, "Preface to *Narcissus*," 93/*OC* II, 959–60.

81. For an earlier version of this argument, see Michael Locke McLendon, "Rousseau, *Amour-Propre*, and Intellectual Celebrity," *Journal of Politics* 71, no. 2 (2009): 506–19.

82. Ibid., 94/*OC* II, 962.

83. As Darnton states, "To become a Voltaire or d'Alembert, that was the sort of glory to tempt young men on the make." See Robert Darnton, *The Literary Underground of the Old Regime* (Cambridge, Mass.: Harvard University Press, 1982), 3.

84. Leo Damrosch, *Jean-Jacques Rousseau: Restless Genius* (New York: Houghton Mifflin, 2005), 40.

85. Jean-Jacques Rousseau, *The Confessions*, in *The Collected Writings of Jean-Jacques Rousseau*, vol. 5, trans. Christopher Kelly (Hanover: University of New England Press, 1995), 237/*OC* I, 283. Granted, he had other reasons for his move to Paris, including his replacement as Mme. Warens's lover. In addition, he denies he sought fame, in his "Letter to Beaumont." See Jean-Jacques Rousseau, "Letter to Christophe de Beaumont," in *The Collected Writings of Jean-Jacques Rousseau*, vol. 9, trans. Christopher Kelly and Judith R. Bush (Hanover: Dartmouth College Press, 2001), 21/*OC* IV, 927. I take his account in the *Confessions* to be more accurate.

86. Rousseau, *Confessions*, 242/*OC* I, 288. See also Lilti, *Figures publiques*, 185.

87. Hont, *Politics in Commercial Society*, 59.

88. Michael Sonenscher, *Sans-Culottes: An Eighteenth-Century Emblem in the French Revolution* (Princeton: Princeton University Press, 2008), 186.

89. It is also possible to trace the claim that "everyone began to look at everyone else and to wish to be looked at himself" to Rousseau's own life. Damrosch reports that during his childhood Rousseau developed "a lifelong tendency to imagine that people were staring at him." See Damrosch, *Jean-Jacques Rousseau: Restless Genius*, 39. This would explain his excessive self-consciousness. It does not, however, address the language of "being best" and the overvaluation of talent.

90. Rousseau, *Confessions*, 239/*OC* I, 284–85. He would later also turn on Rameau, who accused him of plagiarizing an opera.

91. Rousseau, "Epistle to M. d l'Taing," in *OC* II, 1150.

92. Rousseau, "Preface to *Narcissus*," 97/*OC* II, 965.

93. In his replies to the *First Discourse*, Rousseau proclaims: "Science in itself is very good, that is obvious." See Rousseau, "Observations," in *The Discourses and Other Early Writings*, 33/*OC* III, 36. See also Rousseau, "Preface to *Narcissus*," 96/*OC* II, 964–65.

94. Rousseau, *First Discourse*, 17/*OC* III, 19. See also "Preface to *Narcissus*," in which Rousseau claims that "a taste for philosophy loosens all the bonds of esteem and benevolence that tie men to society." Rousseau, "Preface to *Narcissus*," 99/*OC* II, 967. In addition, note Rousseau's comment in *The Reveries* that the intellectuals were "ardent missionaries of Atheism." See Jean-Jacques Rousseau, *The Reveries of a Solitary Walker*, in *The Collected Writings of Jean-Jacques Rousseau*, vol. 8, trans. Charles E. Butterworth (Hanover: Dartmouth College Press, 2000), 21/*OC* I, 1016. For a good discussion of Rousseau's arguments on religion, see Christopher Kelly, *Rousseau as Author: Consecrating One's Life to the Truth* (Chicago: University of Chicago Press, 2003), 148–51.

95. David Hume, "Of Commerce," in *Selected Essays*, ed. Stephen Copley and Andrew Edgar (Oxford: Oxford University Press, 1996), 160–63.

96. Rousseau, *First Discourse*, 18/*OC* III, 19; Jean-Jacques Rousseau, "Last Reply," in *The Discourses and Other Early Writings*, 65–66/*OC* III 74; Rousseau, "Preface to *Narcissus*," 97–98/*OC* II, 965–66.

97. See Rousseau, "Preface to *Narcissus*," 97–98/*OC* II, 966; Rousseau, *First Discourse*, 20–21/*OC* III, 22–23; Rousseau, *Moral Letters*, 182/*OC* IV, 1089. See also Jean-Jacques Rousseau, *J. J. Rousseau Citizen of Geneva to Monsieur d'Alembert*, in *The Collected Writings of Jean-Jacques Rousseau*, vol. 9, trans. and ed. Allan Bloom and Christopher Kelly, 326 and 334/*OC* V, 92 and 102–3.

98. Voltaire, "Letter #XXIII," in *Letters Concerning the English Nation*, ed. Nicholas Cronk (Oxford: Oxford University Press, 1994), 112–15.

99. Rousseau, *First Discourse*, 19/*OC* III, 21. See also Rousseau, *The Reveries of a Solitary Walker*, 64/*OC* I, 1069. In his own life, Rousseau thought his intellectual friends, the d'Holbach coterie, were jealous of his successes. Although they could all write, he believed none of them, save Duclos, could forgive him for the success of his opera. See Rousseau, *Confessions*, 325/*OC* I, 387.

100. In *The Confessions*, he contends: "It is too difficult to think nobly when one thinks for a living." See Rousseau, *Confessions*, 338/*OC* I, 403.

101. Rousseau, "Observations," 45–49/*OC* III, 50–55.

102. Rousseau, "Letter to Beaumont," 55/*OC* IV 971.

103. See also Rousseau, *The Reveries of a Solitary Walker*, 18 and 64/*OC* I, 1013 and 1069; Rousseau, "Preface to *Narcissus*," 97/*OC* II, 965; Rousseau, *First Discourse*, 19/*OC* III, 21. Rousseau, of course, claims he is much less affected by such vanity. As early as "Preface to *Narcissus*," marking the first of many such proclamations, he asserts that he has learned to do without the esteem of others. Rousseau, "Preface to *Narcissus*," 92/*OC* II, 959. In one of his fragments, he cites his ability to live alone as evidence for his superior temperament: "Proof that I have less *amour propre* than other men, or that mine affects me less, is that I have the capability of living alone." See Jean-Jacques Rousseau, "My Portrait," in *The Collected Writings of Jean-Jacques Rousseau*, vol. 12, trans. Christopher Kelly, #12, 40/*OC* I, 1124.

104. Rousseau, "Preface to *Narcissus*," 102/*OC* II, 970. As Jason Neidleman has stated, Rousseau believes that "we are far more likely to be harmed by an excess of learning than by the

absence of it." Jason Neidleman, *Rousseau's Ethics of Truth: A Sublime Science of Simple Souls* (New York: Routledge, 2016), 21.

105. Ibid., 24/*OC* III, 26.

106. Ibid., 23/*OC* III, 25. See also "Preface to *Narcissus*," in which Rousseau continues this line: "Once talents preempt the honors owed to virtue . . . everyone wants to be an agreeable man, and no one cares to be a good man." See Rousseau, "Preface to *Narcissus*, 98/*OC* II, 966.

107. Rousseau, *First Discourse*, 26/*OC* III, 29.

108. Ibid.

109. Rousseau, "Preface to *Narcissus*," 98/*OC* II, 966.

110. Rousseau, *First Discourse*, 28/*OC* III, 30.

111. I imagine Rousseau would approve of Horace's famous epigram "To state I awe of nothing, Numicus, is practically the only way to feel really good about yourself." See Horace, "Letter to Numicius, on How to Be Happy," in *Epistles*, in *The Complete Works of Horace*, ed. Casper J. Kraemer Jr. and trans. Francis Howes (New York: Random House, 1936), I, 6, p. 321.

112. Rousseau, "Preface to *Narcissus*," 97/*OC* II, 965.

113. Rousseau, *Emile*, 592/*OC* IV, 769.

114. Rousseau, "My Portrait," 44/*OC* I, 1129.

115. Rousseau, *J. J. Rousseau Citizen of Geneva to Monsieur d'Alembert*, 295/*OC* V, 55. See also *Emile*, 345–53/*OC* IV, 470–80.

116. Adam Ferguson, *An Essay on the History of Civil Society*, ed. Fania Oz-Salzberger (Cambridge: Cambridge University Press, 1995), 173.

117. Ibid., 176.

118. Ibid., 174.

119. Adam Smith, *Lectures on Jurisprudence*, ed. R. L. Meek, D. D. Raphael, and P. G. Stein (Oxford: Clarendon Press, 1978), B, 328–29, p. 539. Italics mine.

120. Adam Smith, *The Wealth of Nations*, ed. Edward Cannan (New York: Random House, 2000), 840. Italics mine.

121. Ferguson, *An Essay on the History of Civil Society*, 177.

122. Ibid., 83. Alexander Welsh claims that even in Homer there is a reluctance to rank the heroes. Victory of one hero over another usually requires divine assistance. See Welsh, *What Is Honor?* 14.

123. In "Preface to *Narcissus*," Rousseau does claim he gave up on the idea of being an author; he had "seen things from close up" and stopped aspiring to be one. See Rousseau, "Preface to *Narcissus*," 95/*OC* II, 962.

124. See Kelly, *Rousseau as Author*, chapter 1.

125. Robert Darnton, "Readers Respond to Rousseau," in *The Great Cat Massacre and Other Episodes in French Cultural History* (New York: Basic Books, 1999), 230–33. Antoine Lilti also addresses this problem. See Lilti, *Figures publiques*, chapter 5. His Rousseau seeks to regain authenticity through solitude.

126. Jean-Jacques Rousseau, *Julie, or The New Heloise: Letters of Two Lovers Who Live in a Small Town at the Foot of the Alps*, in *The Collected Writings of Jean-Jacques Rousseau*, vol. 6, trans. Philip Stewart and Jean Vaché (Hanover: Dartmouth College Press, 1997), 11/*OC* II, 14–17; Darnton, "Readers Respond to Rousseau," 230.

127. Jean le Rond d'Alembert, *Discours préliminaire de l'Encyclopédie*, in *Oeuvres complètes*, vol. I (Geneva: Slatkine Reprints, 196), 82. Hereafter referred to as the *Preliminary Discourse*. See also Darnton, "Philosophers Trim the Tree of Knowledge," in *The Great Cat Massacre and Other Episodes in French Cultural History*, 207; Kelly, *Rousseau as Author*, 3.

128. See Arthur M. Wilson, *Diderot* (Oxford: Oxford University Press, 1972), 114–15; P. N. Furbank, *Diderot: A Critical Biography* (New York: Alfred A. Knopf, 1992), 51–52; Maurice Cranston, *Jean-Jacques Rousseau: The Early Life and Work of Jean-Jacques Rousseau, 1712–54* (Chicago: University of Chicago Press, 1982), 229; Raymond Trousson, *Jean-Jacques Rousseau: La marche à la gloire* (Paris: Tallendier, 1988), 256–63; Damrosch, *Jean-Jacques Rousseau: Restless Genius*, 213–14. Diderot's claims continue to be a source of controversy. On the Diderot side, Furbank believes Diderot did in fact supply Rousseau with his grand idea. Wilson is more circumspect and refuses to comment either way. The primary Anglophone Rousseau biographers—Cranston and Damrosch—deny Diderot's claim. Damrosch calls it "highly improbable," and Cranston claims "there is no evidence among his papers to justify our believing that he made it." See Damrosch, *Jean-Jacques Rousseau: Restless Genius*, 213–14; Cranston, *Jean-Jacques: The Early Life and Work of Jean-Jacques Rousseau, 1712–54*, 229. Trousson, the most authoritative of Rousseau's French biographers, states "without a doubt, he [Diderot] did not inspire the main idea." See Trousson, *Jean-Jacques Rousseau: La marche à la gloire*, 263. As for Diderot's attitude, Cranston thinks he did not see it as a frontal assault on the Enlightenment and may have viewed it as "an entertaining paradox." See Cranston, *Jean-Jacques: The Early Life and Work of Jean-Jacques Rousseau, 1712–54*, 229.

129. Rousseau, *Confessions*, 304/ *OC* I, 363

130. Trousson, *Jean-Jacques Rousseau: La marche à la gloire*, 277.

131. Rousseau, "Preface to *Narcissus*," 93–94/ *OC* II, 961.

132. D'Alembert, *Preliminary Discourse*, 41.

133. Ibid., 112.

134. Denis Diderot, "Art," in *Encyclopedia Selections*, trans. Nelly S. Hoyt and Thomas Cassirer (Indianapolis: Bobbs-Merrill, 1965), 5.

135. See Wilson, *Diderot*, 269–70.

136. Julien Offray de La Mettrie, *Man a Machine*, in *Man a Machine and Man a Plant*, trans. Richard A. Watson and Maya Rybalka (Indianapolis: Hackett, 1994), 45.

137. D'Alembert, *Preliminary Discourse*, 82.

138. D'Alembert, "Lettre à J. J. Rousseau, Citoyen de Genève," in *Oeuvres complètes*, IV, 436.

139. D'Alembert, *Preliminary Discourse*, 51.

140. Denis Diderot, "Encyclopedia," in *Rameau's Nephew and Other Works*, trans. Jacques Barzun and Ralph H. Bowen (Indianapolis: Hackett, 1956), 300.

141. Ibid., 301.

142. For a general discussion of this phenomenon in seventeenth and eighteenth century French intellectual life, see Élisabeth Badinter, *Les passions intellectuelles: Désirs de gloire (1735–1751)* (Paris: Fayard, 1999), vol. I, part I, chapters 2–3.

143. Diderot, "Encyclopedia," 283. See also 296–97.

144. Ibid., 296–97.

145. Even Voltaire has a soft spot in his heart for mechanical labor. At the end of *Candide*, earthly happiness is attained through devotion to mechanical arts such as carpentry, baking, embroidering, laundering, and other occupations Rousseau would consider suitable for Emile. Such work, it is claimed, "keeps at bay the three great evils: boredom, vice, and necessity." See Voltaire, *Candide, or Optimism*, trans. Theo Cuffe (New York: Penguin Books, 2005), 92. Although it is unlikely that Voltaire adopted these attitudes in response to Rousseau—Peter Gay has commented that throughout his life Voltaire "preached the gospel of work"—his vision of the good life has more in common with Rousseau's than is sometimes appreciated. See Peter Gay, *Voltaire's Politics: The Poet as Realist* (New Haven: Yale University Press, 1988), 22.

146. One of the most important scholars of *The Encyclopedia*, R. J. White, takes d'Alembert and Diderot at face value and believes their appreciation of the mechanical arts and sympathy for the working classes are genuine and sincere. See R. J. White, *The Anti-Philosophers: A Study of the Philosophes in Eighteenth-Century France* (New York: St. Martin's Press, 1970), 124–25. He writes: "As for the ploughman, the laborer, the Encyclopedia speaks for him with all the fervor of the Physiocrats, allies of the Philosophes, with their economic doctrine that the land was the source of all wealth, and that consequently, the farmers, great and small, were the most valuable element of society." Jonathan Israel likewise cites Diderot's positive entries on the mechanical arts as a step toward egalitarianism. See Jonathan Israel, *A Revolution of the Mind: Radical Enlightenment and the Intellectual Origins of Modern Democracy* (Princeton: Princeton University Press, 2010), 100.

147. D'Alembert, *Preliminary Discourse*, 82. Granted, in his *Letter to d'Alembert on the Theater*, Rousseau somewhat mocks the contention that the arts and sciences have their uses in corrupt societies. In Paris, he sarcastically comments, the theater ought to be maintained because it serves as a potential distraction for criminals. The two hours they spend in the theater is two hours they cannot do mischief, thereby reducing crime by one-twelfth. See Rousseau, *J. J. Rousseau Citizen of Geneva to Monsieur d'Alembert*, 294/*OC* V, 54. In "Preface to *Narcissus*," he similarly argues that colleges, libraries, spectacles, and so on are not designed to promote goodness but designed to provide distractions from doing evil. See Rousseau, "Preface to *Narcissus*," 104/*OC* II, 972.

148. Ibid., 41.

149. D'Alembert, "Lettre à J. J. Rousseau, Citoyen de Genève," 433.

150. Denis Diderot, "Lettre à Mme Volland, LXVIII (7.31.1762)," in *Oeuvres complètes*, vol. XIX, ed. J. Assézat and Maurice Tourneux (Nendeln, Lichtenstein: Kraus Reprint, 1966), 87.

151. Herbert Dieckmann, "Diderot's Conception of Genius," *Journal of the History of Ideas* 2, no. 2 (1941): 159.

152. France, *Diderot: Past Masters* (Oxford: Oxford University Press, 1983), 85–86.

153. D'Alembert, Diderot, and Voltaire actually argue they are superior to the Renaissance thinkers and go out of their way to criticize them for their obsession with antiquity and congratulate themselves for being more forward looking in the *Preliminary Discourse*, "Encyclopedia," and "Men of Letters," respectively. See d'Alembert, *Preliminary Discourse*, 53–61; Diderot, "Encyclopedia," 298; Voltaire, "Men of Letters," in *Encyclopedia Selections*, 248.

154. Darnton, "Philosophers Trim the Tree of Knowledge," 199. Élisabeth Badinter makes a similar claim in references to the scientists in l'Académie des sciences: "Charged with deciphering the mysteries of nature, *le savant philosophe* could believe himself a demiurge." See Badinter, *Les passions intellectuelles*, vol. I, 13. Translation mine.

155. See Dieckmann, "Diderot's Conception of Genius,"153; Dena Goodman, *The Republic of Letters: A Cultural History of the French Enlightenment* (Ithaca: Cornell University Press, 1994), 35–39; Mark Hulliung, *The Autocritique of Enlightenment: Rousseau and the Philosophes* (Cambridge, Mass.: Harvard University Press, 1994), 77–78. Both Huilling and Goodman note that the early works of Rousseau, and indeed his use of *amour-propre* in the *Second Discourse*, are in part a response to this project to glorify the intellectuals. Goodman argues that the *Second Discourse* was a direct reply to d'Alembert.

156. For a good discussion, see Ronald Grimsley, *Jean d'Alembert* (Oxford: Clarendon Press, 1963), 125–31. D'Alembert was annoyed that Voltaire in his personal life was too friendly with the aristocrats and the clergy.

157. D'Alembert, "Essai sur la société des gens de lettres et des grands," in *Oeuvres complètes*, vol. IV, 357.

158. D'Alembert, "Préface du troisième volume de l'Encyclopédie," in *Oeuvres complètes*, vol. IV, 389. The last clause, about the vanity of men, appears to be directed at Rousseau.

159. Hulliung, *The Autocritique of Enlightenment*, 133.

160. Denis Diderot, *Le fils naturel*, in *Oeuvres de théâtre de M. Diderot: Avec un discours sur la poésie dramatique*, vol. 2 (Amsterdam: M. M. Rey, 1772), 93.

161. Darnton, *The Literary Underground of the Old Regime*, 12–13.

162. D'Alembert, "Essai sur la société des gens de lettres et des grands," 354.

163. Darnton, *The Literary Underground of the Old Regime*, 13.

164. Grimsley, *Jean d'Alembert*, 118.

165. See Israel, *A Revolution of the Mind*, 5–6.

166. Such a reading, however, should not be considered controversial. As Peter France notes, Rousseau "was always a point of reference for Diderot." See France, *Diderot: Past Masters*, 81.

167. According to Wilson, Diderot was fascinated by genius and thought it "is the highest gift of all." See Wilson, *Diderot*, 414–15. See also Peter Gay, *The Enlightenment: An Interpretation, Volume II, The Science of Freedom* (New York: W. W. Norton, 1969), 287.

168. Diderot, *Rameau's Nephew*, in *Rameau's Nephew and Other Writings*, 15.

169. Ibid., 17.

170. Ibid., 34.

171. Ibid.

172. Ibid., 73.

173. Ibid., 76.

174. Julia Kristeva argues that the nephew's rejection of the virtues of ancient cynicism is perhaps the greatest expression of cynicism. He "is the cynic's cynic" and "carries it [cynicism] to its peak." See Julia Kristeva, *Strangers to Ourselves*, trans. Leon S. Roudiez (New York: Columbia University Press, 1991), 138.

175. France, *Diderot: Past Masters*, 81; Sonenscher, *Sans-Culottes*, chapter 3.

176. Cranston, *Jean-Jacques Rousseau: The Early Life and Work of Jean-Jacques Rousseau, 1712–54*, 313.

177. See ibid., 313, and Damrosch, *Jean-Jacques Rousseau: Restless Genius*, 251–52. Damrosch adds slightly to Cranston's analysis by speculating that Rousseau was projecting his own insecurities onto the abbé. Furbank, a Diderot biographer, also has little to say about the event. His only concern is that it did not break up Diderot and Rousseau's friendship. See Furbank, *Diderot: A Critical Biography*, 117–18. Wilson takes the standard line that it is a sign of souring relationships between Rousseau and the *philosophes*, though, nearer to my point, he does suggest it has much to do with Rousseau's belief that philosophy diminishes civic friendship. See Wilson, *Diderot*, 181–82.

178. Rousseau, *First Discourse*, 26/*OC* III, 29.

179. Rousseau, "Preface to *Narcissus*," 98/*OC* II, 966.

180. See Augustine, *City of God*, vol. II, trans. Philip Levine (Cambridge, Mass.: Harvard University Press/Loeb Classical Library, 1966), V, 18, p. 235.

181. Michael Young, *The Rise of the Meritocracy, 1870–2033: An Essay on Education and Equality* (New York: Penguin Books, 1975), 15.

CHAPTER 2

1. Recently, Christopher Brooke and Robin Douglass have done so. Brooke begins his consideration of pride from Lipsius to Rousseau with Augustine. See Christopher Brooke, *Philosophic Pride: Stoicism in Political Thought from Lipsius to Rousseau* (Princeton: Princeton University Press, 2012). Douglass argues that one can trace Rousseau's Augustinianism, as I will shortly, to Pierre Nicole and seventeenth-century neo-Augustinians. See Robin Douglass, *Hobbes and Rousseau: Nature, Free Will, and the Passions* (Oxford: Oxford University Press, 2015), 152–60.

2. Rousseau, "Letter to Beaumont," 29–30/ *OC* IV, 936–38. For a good brief discussion, see Sonenscher, *Sans-Culottes*, 111–12.

3. Rousseau, *Emile*, 161/ *OC* IV, 245.

4. Rousseau, "Observations," 36/ *OC* III, 39.

5. See Rousseau, "Pastoral Letter of His Grace the Archbishop of Paris," in *The Collected Writings of Jean-Jacques Rousseau*, vol. 9, 7, 14; Rousseau, "Letter to Beaumont," 19/ *OC* IV, 25.

6. For structural similarities of both works, see Ann Hartle, *The Modern Self in Rousseau's Confessions: A Reply to St. Augustine* (Notre Dame: University of Notre Dame Press, 1983), 26–27.

7. Hartle argues, too strongly I think, that Rousseau's *Confessions* serves as a "response" to Augustine's. See Hartle, *The Modern Self in Rousseau's* Confessions, 9. For a critique of Hartle's dichotomy, see Patrick Riley, "The Inversion of Conversion: Rousseau's Rewriting of Augustinian Autobiography," *Studies in Eighteenth-Century Culture* 28, no. 1 (1999): 229–55.

8. For the connection between the doctrine of the two loves and *amour-propre*, see Nigel Abercrombie, *Saint Augustine and French Classical Thought* (New York: Russell and Russell, 1938), 91; Anthony Levi, *French Moralists: The Theory of the Passions, 1585–1649* (Oxford: Clarendon Press, 1964), 225; Alexander Sedgwick, *Jansenism in Seventeenth-Century France: Voices from the Wilderness* (Charlottesville: University Press of Virginia, 1977), 47–48; Keohane, *Philosophy and the State in France*, 184; Douglass, *Hobbes and Rousseau*, 153–54.

9. Keohane, *Philosophy and the State in France*, 194–95.

10. Rousseau, *Confessions*, 203/ *OC* I, 242.

11. See Rousseau, "Letter to Beaumont," 25–26 and 54 *OC* IV, 932–33 and 969; Rousseau, *Confessions*, 477/ *OC* I, 570; Rousseau, *Letters Written from the Mountain*, 186/ *OC* III, 753; Rousseau, *Julie; or, the New Heloise*, 563/ *OC* II, 685.

12. See François Fénelon, "On Pure Love," in *Oeuvres complètes,* vol. I, ed. Jacques Le Brun (Paris: Gallimard, 1983), 656–71.

13. See Patrick Riley, "Rousseau, Fénelon, and the Quarrel Between the Ancients and the Moderns," in *The Cambridge Companion to Rousseau*, ed. Patrick Riley (Cambridge: Cambridge University Press, 2001), 82–85. My approach differs from that of Riley, but his work serves as precedent that Rousseau employs Augustine's doctrine of the two loves for secular purposes.

14. Rousseau, *Emile*, 59–99/ *OC* IV, 775–78.

15. Pierre Bayle, *Various Thoughts on the Occasion of a Comet*, trans. Robert C. Bartlett (Indianapolis: Hackett, 2000), §84, p. 106.

16. See ibid., §172, p. 212, and §179, p. 223.

17. Jacques Abbadie, *The Art of Knowing One's Self: Or, A Diligent Search After the Spring of Morality*, trans. P. Hanbury (London: Edward Jones, 1696), II, 14, p. 146. Italics mine.

18. Bernard Mandeville, "The Third Dialogue Between Horatio and Cleomenes," in *The Fable of the Bees*, vol. II, ed. F. B. Kaye (Indianapolis: Liberty Fund, 1988), 130. Italics mine.

19. Charles-Louis de Secondat, baron de Montesquieu, *My Thoughts*, trans. and ed. Henry C. Clark (Indianapolis: Liberty Fund, 2013), #1871, p. 557. See also #2064, p. 635.

20. See Welsh, *What Is Honor?* 93; Michael Sonenscher, *Before the Deluge: Public Debt, Inequality, and the Origins of the French Revolution* (Princeton: Princeton University Press, 2009), 232.

21. See Paul Anthony Rahe, *Montesquieu and the Logic of Liberty: War, Religion, Commerce, Climate, Terrain, Technology, Uneasiness of Mind, the Spirit of Political Vigilance, and the Foundations of the Modern Republic* (New Haven: Yale University Press, 2010), 108–9.

22. See Rousseau, "Preface to *Narcissus*," 99/ *OC* II, 967; d'Alembert, "Essai sur la société des gens de lettres et des grands," in *Oeuvres complètes*, vol. IV, 340–42.

23. Voltaire, "Self-Love (Amour-Propre)," in *A Pocket Philosophical Dictionary*, trans. John Fletcher (Oxford: Oxford University Press, 2011), 23.

24. Voltaire, "Letter XX, On Paschal's Thoughts Concerning Religion, &c.," in *Letters Concerning the English Nation*, 123. Voltaire's hatred of Jansenism is personal as well as philosophical. His brother Armand, whom he detested, was a Jansenist priest on the fringes of the religion. See Ian Davidson, *Voltaire: A Life* (New York: Pegasus Books, 2010), 14.

25. Denis Diderot, "Lettre à Mme Volland, XLI (September 30, 1762), in *Oeuvres complètes*, XVIII, 476. In another letter, he essentially calls Pascal's God a tyrant. See ibid., III (August 3, 1759), 21. See also Diderot, *Rameau's Nephew*, 66.

26. Carl Becker has also noted the latent Augustinianism in the Enlightenment. In a well-known argument, he claims that the *philosophes* relied heavily on Augustinian concepts and narratives. They relied on natural law, constructed closed and unquestionable narratives, had faith in reason, and offered a new version of salvation. See Carl L. Becker, *The Heavenly City of the Eighteenth-Century Philosophers* (New Haven: Yale University Press, 1960). He writes nothing, however, of *amour-propre* and moral psychology.

27. Oliver O'Donnell, *The Problem of Self-Love in Saint Augustine* (New Haven: Yale University Press, 1988), 1. See also Christopher Brooke, "Rousseau's Political Philosophy: Stoic and Augustinian Origins," in *The Cambridge Companion to Rousseau*, 114.

28. Peter Brown, *Augustine of Hippo: A Biography* (Berkeley: University of California Press, 2000), 307.

29. Ibid., 310.

30. See John M. Rist, *Augustine: Ancient Thought Baptized* (Cambridge: Cambridge University Press, 1994), 221.

31. Ibid., 190.

32. Augustine, *Ten Homilies on the First Epistle of John to the Parthians* (*In epistolam Joannis ad Parthos tracatus decem*), trans. Rev. H. Browne (London: Aeterna Press, 2014), 8.9, p. 86.

33. Brooke, *Philosophic Pride*, 7. See also Augustine, *City of God*, vol. III, trans. David S. Wiesen (Cambridge: Harvard University Press/ Loeb Classical Library, 1968), IX, 4, and Augustine, *City of God*, vol. IV, trans. Philip Levine (Cambridge: Harvard University Press/ Loeb Classical Library, 1966), XIX, 4.

34. Augustine, *City of God*, vol. IV, XIV, 3, p. 273.

35. I am basing my interpretation of Augustine's doctrine of the Fall on book XIV, chapter 13 of *City of God* and its relation to the doctrine of the two loves. In this chapter, Augustine claims that the Fall occurs because Adam and Eve are secretly corrupted by pride and the desire for "perverse elevation." See Augustine, *City of God*, vol. IV, XIV, 13, p. 335. Importantly, Augustine does not blame sexuality, which predates the Fall and is originally part of human nature in Eden. The sins of the body are caused by the sins of the soul. See Augustine, *City of God*, vol. IV, XIV, 26,

pp. 397–99; *Brown, Augustine of Hippo: A Biography*, 501–3; Nussbaum, *Upheavals of Thought*, 554. For an alternative view, see Stephen Greenblatt, *The Rise and Fall of Adam and Eve* (New York: W.W. Norton, 2017), 81–119. He interprets Augustine's doctrine of the Fall in sexual terms and only once references pride. Notably, he does not reduce sexual corruption to pride, and claims both are responsible for the Fall. See Greenblatt, *The Rise and Fall of Adam and Eve*, 119.

36. Michael Bakunin interprets the Fall in a similar manner. See Michael Bakunin, *God and State* (New York: Dover, 1970), 10–14.

37. Augustine, *Confessions*, vol. II, trans. William Watts (Cambridge, Mass.: Harvard University Press/ Loeb Classical Library, 1951), X, 35, p. 177.

38. Augustine, *City of God*, vol. II, V, 20, p. 249.

39. Ibid., vol. IV, XIV, 28, pp. 405–7.

40. Augustine, *Eighty-Three Different Questions*, trans. David A. Mosher (Washington, D.C.: Catholic University Press of America, 1977), Q.79.1, p. 201.

41. Augustine, "To Bishop Aurelius, from Augustine, Priest (no. 8, Ep. XXII)," in *Select Letters*, trans. James H. Baxter (Cambridge, Mass.: Harvard University Press/ Loeb Classical Library, 1930), 51.

42. See Brown, *Augustine of Hippo: A Biography*, 55–56.

43. Ibid., 55.

44. Larry Siedentop, *Inventing the Individual: The Origins of Western Liberalism* (Cambridge, Mass.: Belknap Press of Harvard University Press, 2014), 101.

45. See Rist, *Augustine: Ancient Thought Baptized*, 189.

46. Augustine, *City of God*, vol. I, trans. George E. McCracken (Cambridge: Harvard University Press/ Loeb Classical Library, 1957), Preface, p. 13.

47. There has yet to be an academic study of this problem. See Katherine Chambers, "Slavery and Domination as Political Ideas in Augustine's *City of God*," *Heythrop Journal* 54, no. 1 (2013): 13, 15.

48. See Hannah Arendt, *Love and Saint Augustine*, ed. Joanna Vecchiarelli Scott and Judith Chelsius Stark (Chicago: University of Chicago Press, 1996), 95; Nussbaum, *Upheavals of Thought*, 551–53.

49. Homer, *The Iliad*, trans. Robert Fagles (New York: Penguin Classics, 1997), 2.225–35, p. 106.

50. See Jean-Luc Marion, *In the Self's Place: The Approach of Saint Augustine*, trans. Jeffrey L. Kosky (Stanford: Stanford University Press, 2012), 254–60.

51. Arendt, *Love and Saint Augustine*, 81.

52. Augustine, *Confessions* vol. II, X, 17, p. 121.

53. Geuss succinctly sums up this point: "I am the history of my loves." See Raymond Geuss, *Public Goods, Private Goods* (Princeton: Princeton University Press, 2001), 59.

54. Augustine, *Confessions*, vol. II, X, 17, p. 121. See also Brian Stock, *Augustine the Reader: Meditation, Self-Knowledge, and the Ethics of Interpretation* (Cambridge, Mass.: Belknap Press of Harvard University Press, 1996), 23.

55. Augustine, *City of God*, vol. IV, XIV, 4, pp. 275–77; Augustine, *On the Trinity*, trans. Stephen McKenna and ed. Gareth B. Matthews (Cambridge: Cambridge University Press, 2002), XIII, 4, 7, pp. 110–12.

56. Augustine, *Confessions*, vol. I, II, 4, p. 79.

57. Ibid., vol. II, X, 17, p. 123.

58. Augustine, *On the Trinity*, XIV, 12, 15, pp. 153–54.

59. Ibid., X, 11, 18, pp. 58–59.

60. See Hartle, *The Modern Self in Rousseau's* Confessions, 103–15.

61. See Brown, *Augustine of Hippo: A Biography*, 234–36.

62. Augustine, *Ten Homilies on the First Epistle of John to the Parthians*, 8.9, p. 86. See also Paul A. Rahe, "Blaise Pascal, Pierre Nicole, and the Origins of Liberal Sociology," in *Enlightenment and Secularism: Essays on the Mobilization of Reason*, ed. Christopher Nadon (Lanham, Md.: Lexington Books, 2013), 134; Rahe, *Montesquieu and the Logic of Liberty*, 109.

63. Augustine, "To Bishop Aurelius, from Augustine, Priest (no. 8, Ep. XXII)," in *Select Letters*, 51.

64. Ibid., vol. II, V, 12, p. 191. See also p. 193: "So it was this eagerness for praise and passion for glory that [men] performed so many marvelous deeds." Incidentally, philosophers also may suffer from love of glory when they wish to be thought wiser and more acute than their peers.

65. Ibid., vol. II, V, 15, p. 217.

66. Augustine, *Confessions*, vol. II, X, 38, p. 193.

67. Ibid., vol. II, V, 12, p. 203.

68. Ibid., vol. II, V, 13, p. 209.

69. Augustine, *City of God*, vol. II, V, 14, p. 211.

70. Ibid., vol. II, V, 19, pp. 239–41.

71. Augustine, *City of God*, vol. II, V, 19, p. 239.

72. Augustine, *Eighty-Three Different Questions*, 35, 1 and 2. See also Arendt, *Love and Saint Augustine*, 9.

73. Herbert A. Deane, *The Political and Social Ideas of Saint Augustine* (New York: Columbia University Press, 1963), 50–51.

74. Augustine, *City of God*, vol. II, V, 14, p. 215.

75. See Keohane, *Philosophy and the State in France*, 183–84.

76. Jean-François Sénault, *De l'Usage des passions* (Paris: Jean Camusat, 1641), 290. All translations mine.

77. Ibid., 59.

78. Blaise Pascal, "Lettre de Pascal a Monsieur et Madame Périer" (9.24.1651), in *Oeuvres complètes*, ed. Jacques Chevalier (Paris: Pléiade, 1954), 496.

79. See Rahe, *Montesquieu and the Logic of Liberty*, 103–5.

80. Blaise Pascal, *Pensées*, in *Pensées and Other Writings*, trans. Honor Levi (Oxford: Oxford University Press, 1995), S 510, p. 122. See also S 152, p. 38.

81. Blaise Pascal, *Trois discours sur la condition des grands*, in *Oeuvres complètes*, 618–19.

82. Jacques Abbadie, *L'art de se connoitre soy-mesme, ou La recherche des sources de la morale* (Rotterdam: Pierre Reinier Leers, 1710), II, 18, p. 195. All translations mine.

83. Ibid., II, 19, p. 203.

84. Pierre Nicole, "De la connaissance de soi-même," in *Oeuvres philosophiques et morales, comprenant un choix de ses essais*, ed. Charles Jourdain (Paris: L. Hachette, 1845), 13. All translations mine except for "idea of me," which I will be using hereafter. It comes from a seventeenth-century translator. See Pierre Nicole, "Of the Knowledge of One's Self, First Part," in *Moral Essays, contain'd in several treatises on many important duties*, 2nd ed., trans. A Person of Quality (London: n.p., 1677), III, vi, p. 4.

85. Ibid.

86. Nicole, "De la faiblesse de l'homme," in *Oeuvres philosophiques et morales*,71

87. According to Keohane, the seventeenth-century neo-Augustinians had ongoing debates with some of the most famous aristocratic writers and philosophers of the age, such as Corneille and Descartes, who put forth an aristocratic ethic of *la gloire* that emphasized the autonomy of

the individual will and celebrated "the ideal of the noble hero, the self-realizing individual." See Keohane, *Philosophy and the State in France*, 186.

88. Thomas Piketty, incidentally, makes the same argument in *Capital in the Twenty-First Century*: "Modern meritocratic society, especially in the United States, is much harder on the losers, because it seeks to justify domination on the grounds of justice, virtue, and merit, to say nothing of the insufficient productivity of those at the bottom." Thomas Piketty, *Capital in the Twenty-First Century*, trans. Arthur Goldhammer (Cambridge, Mass.: Belknap Press of Harvard University Press, 2014), 416.

89. Nicole, "De la grandeur," in *Oeuvres philosophiques et morales*, 396.

90. Ibid.

91. Nicole, "Danger des entretiens," in *Oeuvres philosophiques et morales*, 373–74.

92. Nicole, "De la faiblesse de l'homme," in *Oeuvres philosophiques et morales*, 89.

93. Nicholas Malebranche, *Traité de morale*, ed. Henri Joly (Paris: Ernest Thorin, 1882), I, 3, XIII, p. 31.

94. Ibid.

95. As Viroli points out, numerous thinkers besides Malebranche influenced Rousseau's love of order. He cites Bernard Lamy's *Entretiens sur les sciences* as particularly important. See Viroli, *Rousseau and the "Well-Ordered Society,"* 29–30, 30n. Still, there is no denying Malebranche was important for Rousseau.

96. Sénault, *De l'usage des passions*, 130.

97. Ibid., 563.

98. Ibid., 441–44.

99. Pascal, *Pensées*, S 243–44, p. 75. See also Rahe, *Montesquieu and the Logic of Liberty*, 103; Rahe, "Blaise Pascal, Pierre Nicole, and the Origins of Liberal Sociology," 133.

100. Abbadie, *L'art de se connoitre soy-mesme*, II, 15, p. 160.

101. Ibid., II, 15, p. 161.

102. Ibid., II, 3, 24.

103. Ibid., II, 18, p. 201.

104. Ibid., II, 15, p. 161.

105. Ibid., II, 15, p. 158.

106. See Ibid., II, 15, pp. 158–60.

107. Smith, *The Theory of Moral Sentiments*, IV, i. 6, p. 180.

108. Mandeville, "The First Dialogue Between Horatio and Cleomenes," 52.

109. Malebranche, *Traité de morale*, II, 14, iv, p. 263.

110. He may have an equal in Jean Domat. Domat claims in his *Traité de lois*, "From amour-propre, which is society's poison, God has made a remedy from which to maintain it." Quoted from Lucien Jaume, *Tocqueville: The Aristocratic Sources of Liberty*, trans. Arthur Goldhammer (Princeton: Princeton University Press, 2008), 177.

111. Keohane, *Philosophy and the State in France*, 297. See also Lionel Rothkrug, *Opposition to Louis XIV: The Political and Social Origins of the French Enlightenment* (Princeton: Princeton University Press, 1965), 50–54. Rothkrug's Nicole is less enthusiastic than Keohane's. See also Dale Van Kley, "Pierre Nicole, Jansenism, and the Morality of Enlightened Self-Interest," in *Anticipations of the Enlightenment in England, France, and Germany*, ed. Alan Charles Kors and Paul J. Korshin (Philadelphia: University of Pennsylvania Press, 1987), 74; J. B. Schneewind, *The Invention of Autonomy: A History of Modern Moral Philosophy* (Cambridge: Cambridge University Press, 1998), 275; Istvan Hont, *Jealousy of Trade: International Competition and the Nation-State in Historical Perspective* (Cambridge, Mass.: Belknap Press of Harvard

University Press, 2005), 47–51; Rahe, "Blaise Pascal, Pierre Nicole, and the Origins of Liberal Sociology," 133–34.

112. Nicole, "De la grandeur," 398. Notably, this is not how Augustine writes of charity in *City of God.* See Augustine, *City of God,* vol. VI, trans. William Chase Greene (Cambridge, Mass.: Harvard University Press/ Loeb Classical Library, 1960), XXI, 27. In the chapter, he claims that acts of charity are insufficient to gain entrance to the City of God.

113. Nicole, "De la charité et de l'amour-propre," in *Oeuvres philosophiques et morales,* 179. Rousseau is suspicious of charity and believes it invariably leads to *amour-propre.* He writes in *The Moral Letters* that "the practice of beneficence naturally gratifies amour-propre by an idea of superiority . . . one still has the force to relieve someone else's [needs.]" See Rousseau, *Moral Letters,* 201/ *OC* IV, 1115.

114. See Schneewind, *The Invention of Autonomy,* 275.

115. Nicole, "De la charité et de l'amour-propre," 181.

116. Nicole, "De la grandeur," 398–99.

117. Nicole, "De la charité et de l'amour-propre," 180–81.

118. Nicole, "Des moyens de conserver la paix avec les hommes," in *Oeuvres philosophiques et morales,* 239.

119. Augustine, *City of God,* vol. VI, XIX, 6.

120. Ibid, vol. II, V, 13, p. 207. For a helpful if brief discussion, see Peter Dennis Bathory, *Political Theory as Public Confession: The Social and Political Thought of St. Augustine of Hippo* (New Brunswick, N.J.: Transaction Books, 1980), 137–38.

121. Given his education in Rotterdam, this is hardly surprising. Mandeville may have been taught by Pierre Bayle and was widely exposed to La Rochefoucauld, Pascal, Nicole, and others. See E. J. Hundert, *The Enlightenment's Fable: Bernard Mandeville and the Discovery of Society* (Cambridge: Cambridge University Press, 2005), 23–24. See also Jonathan Israel, *Radical Enlightenment: Philosophy and the Making of Modernity, 1650–1750* (Oxford: Oxford University Press, 2001), 623. For Mandeville's relationship to neo-Augustinians, see Thomas Horne, *The Social Thought of Bernard Mandeville: Virtue and Commerce in Early Eighteenth-Century England* (New York: Columbia University Press, 1978), chapter 2; M. M. Goldsmith, *Private Vice, Public Benefits: Bernard Mandeville's Social and Political Thought* (Cambridge: Cambridge University Press, 1985), chapter 1; Laurence Dickey, "Pride, Hypocrisy, and Civility in Mandeville's Social and Historical Theory," *Critical Review* 4, no. 3 (1990): 387–431.

122. See Hundert, *The Enlightenment's Fable,* 31–55. He also stresses the importance of La Rochefoucauld.

123. See Mandeville, "The Fifth Dialogue Between Horatio and Cleomenes," 197–99.

124. Ibid.

125. Mandeville, "The Fifth Dialogue Between Horatio and Cleomenes," 211. See also Mandeville, "An Enquiry into the Origin of Moral Virtue," in *The Fable of the Bees,* vol. I, 41.

126. This position has been rejected by contemporary adherents to evolution, who believe humans naturally live in groups. As E. O. Wilson succinctly states, "People must have a tribe." See Edward O. Wilson, *The Social Conquest of the Earth* (New York: Liveright, 2012), 57.

127. See Mandeville, "An Enquiry into the Origin of Honor," 6; Hundert, *The Enlightenment's Fable,* 54.

128. Mandeville, "The Third Dialogue Between Horatio and Cleomenes," 130.

129. Mandeville, "The Sixth Dialogue Between Horatio and Cleomenes," in *The Fable of the Bees,* vol. II, 296.

130. In "An Enquiry into the Origin of Moral Virtue," a single lawgiver manipulates people

into obedience. In "Dialogues Between Horatio and Cleomenes," human society evolves over generations, and no one lawgiver is responsible for establishing society.

131. Mandeville, "An Enquiry into the Origin of Moral Virtue," 51.

132. Hont suggests Locke might be Mandeville's source here. Through his "law of fashion," Locke argues that peer pressure is a great motivator to follow the laws. That is, people often follow the natural law to avoid public condemnation and follow it for praise or public commendation. See Locke, *An Essay Concerning Human Understanding*, II, xxviii, 12, pp. 356–67.

133. La Rochefoucauld succinctly expresses this point: "We refuse praise from a desire to be praised twice." See François Duc de La Rochefoucauld, *Maxims*, trans. Louis Kronenberger (New York: Random House, 1959), #149, p. 60.

134. Mandeville, "The Third Dialogue Between Horatio and Cleomenes," 131. See also Mandeville, "An Enquiry into the Origin of Moral Virtue," 44. Similarly, Sénault thinks bulls fight for glory. See Sénault, *De l'usage des passions*, 89.

135. Erving Goffman, *The Presentation of the Self in Everyday Life* (New York: Anchor Books, 1959), 9. On p. 251, Goffman's language is similar to Mandeville's: "But, *qua* performers, individuals are concerned not with the moral issue of realizing these [moral] standards, but the amoral issue of engineering a convincing impression that these standards are being realized."

136. Mandeville, "The Sixth Dialogue Between Horatio and Cleomenes," 296.

136. Ibid., 284.

137. See Horne, *The Social Thought of Bernard Mandeville*, chapter 2.

138. Mandeville, "The First Dialogue Between Horatio and Cleomenes," in *The Fable of the Bees*, vol. II, 60.

139. Ibid., 48. In "Remark N," Mandeville discusses the envy of the "Men of Letters." See Mandeville, "Remark N," in *The Fable of the Bees*, vol. I, 136–37.

140. Mandeville, "Remark R," in *The Fable of the Bees*, vol. I, 213–14.

141. Malcolm Jack, *Corruption and Progress: The Eighteenth-Century Debate* (New York: AMS Press, 1989), 23–24.

142. See Istvan Hont, "The Early Enlightenment Debate on Commerce and Luxury," in *The Cambridge History of Eighteenth-Century Political Thought*, ed. Mark Goldie and Robert Wokler (Cambridge: Cambridge University Press, 2005), 377–418. See also Brooke, *Philosophic Pride*, 157. See also Hundert, *The Enlightenment's Fable*, 122–26.

143. See Horne, *The Social Thought of Bernard Mandeville*, 43–44.

144. Ibid., 177.

145. Ibid., 136–37.

146. Mandeville, "An Essay on Charity Schools," in *The Fable of the Bees*, vol. I, 190.

147. See Hundert, *The Enlightenment's Fable*, 37.

CHAPTER 3

1. Keohane, *Philosophy and the State in France*, 297.

2. Rousseau, *Second Discourse*, 184/ *OC* III, 189.

3. Rousseau, *Emile*, 400/ *OC* IV, 536.

4. See Hundert, *The Enlightenment's Fable*, 105–17; Force, *Self-Interest Before Adam Smith*, 18–20, 34–35. Hundert, however, focuses mostly on Rousseau's theory of language. Rosenblatt argues that the *Second Discourse* is a deconstruction of the modern natural law theories of Grotius and Pufendorf. See Rosenblatt, *Rousseau and Geneva*, chapter 4. While I think she is

correct that Rousseau had concerns beyond Paris, Genevan aristocrats are not his primary targets.

5. See Brooke, *Philosophic Pride*, 201. Furthermore, as Brooke notes, Neuhouser's central insight, as reflected in the title of his work, is that Rousseau is writing a secular theodicy.

6. Rousseau, "Letter to Beaumont," 29–30/ *OC* IV, 936–38. For a good brief discussion, see Sonenscher, *Sans-Culottes*, 111–12.

7. Rousseau, *Emile*, 641/ *OC* IV, 827.

8. The third similarity is that justice and law comes from deception and chicanery. For Mandeville, to recall an earlier discussion, the state is the achievement of a lawgiver who manipulates vanity to tame the discordant passions of humans. It is "a trick played on fools by knaves." Goldsmith, *Private Vices, Public Benefits*, 53. In the *Second Discourse*, justice results from a bogus social contract concocted by the wealthy to solidify their ill-gotten gains.

9. Adam Smith, "A Letter to the Authors of the Edinburgh Review," in *Essays on Philosophical Subjects*, ed. W. P. D. Wightman and J. C. Bryce (Indianapolis: Liberty Fund, 1980), 250.

10. Brooke notes that the French translation of *The Fable of the Bees* that appeared in 1740 rendered self-love and self-liking as "vanité" and "estime de soi-même," respectively. Rousseau opted for the more traditional *amour de soi-même* and *amour-propre* first articulated earlier in the century. See Brooke, *Philosophic Pride*, 183. For a linkage between Mandeville and Rousseau on this point, see also Malcolm Jack, "One State of Nature: Mandeville and Rousseau," *Journal of the History of Ideas* 39, no. 1 (1978): 119–24.

11. Brooke, *Philosophic Pride*, 183–84.

12. Rousseau, *Dialogues*, 206/ *OC* I, 926.

13. Rousseau *Second Discourse*, 155/ *OC* III, 158.

14. Ibid., 165/ *OC* III, 169. In *Emile*, Rousseau more tightly connects sexuality and *amour-propre*, as Emile's adolescent sexuality drives him to seek and consider others. Sexuality, furthermore, is dramatically altered by *amour-propre*, as it makes it a social phenomenon. In this modified form, it compels people and teaches them how to compare and evaluate themselves against others. Thus, it serves as a catalyst and precondition of *amour-propre*. His discussion is uneven at best, however, and sometimes Rousseau rejects the connection between sexual rivalry and *amour proper*. See Timothy O'Hagan, *Rousseau* (London: Routledge, 1999), 164–65.

15. Rousseau, *Second Discourse*, 152/ *OC* III, 155–56.

16. Ibid., 141/ *OC* III, 42.

17. Ibid., 164–65/ *OC* III, 168.

18. Ibid., 167/ *OC* III, 171.

19. Ibid., 164/ *OC* III, 168.

20. John Plamenatz, *Man and Society: A Critical Examination of Some Important Social and Political Theories from Machiavelli to Marx*, vol. I (London: Longman's, 1963), 368.

21. It is important not to confuse *amour-propre* with sexuality. If sexuality can lead to conditions that catalyze *amour-propre*, not all expressions of *amour-propre* have something to do with sexuality. See Cooper, *Rousseau, Nature, and the Problem of the Good Life*, 157.

22. Ibid., 116.

23. In *Theory of Moral Sentiments*, Smith contends that the poor suffer one of the worst indignities for a species that needs sympathy: being ignored. See Smith, *The Theory of Moral Sentiments*, I, iii, 2, p. 51.

24. Rousseau, *Second Discourse*, 166/ *OC* III, 170.

25. Ibid., 169/ *OC* III, 174.

26. Ibid.

27. Ibid., 183–84/ *OC* III, 189.

28. Ibid., 184/ *OC* III, 189.

29. Ibid., 131/ *OC* III, 131.

30. Ibid., 188/ *OC* III, 193–94.

31. Rousseau, *First Discourse*, 27/ *OC* III, 29–30; Rousseau, *The Social Contract*, III, v, 93/ *OC* III, 407; Rousseau, *Plan for a Constitution for Corsica*, 128/ *OC* III, 907.

32. See Maurice Cranston, "Rousseau on Equality," *Social Philosophy and Policy*, vol. II, no. 1 (October 1984): 120–22; Dent, *Rousseau*, 68; Robert Derathé, "La place et l'importance de la notion d'égalité dans la doctrine politique de Jean-Jacques Rousseau," in *Rousseau After Two Hundred Years: Proceedings of the Cambridge Bicentennial Colloquium*, ed. R. A. Leigh (Cambridge: Cambridge University Press, 1982), 57–60; Sonenscher, *Before the Deluge: Public Debt, Inequality*, 232; Neuhouser, *Rousseau's Critique of Inequality*, chapters 1 and 2.

33. Dent, *Rousseau*, 68.

34. Neuhouser, *Rousseau's Critique of Inequality*, 141.

35. For an earlier version of this argument, see McLendon, "Rousseau, *Amour-Propre*, and Intellectual Celebrity," *Journal of Politics*, 71 no. 2 (2009): 516–17.

36. Rousseau, *Second Discourse*, 170/ *OC* III, 174.

37. Incidentally, Augustine also connects hypocrisy to honor. In a letter to Bishop Aurelius, he contends that the clergy are more factious and envious than the laity, since "evils are the offspring of pride and eagerness for the praise of men, which often begets hypocrisy as well." Augustine, "To Bishop Aurelius, from Augustine, Priest (no. 8, Ep. XXII)," in *Select Letters*, 51.

38. See Viroli, *Rousseau and the "Well-Ordered Society,"* 5. In general, Viroli's argues that Rousseau blends a belief in natural hierarchy and a desire to limit *amour-propre* inspired by inequality. See Viroli, *Rousseau and the "Well-Ordered Society,"* 87–106. Niko Kolodny makes a similar argument, holding that natural inequalities do not inflame *amour-propre* provided people accept natural standards of their value. Although he does not mention Malebranche by name, his contention appears to rely on this aspect of Rousseau's thought. See Niko Kolodny, "The Explanation of Amour-Propre," *Philosophical Review* 119, no. 2 (2010): 165–200.

39. He specifically mentions the love of order a few times in his oeuvre. In the "Letter to Beaumont," he states: "The goodness of God is the love of order." Rousseau, "Letter to Beaumont," 46/ *OC* IV, 959. In *Julie*, he claims: "My only active principle is a natural taste for order." Rousseau, *Julie; or, the New Heloise*, 403/ *OC* II, 490. Sonenscher makes much of the love of order in Rousseau. See Sonenscher, *Sans-Culottes*, 112–14; Michael Sonenscher, "Sociability, Perfectibility and the Intellectual Legacy of Jean-Jacques Rousseau," *History of European Ideas* 41, no. 5 (2015): 688–89.

40. In "Letter to Beaumont," Rousseau divides up the psychological degeneration of humans into three stages: *amour de soi-même*, *amour-propre*, and corrupted *amour-propre* that turns people against each other. I interpret the third stage as composed of "*amour-propre* interested" and Rousseau's equivalent of *libido dominandi*. See Rousseau, "Letter to Beaumont," 28–30/ *OC* IV, 935–37

41. The "commercial *amour-propre*" theorists, such as Keohane and Hont, rightly emphasize this development but fail to distinguish between *amour-propre*, *amour-propre* interested, and *amour-propre* as *libido dominandi*.

42. Rousseau, *Second Discourse*, 167/ *OC* III, 171.

43. Ibid., 170/ *OC* III, 174.

44. Pierre Force succinctly sums up this point: "A contamination between material needs . . . and symbolic needs (the desire to be approved of)." Force, *Self-Interest Before Adam Smith*, 129–30.

45. Rousseau, *Second Discourse*, 218/ *OC* III, 219.

46. Ibid., 170/ *OC* III, 174.

47. Ibid., 170/ *OC* III, 175.

48. Ibid., 198, n. 9/ *OC* III, 204.

49. Rousseau, "Letter to Beaumont," 29/ *OC* IV, 937.

50. In *Emile*, Rousseau describes such boredom in Pascalian terms. Far from producing happiness, he claims that luxuries and entertainments lead to inconstancy and boredom: "The restlessness of desire produces curiosity and inconstancy. The emptiness of turbulent pleasures produces boredom. One is never bored with his condition when one knows none more agreeable." Rousseau, *Emile*, 382/ *OC* IV, 514.

51. Rousseau, *Second Discourse*, 184/ *OC* III, 189. Other Augustinian theorists make this claim. Thomas More, in *Utopia*, remarks that "pride measures prosperity not by her own good fortune but rather by the ill-fortune of others." Thomas More, *Utopia*, trans. Paul Turner (New York: Penguin Classics, 2003), 121. Sénault makes a similar claim as well: "The Avaricious suffer, for all their property; they have custody of it and do not use it . . . and their only satisfaction they derive from it is preventing others from owning it." Sénault, *De l'usage des passions*, 511. Even Voltaire, who enjoyed his life at the top of French society and had lifelong aristocratic friends from his schooldays at the college Louis-le-Grand, was fully aware of the brutal nature of social class relations in the eighteenth century: "In our unhappy world, it's impossible for people living in society not to be divided into two classes, the oppressors on one hand and the oppressed on the other." Voltaire, "Equality," in *A Pocket Philosophical Dictionary*, 124.

52. Ibid., 171/ *OC* III, 175.

53. Ibid., 171/ *OC* III, 175–76.

54. Ibid., 199/ *OC* III, 203. Italics mine.

55. Rousseau, *Dialogues*, 9/ *OC* I, 669.

56. Jean-Jacques Rousseau, "On Wealth and Fragments on Taste," in *The Collected Writings of Jean-Jacques Rousseau*, vol. 11, trans. Christopher Kelly, 11/ *OC* V, 475.

57. Ibid.

58. Ibid., 12/ *OC* V, 476.

59. Although Neuhouser is partially correct in arguing that Rousseau wants to eliminate domination in order to allow room for free will and agency to grow, he wrongly deemphasizes Rousseau's primary concern: protecting the lives and limbs of the people against the brutality and cruelty of the powerful. See Neuhouser, *Rousseau's Critique of Inequality*, 128.

60. Peter Brown, *Through the Eye of a Needle: Wealth, the Fall of Rome, and the Making of Christianity in the West, 350–550 AD* (Princeton: Princeton University Press, 2014), 349.

61. Rousseau, *Second Discourse*, 172/ *OC* III, 176.

62. Ibid., 173/ *OC* III, 177.

63. Christopher Brooke and David Lay Williams both have made compelling Rousseau-Rawls linkages. See Christopher Brooke, "Rawls on Rousseau and the General Will," in *The General Will: The Evolution of a Concept*, ed. James Farr and David Lay Williams (Cambridge: Cambridge University Press, 2015), 429–46; see David Lay Williams, *Rousseau's Social Contract: An Introduction* (Cambridge: Cambridge University Press, 2014), 238–43.

64. Rawls, *A Theory of Justice*, §12, p. 74.

65. Ibid., §11, p. 62.

66. John Rawls, *Lectures on the History of Political Philosophy*, ed. Samuel Freeman (Cambridge, Mass.: Belknap Press of Harvard University Press, 2007), 199–200. See also Brooke, "Rawls on Rousseau and the General Will," 432.

67. For an earlier version of this section, see Michael Locke McLendon, "Rousseau and the Minimal Self: A Solution to the Problem of Amour-Propre," *European Journal of Political Theory* 13, no. 3 (2014): 347–51.

68. Rousseau, *First Discourse*, 27/ *OC* III, 29–30.

69. Rousseau, *The Social Contract*, III, 93/ *OC* III, 407; Jean-Jacques Rousseau, *Letters Written from the Mountain*, in *The Collected Works of Jean-Jacques Rousseau*, vol. 9, trans. Judith R. Bush and Christopher Kelly, 233/ *OC* III, 809; Rousseau, *Plan for a Constitution for Corsica*, 128/ *OC* III, 907.

70. Rousseau, *Emile*, 164/ *OC* IV, 249.

71. Rousseau, *Second Discourse*, 120/ *OC* III, 117.

72. D'Alembert, "Essai sur la société des gens de lettres et des grands," 356; see also Hulliung, *The Autocritique of Enlightenment*, 91–92.

73. Even the *philosophes* who tried to influence political authorities knew the source of their power was public opinion.

74. Diderot, *Le fils naturel*, 93.

75. Rousseau, "My Portrait," 44/ *OC* I, 1129.

76. Badinter, *Les passions intellectuelles*, I, 9. In the third volume of the series, *Volonté de pouvoir (1762–1778)*, she contends that the *philosophes* are driven by a *libido dominandi*. She never connects this theme with Rousseau's *Second Discourse*, however. Furthemore, she believes it is only "the will to impose their views." See Élisabeth Badinter, *Les passions intellectuelles, Volume III: Volonté de pouvoir (1762–1778)* (Paris: Fayard, 2007), 9. She thus does not think that it leads to cruelty, as does Rousseau. Her intellectuals want to influence kings and princes, or even become politicians themselves. Still, in her three-volume set, *Les passions intellectuelles*, Badinter characterizes the progression of the psychology of French intellectuals in the same Augustinian terms as Rousseau. That is, the desire for glory leads to the desire for power and to control others.

77. Rousseau, *The Social Contract*, I, vii, 51–52/ *OC* III, 363.

78. Rousseau, *The Social Contract*, I, i, 41/ *OC* III, 351. See also Williams, *Rousseau's Social Contract: An Introduction*, 36–37.

79. Rousseau, *Letters Written from the Mountain*, 260–61/ *OC* III, 841. Similarly, Emile "conceives of no ill greater than servitude." See Rousseau, *Emile*, 400/ *OC* IV, 536.

80. Rousseau, *The Social Contract*, I, viii, 53/ *OC* III, 364.

81. Ibid., II, x, pp. 77–78/ *OC* III, 391–92.

82. For a helpful discussion, see Jonathan Marks, *Perfection and Disharmony in the Thought of Jean-Jacques Rousseau* (Cambridge: Cambridge University Press, 2005), 79–80.

83. Rousseau, *The Social Contract*, II, iv, 61/ *OC* III, 374.

84. Ibid., II, iv, 63/ *OC* III, 375.

85. For a helpful, in-depth treatment of this passage, see Dennis C. Rasmussen, "If Rousseau Were Rich: Another Model of the Good Life," *History of Political Thought* 36, no. 3 (2015): 499–520.

86. Rousseau, *Emile*, 517–22/ *OC* IV, 678–83.

87. It is worth pointing out that Rousseau follows Augustine in conflating love and morals. In book IV of *The Social Contract*, he writes: "It is useless to draw a distinction between a nation's morals and the objects of its esteem." Rousseau, *The Social Contract*, 141/ *OC* III, 458.

88. Ibid., III, xv, 113/ *OC* III, 429.

89. Rousseau, *Emile*, 521/ *OC* IV, 682–83.

90. Recall Rousseau's criticism of Diderot's conceptualization of the general will, as

discussed in his essay "Natural Right," in "The Geneva Manuscripts." The claim by Diderot that reason gives rise to the ability to conceive of a general will leaves him unable to supply motive to follow it. It is wrong to suppose, he thinks, that a reason-inspired general will can reliably overpower natural instincts to survive. See Rousseau, "The Geneva Manuscript," in *The Social Contract and Other Later Writings*, I, ii, p. 156/ *OC* III, 284–85.

91. Arthur Schopenhauer, "Pride," in *The Essays of Arthur Schopenhauer*, trans. Ben Ray Redman (New York: Walter J. Black, 1932), 57.

92. See Patrick Riley, *The General Will Before Rousseau: The Transformation of the Divine into the Civic* (Princeton: Princeton University Press, 1986).

93. James Boswell, *Life of Johnson*, ed. R. W. Chapman (Oxford: Oxford University Press, 1994), 615.

94. Rousseau, *The Social Contract*, II, vii, 71/ *OC* III, 384. In this passage, he calls the existence of a lawgiver a "true miracle."

95. See Williams, *Rousseau's Platonic Enlightenment*.

96. Sonenscher, *Sans-Culottes*, chapter 3.

97. Ibid., 170–78; Sonenscher, *Before the Deluge*, 225–26; Christopher Brooke, "Rousseau's *Second Discourse*: Between Epicureanism and Stoicism," in *Rousseau and Freedom*, ed. Christie McDonald and Stanley Hoffman (Cambridge: Cambridge University Press, 2010), 44–57. Leo Strauss and Victor Goldschmidt are the most renowned scholars to describe Rousseau as Epicurean, though Goldschmidt relies on Buffon rather than Hobbes. See Leo Strauss, *Natural Right and History* (Chicago: University of Chicago Press, 1953), 264, 279; Goldschmidt, *Anthropologie et politique*, 231–40;

98. See Force, *Self-Interest Before Adam Smith*, chapter 2; Christopher Brooke, "Rousseau's Political Philosophy: Stoic and Augustinian Origins," in *The Cambridge Companion to Rousseau*, 94–123. Brooke, *Philosophic Pride*, chapter 8. Brooke backs off from this position and later decides Rousseau is more Epicurean than Stoic. See Brooke, "Rousseau's *Second Discourse*: Between Epicureanism and Stoicism," 44–57.

99. See Brooke, "Rousseau's *Second Discourse*: Between Epicureanism and Stoicism," 53–54.

100. Rousseau, *Emile*, 376/ *OC* IV, 507.

101. Ibid., 389n./ *OC* IV, 523n.

102. Ibid., 166/ *OC* IV, 252.

103. Ibid., 373/ *OC* IV, 504.

104. Hutcheson argues against Mandeville's rigorism by claiming that people have a moral sense that overrides considerations of vanity: "But shall any Man ever really love the Publick, or study the good of others in his heart, if Self-love be the only spring of his actions? No: that is impossible. Or shall we really love Men who appear to love the Publick, without a moral sense? No . . . we should hate them as Hypocrites, and our Rivals in Fame." Francis Hutcheson, *An Inquiry into the Original of Our Ideas of Beauty and Virtue*, rev. ed., ed. Wolfgang Leidhold (Indianapolis: Liberty Fund, 2008), 154. Smith adopts this critique of Mandeville in *The Theory of Moral Sentiments*, asserting that "the desire of doing what is honorable and noble . . . cannot with any propriety be called vanity." Smith, *The Theory of Moral Sentiments*, 363. Neuhouser is effective on this point as well. See Neuhouser, *Rousseau's Theodicy of Self-Love*, 241.

105. In the *Plan for a Constitution for Corsica*, Rousseau claims "esteeming oneself based on truly estimable goods" is appropriately considered pride, not vanity. Cooper makes much of this distinction. See Cooper, *Rousseau, Nature, and the Problem of the Good Life*, 160–72. Applied to Emile, he will experience pride rather than the bad form of *amour-propre*. Rousseau, *Plan for a Constitution for Corsica*, 154/ *OC* III, 938.

106. Rousseau, *Emile*, 352/ *OC* IV, 479.

107. Ibid., 400/ *OC* IV, 537.

108. See Viroli, *Rousseau and the "Well-Ordered Society,"* 57, 94–95.

109. Rousseau, *Dialogues*, 147/ *OC* I, 850. See also Rousseau, *Plan for a Constitution for Corsica*, 126/ *OC* III, 905.

110. Emile, however, has considerable pride in his virtues, such as sobriety and temperance. See *Emile*, 506/ *OC* IV, 665.

111. Cohen rightly criticizes Durkheim, Cassirer, and Bloom for failing to recognize Rousseau's commitment to individuality. See Cohen, *Rousseau: A Free Community of Equals*, 35–40. He understates, however, Rousseau's concern of the dangers of individuality.

112. Rousseau does not make consistent use of the term. Most of the time, it seems to refer to *amour de soi-même* and a consciousness bereft of a sense of identity. At the end of the *Second Discourse*, however, he seems to conflate it with the "sentiment of identity." See Rousseau, *Second Discourse*, 187/ *OC* III, 193.

113. Rousseau, *The Reveries of the Solitary Walker*, 46/ *OC* I, 1047; see also Rousseau, *Emile*, 372/ *OC* IV, 503; Rousseau, *Julie; or, the New Heloise*, 9/ *OC* II, 14.

114. He found another way to enter the "sentiment of existence." In the "Second Walk," while walking on the side of a road, he was knocked out by a Great Dane and suffered temporary amnesia. His description of the event is nothing short of remarkable: "Entirely absorbed in the present moment, I remembered nothing; I had no distinct notion of my person nor the least idea of what had just happened to me; I knew neither who I was nor where I was; I felt neither injury, fear, nor worry. I watched my blood flow as I would have watched a brook flow; without even suspecting that his blood belonged to me in any way. I felt a rapturous calm in my whole being; and each time I remember it, I find nothing comparable to it in all the activity of known pleasures." Rousseau, *The Reveries of the Solitary Walker*, 12/ *OC* I, 1005.

115. Cooper, *Rousseau, Nature, and the Problem of the Good Life*, 178.

116. Rousseau, "My Portrait," #21, p. 40/ *OC* I, 1124.

117. Rousseau, "Preface to *Narcissus*," 92/ *OC* II, 959.

118. Rousseau, *The Reveries of the Solitary Walker*, 47/ *OC* I, 1048. For a good discussion, see David Lay Williams, "The Platonic Soul of the *Reveries*: The Role of Solitude in Rousseau's Democratic Politics," *History of Political Thought* 34, no. 1 (2012): 111–14.

119. Rousseau, *Second Discourse*, 167/ *OC* III, 171.

120. Ibid.

121. Rousseau, *Emile*, 228/ *OC* IV, 326.

122. Ibid., 187/ *OC* IV, 277.

123. Ibid., 661/ *OC* IV, 850.

124. Ibid.

125. Rousseau, *Julie; or, the New Heloise*, 3/ *OC* II, 9.

126. Rousseau, *Plan for a Constitution for Corsica*, 132/ *OC* III, 911.

127. Rousseau, *Julie; or, the New Heloise*, 14/ *OC* II, 20.

128. Rousseau, *The Social Contract*, IV, i, 121/ *OC* III, 437. Granted, in *Emile* he does belittle peasants as being thoughtless and attached to habit. See Rousseau, *Emile*, 255–56/ *OC* IV, 360.

129. Rousseau, *Dialogues*, 213/ *OC* I, 935. This argument was put to rest by Arthur Lovejoy some time ago. See Arthur Lovejoy, "The Supposed Primitivism of Rousseau's 'Second Discourse,'" in *Essays in the History of Ideas* (Baltimore: Johns Hopkins University Press, 1948), 14–37.

130. Rousseau, *Letters Written from the Mountain*, 292/ *OC* III, 881. In fact, Rousseau argues that to compare oneself to such an illustrious past is an expression of *amour-propre*.

131. See the section "From *Amour-Propre* to *Amour-Propre* Interested to *Libido Dominandi*."

132. Rousseau's description of the patriotism of the Saint Gervais Festival is evidence for this claim. See Rousseau, *J. J. Rousseau Citizen of Geneva to Monsieur d'Alembert*, 351n/ *OC* V, 124.

133. Rousseau, *Plan for a Constitution for Corsica*, 127/ *OC* III, 905.

134. See Axel Honneth, *The Struggle for Recognition: The Moral Grammar of Social Conflicts*, trans. Joel Anderson (Cambridge, Mass.: MIT Press, 1995), 88; See George Herbert Mead, *Mind, Self, and Society*, ed. Charles W. Morris (Chicago: University of Chicago Press, 1967), 208.

135. Mead, *Mind, Self, and Society*, 208.

136. Neuhouser, *Rousseau's Theodicy of Self-Love*, 169.

137. Neuhouser is well aware of Rousseau's response. See ibid., 5.

CHAPTER 4

1. For an earlier version of this summary of Rousseau's influence on Tocqueville, see Michael Locke McLendon, "The General Will After Rousseau: The Case of Tocqueville," in *The General Will: The Evolution of a Concept*, 402–5.

2. For example, see John Koritansky, *Alexis de Tocqueville and the New Science of Politics* (Durham, N.C.: Carolina Academic Press, 1986), 26; Cheryl B. Welch, *De Tocqueville* (Oxford: Oxford University Press, 2001), 170–71; Sheldon S. Wolin, *Tocqueville Between Two Worlds: The Making of a Theoretical and Political Life* (Princeton: Princeton University Press, 2001), 204–5; Leo Damrosch, *Tocqueville's Discovery of America* (New York: Farrar, Straus and Giroux, 2010), 70–71.

3. André Jardin, *Tocqueville: A Biography*, trans. Lydia Davis with Robert Hemenway (Baltimore: Johns Hopkins University Press, 1998), 243–44. Welch, *De Tocqueville*, 70; Michael Drolet, *Tocqueville, Democracy and Social Reform* (London: Palgrave Macmillan, 2003), 136–37; Richard Swedberg, *Tocqueville's Political Economy* (Princeton: Princeton University Press, 2009), 137.

4. Wolin, *Tocqueville Between Two Worlds*, 179. See also George Wilson Pierson, *Tocqueville in America* (Baltimore: Johns Hopkins University Press, 1996), 410.

5. Aurelian Craiutu, *Liberalism Under Siege: The Political Thought of the French Doctrinaires* (Lanham, Md.: Lexington Books, 2003), 91. See also Tracy B. Strong, "Seeing Differently, Seeing Further: Rousseau and Tocqueville," in *Friends and Citizens: Essays in Honor of Wilson Carey McWilliams*, ed. Peter Dennis Bathory and Nancy L. Schwartz (Lanham, Md.: Rowman and Littlefield, 2001), 106–7.

6. Koritansky, *Alexis de Tocqueville and the New Science of Politics*, 129–30.

7. Allan Bloom, *Giants and Dwarfs: Essays 1960–1990* (New York: Simon and Schuster, 1990), 312.

8. Damrosch, *Tocqueville's Discovery of America*, 72.

9. The best discussion of Tocqueville's Jansenism comes from Jaume, *Tocqueville: The Aristocratic Sources of Liberty*, chapter 9.

10. See Jardin, *Tocqueville: A Biography*, 40, 42, 82, and 182; Jean-Claude Lamberti, *Tocqueville and the Two Democracies*, trans. Arthur Goldhammer (Cambridge, Mass.: Harvard University Press, 1989), 48.

11. Jardin, *Tocqueville: A Biography*, 269.

12. Tocqueville is hardly unique among nineteenth-century theorists in denigrating the

masses as ordinary and uninspiring, and in noting the cultural production of weak personalities in commercial democracies. The argument finds expression in mid- to late eighteenth-century intellectuals such as Ferguson, Goethe, and others and becomes wildly popular in the nineteenth century. Numerous thinkers of a variety of political stripes—the Russian socialist Alexander Herzen, liberals like J. S. Mill, the American transcendentalists Ralph Waldo Emerson and Henry David Thoreau, and even the Christian existentialist Søren Kierkegaard—agree that bourgeois institutions produce a mediocre, timid, thoughtless population and give rise to a soul-crushing conformity. For example, Herzen contends that the bourgeoisie "have no need of strongly marked characters or original minds," while Kierkegaard similarly asserts that they "have never felt enthusiasm for greatness." See Alexander Herzen, *My Past and Thoughts*, trans. Constance Garnett (Berkeley: University of California Press, 1973), 660; Søren Kiekegaard, *Journals*, trans. and ed. Alexander Dru (London: Oxford University Press, 1938), #149, p. 49. In addition, J. S. Mill, a friend of Tocqueville's, borrows the tyranny of the majority argument Tocqueville offers and makes it a central part of his argument in *On Liberty*. Finally, Nietzsche also might be included here. Despite its tracing modern corruptions to the Jews of ancient Egypt, his "slave revolt of morality" has been interpreted as a variant of this bourgeois mediocrity argument. See Georg Simmel, "The Metropolis and Mental Life," in *The Sociology of Georg Simmel*, ed. and trans. Kurt H. Wolff (Glencoe, Ill.: Free Press, 1950), 422.

13. Some less sympathetic commentators think his commitment to equality amounts to little more than a hedge against the rising bourgeois liberalism. Brogan, for example, claims that *Democracy* "is the work of a man who regards the egalitarian phantom which he has conjured up with deep hostility and dread, and wants to rally his caste to control it if not defeat it." Hugh Brogan, *Alexis de Tocqueville: A Life* (New Haven: Yale University Press, 2006), 359.

14. Alexis de Tocqueville, *The Old Regime and the Revolution*, trans. Alan S. Kahan (Chicago: University of Chicago Press, 1998), III, 1–2, 195–209/ Alexis de Tocqueville, *L'Ancien Régime et la Révolution*, in *Oeuvres complètes*, vol. II, ed. J. P. Mayer (Paris: Gallimard, 1953), 193–208.

15. Wilhelm Hennis, "Tocqueville's Perspective: *Democracy in America* in Search of the 'New Science of Politics,'" in *Interpretation* 16, no. 1 (Fall 1988): 62 and 70.

16. Koritansky, *Alexis de Tocqueville and the New Science of Politics*, 12.

17. See Sanford Lakoff, "Tocqueville's Response to Rousseau," in *Lives, Liberties and the Public Good: New Essays in Political Theory for Maurice Cranston*, ed. George Feaver and Frederick Rosen (London: Palgrave Macmillan, 1987),116; Melvin Richter, "Rousseau and Tocqueville on democratic legitimacy and illegitimacy," in *Rousseau and Liberty*, ed. Robert Wokler (Manchester: Manchester University Press, 1995), 86; see Jason Andrew Neidleman, *The General Will Is Citizenship: Inquiries into French Political Thought* (Lanham, Md.: Rowman and Littlefield, 2001), chapter 7; Michael Locke McLendon, "The General Will After Rousseau: The Case of Tocqueville," 405–8.

18. Even if politics is merely a function of philosophy, it is probably as foolish to read Tocqueville primarily as a Rousseauian as it is to read interpret Rousseau chiefly as an Epicurean or a Stoic or an Augustinian. Interesting philosophers have a variety of influences and are not easily categorized.

19. Alexis de Tocqueville, *Democracy in America*, trans. Arthur Goldhammer (New York: Library of America, 2004), II, ii, 14, p. 630. See also II, iii, 21/ Alexis de Tocqueville, *De la démocratie en Amérique*, vol. II, in *Oeuvres complètes*, vol. I, ed. J. P. Mayer (Paris: Gallimard, 1961), 147. Vol. I is divided into two volumes. I cite the work along with the English translation as *OC* followed by volume and page number.

20. Alexis de Tocqueville, *Recollections: The French Revolution of 1848*, trans. George Lawrence (New Brunswick, N.J.: Transaction Press, 1987), 5/ Alexis de Tocqueville, *Souvenirs*, in *Oeuvres complètes*, vol. XII, ed. Luc Monnier (Paris: Gallimard, 1964), 31. Italics mine.

21. Tocqueville, *Democracy in America*, II, ii, 8, p. 611/ *OC* I-ii, 128.

22. For a good brief discussion, see Jon Elster, *Alexis de Tocqueville, the First Social Scientist* (Cambridge: Cambridge University Press, 2009), 49–50.

23. *Democracy in America*, I, i, 9, p. 351/ *OC* I-i, 318.

24. Ibid., II, ii, 8, p. 611/ *OC* I-ii, 128.

25. Ibid., I, ii, 5, p. 256/ *OC* I-i, 233.

26. Ibid., I, ii, 5, p. 231/ *OC* I-i, 209.

27. Ibid., I, ii, 3, pp. 212–13/ *OC* I-i, 192.

28. Ibid., I, ii, 10, p. 465/ *OC* I-i, 421.

29. Ibid., II, iii, 18, p. 731/ *OC* I-ii, 244. Italics mine.

30. Ibid., I, i, 3, p. 60/ *OC* I-i, 52.

31. Ibid., II, iii, 21, p. 750/ *OC* I-ii, 261

32. Ibid., II, iii, 15, p. 715/ *OC* I-ii, 229–30.

33. Ibid., I, ii, 5, p. 226/ *OC* I-i, 204.

34. Ibid., I, ii, 10, p. 442/ *OC* I-i, 400.

35. In another passage, he appears to contradict himself by claiming that Americans seek out talented politicians and persuasive orators. I do not believe this undermines his earlier claims, and is yet another instance in which democrats hold contrary views. See ibid., II, i, 21, p. 576/ *OC* I-ii, 95.

36. Of course, this comes from the same man who insists that French aristocrats are the true founders of modern democracy.

37. Tocqueville, *Democracy in America*, II, I, 21, pp. 575–76/ *OC* I-ii, 94.

38. Ibid., II, ii, 4, p. 591/ *OC* I-ii, 110.

39. Ibid., II, ii, 2, p. 585/ *OC* I-ii, 105. The translator uses the term "selfishness" instead of "egoism." I have opted for the more literal interpretation "egoism" for Tocqueville's term "egoïsme." Selfishness and egoism are not synonyms, as the egoism implies some measure of vanity or *amour-propre*. Tocqueville's democrats are egotistical, not merely selfish.

40. See Bloom, *Giants and Dwarfs*, 313.

41. Tocqueville, *Democracy in America*, II, ii, 2, p. 585/ *OC* I-ii, 105.

42. Ibid., II, iii, 16, p. 720/ *OC* I-ii, 234.

43. Ibid., I, i, 3, pp. 56–57/ *OC* I-i, 48.

44. Mark Reinhardt, *The Art of Being Free: Taking Liberties with Tocqueville, Marx, and Arendt* (Ithaca: Cornell University Press, 1997), 43.

45. Tocqueville, *Democracy in America*, II, iii, 5, p. 670/ *OC* I-ii, 186.

46. Tocqueville, *Recollections*, 157/ *OC* XII, 170–71.

47. Alexis de Tocqueville, *Journey to America*, trans. George Lawrence (New Haven: Yale University Press, 1962), notebook I, 259/ Alexis de Tocqueville, *Voyages en Sicile et aux États-Unis*, in *Oeuvres complètes*, vol. V, part i, ed. J. P. Mayer (Paris: Gallimard, 1957), 279.

48. Ibid., 260/ *OC* V-i, 280.

49. Aristotle, *Politics*, in *The Basic Works of Aristotle*, ed. Richard McKeon and trans. Benjamin Jowett (New York: Random House, 1941), 1280a25.

50. Claude Lefort, *Democracy and Political Theory*, trans. David Macey (Minneapolis: University of Minnesota Press, 1988), 186. Italics mine.

51. Tocqueville, *Democracy in America*, I, "Introduction," p. 3/ *OC* I-i, 1.

52. Boswell, *Life of Johnson*, 360.

53. Diderot, *Rameau's Nephew*, in *Rameau's Nephew and Other Writings*, 24.

54. Tocqueville, *Democracy in America*, II, ii, 13, p. 627/ *OC* I-ii, 144–45.

55. Beaumont concisely states Tocqueville's conception of economic equality. While there are rich people in America, there are not any "whose sole occupation is spending their fortune, who live on unearned income." See Gustave de Beaumont, "Letter to His Brother Jules, July 4, 1831," in *Letters from America*, ed. and trans. Frederick Brown (New Haven: Yale University Press, 2010), 53.

56. Tocqueville, *Democracy in America*, I, ii, 5, p. 226/ *OC* I-i, 204. See also ibid., II, ii, 13, pp. 513–14/ *OC* I-ii, 144. Interestingly, Tocqueville's analysis of American political economy goes beyond its spectacular productivity and emphasizes various social and psychological consequences of competition. As Swedberg notes, Tocqueville "soon came to realize that there were forces that generated tensions and problems for the population in the midst of all the wealth and consumer goods." See Swedberg, *Tocqueville's Political Economy*, 33.

57. Tocqueville, *Democracy in America*, I, ii, 5, p. 226/ *OC* I-i, 204.

58. Ibid., II, iii, 16, p. 720/ *OC* I-ii, 234.

59. Lamberti, *Tocqueville and the Two Democracies*, 46.

60. See Derathé, "La place et l'importance de la notion d'égalité dans la doctrine politique de Jean-Jacques Rousseau," in *Rousseau After Two Hundred Years: Proceedings of the Cambridge Bicentennial Colloquium*, 63; Lakoff, "Tocqueville's Response to Rousseau," 114.

61. There is also a version of it in *The Old Regime and the Revolution*. See Tocqueville, *The Old Regime and the Revolution*, II, 11, 171–79/ *OC* II, 168–77.

62. Tocqueville, *Democracy in America*, I, i, 5, p. 75/ *OC* I-i, 66.

63. Ibid., II, ii, 4, pp. 590–91/ *OC* I-ii, 110.

64. Ibid, 591/ *OC* I-ii, 110.

65. Ibid., II, ii, 5, p. 598/ *OC* I-ii, 115–16.

66. Rousseau, *The Social Contract*, I, 8, p. 53/ *OC* III, 364. To be sure, he might have also gotten this language from Constant's essay "The Liberty of the Ancients Compared with That of the Moderns." Constant writes: "Political liberty . . . enlarges their spirit, ennobles their thoughts, and establishes among them a kind of intellectual equality which forms the glory and power of a people." See Benjamin Constant, *Political Writings*, ed. and trans. Biancamaria Fontana (Cambridge: Cambridge University Press, 1988), 327. Still, Constant may have derived his language from Rousseau.

67. Reinhardt, *The Art of Being Free*, 22.

68. Tocqueville, *Democracy in America*, II, ii, 8, p. 612/ *OC* I-ii, 129.

69. Émile Faguet, *Politicians and Moralists of the Nineteenth Century* (Freeport, N.Y.: Books for Libraries Press, 1970), 86.

70. Ibid., 280.

71. Ibid.

72. Alexis de Tocqueville, "Letter to Ernest de Chabrol, June 9, 1831," in *Letters from America*, 66.

73. Neidleman, *The General Will Is Citizenship*, 152.

74. Tocqueville, *Democracy in America*, II, "Notice," p. 480/ *OC* I-ii, 8.

75. In a letter, he claims that that when he speculates on his lineage it "sometimes stirs in him a childish enthusiasm of which afterwards I am ashamed." See Alexis de Tocqueville, *Journeys to England and Ireland*, ed. J. P. Mayer (London: Faber and Faber, 1953), 21. There were

limits to his aristocratic prejudices. Tocqueville never wanted to take his title of viscount and signed his name simply "Alexis de Tocqueville, sans title."

76. Brogan, *Alexis de Tocqueville: A Life*, 4.

77. Tocqueville, *Democracy in America*, I, i, 1, p. 27/ *OC* I-i, 23.

78. Ibid., 28.

79. See Tocqueville, *The Old Regime and the Revolution*, II, 3, and II, 11–12.

80. Ibid., II, 11, p. 179/ *OC* II, 176.

81. Tocqueville, *Democracy in America*, I, "Introduction," p. 8/ *OC* I-i, 6.

82. Ibid., 9.

83. See Jon Elster, *Political Psychology* (Cambridge: Cambridge University Press, 1993), 104–5; Jon Elster, *Alchemies of the Mind* (Cambridge: Cambridge University Press, 1999), 19; Claus Offe, *Reflections on America: Tocqueville, Weber and Adorno in the United States*, trans. Patrick Camiller (Malden, Mass.: Polity Press, 2005), 15.

84. James T. Kloppenberg, *The Virtues of Liberalism* (Oxford: Oxford University Press, 1998), chapter 5.

85. Quoted from ibid., 73.

86. Frances Trollope, *Domestic Manners of Americans*, ed. Donald Smalley (New York: Alfred A. Knopf, 1949), 16.

87. Ibid. Elias addresses the European cultural hang-up against spitting. By the late eighteenth century, Europeans considered it disgusting—a sign of uncleanliness and incivility. Elias writes: "By 1774 the whole practice, and even speaking about it, had become considerably more distasteful." See Elias, *The Civilizing Process*, 129.

88. Tocqueville, *Democracy in America*, "Author's Introduction," p. 4/ *OC* I-i, 2.

89. In *The Old Regime and the Revolution*, he claims the feudal aristocracy in part is defined by legal uniformity. See Tocqueville, *The Old Regime and the Revolution*, I, 4.

90. Ibid.

91. Tocqueville, *Democracy in America*, I, I, 4, p. 65/ *OC* I-i, 56.

92. Ibid., I, ii, 2, p. 203/ *OC* I-i, 183.

93. Ibid., I, i, 4, p. 63/ *OC* I-i, 55.

94. Ibid. I, ii, 2, p. 204/ *OC* I-i, 184.

95. The other reason is a lack of enlightenment. Later in the text, he argues that public officials get paid poorly, which is a major disincentive for a people obsessed with money.

96. Tocqueville, *Journey to America*, 95/ *OC* V-i, 128.

97. Tocqueville, *Democracy in America*, I, ii, 5, p. 253/ *OC* I-i, 230.

98. Ibid., I, i, 3, p. 58/ *OC* I-i, 51.

99. Ibid., I, ii, 7, p. 284/ *OC*, I-i, 258.

100. Ibid., I, ii, 5, p. 228/ *OC* I-i, 206.

101. Ibid., II, i, 9, p. 516/ *OC* I-ii, 41.

102. Ibid., 521/ *OC* I-i, 45.

103. Ibid., I, ii, 1, p. 197/ *OC* I-i, 177.

104. Ibid., I, ii, 7, p. 294/ *OC* I-i, 267.

105. Faguet, *Politicians and Moralists of the Nineteenth Century*, 83.

106. It is worth noting that Tocqueville is not original in his critique of the tyranny of the majority or of American conformity. Lucien Jaume claims that James Fenimore Cooper may have been the source of Tocqueville's analysis. See Jaume, *Tocqueville: The Aristocratic Sources of Liberty*, 9, 144. Richard Boyd suggests Stendhal predates Tocqueville in this critique. See Richard

Boyd, "Politesse and Public Opinion in Stendhal's Red and Black," *European Journal of Political Theory* 4, no. 4 (2005), 368–69. Boyd's case is easy to prove. In the opening chapter of *Red and Black*, published the very year Tocqueville sailed to America, Stendhal compares the tyranny of opinion in provincial French life to that of America: "The tyranny of opinion—and such an opinion!—is every bit as idiotic in the small towns of France as it is in the United States of America." Stendhal, *The Red and the Black*, trans. Burton Raffel (New York: Modern Library, 2003), 6.

107. Tocqueville, *Democracy in America*, I, ii, 7, p. 297/ *OC* I-i, 269.

108. Ibid., I, ii, 7, pp. 297–98/ *OC* I-i, 270.

109. See Hume, "The Idea of a Perfect Commonwealth," in *Selected Essays*, 301–15.

110. Tocqueville, *Democracy in America*, I, ii, 8, p. 305/ *OC* I-i, 275.

111. Ibid., I, ii, 8. p. 307/ *OC* I-i, 278.

112. Ibid., II, iv, 6, p. 817/ *OC* I-ii, 323.

113. Swedberg, *Tocqueville's Political Economy*, 126.

114. Tocqueville, *Democracy in America*, II, ii, 20, p. 649/ *OC*, I-ii, 164.

115. Ibid., II, ii, 20, p. 650/ *OC* I-ii, 165.

116. Ibid.

117. Ibid., 651/ *OC* I-ii, 166.

118. Smith, *Wealth of Nations*, V, I, i, p. 766.

119. Tocqueville, *Democracy in America*, II, iii, 21, p. 652/ *OC* I-ii, 167.

120. Brogan, *Alexis de Tocqueville: A Life*, 306.

121. Tocqueville, *Journeys to England and Ireland*, 104/ Alexis de Tocqueville, *Voyages en Angleterre, Irlande, Suisse et Algérie*, in *Oeuvres complètes*, vol. V, part ii, ed. J. P. Mayer and André Jardin, 5th ed. (Paris: Gallimard, 1958), 78.

122. Ibid., 104 and 108/ *OC* V-ii, 78 and 83.

123. Ibid, 108/ *OC* V-ii, 82.

124. Tocqueville, *Democracy in America*, II, iii, 21, p. 652/ *OC* I-ii, 167.

125. Ibid., II, i, 8, p. 514/ *OC* I-ii, 39.

126. Ibid., II, ii, 5, p. 596/ *OC* I-ii, 114. In volume I, Tocqueville makes a similar point, claiming equality makes it so no one is "strong enough to fight alone with advantage." Ibid., I, i, 3, p. 60/ *OC* I-i, 53.

127. Ibid., II, iii, 4, p. 667/ *OC* I-ii, 183.

CONCLUSION

1. See Frankfurt, *On Inequality*, 11–12; Pankaj Mishra, *The Age of Anger: A History of the Present* (New York: Farrar, Straus and Giroux, 2017), 112. See also Deirdre N. McCloskey, *Bourgeois Equality: How Ideas, Not Capital or Institutions, Enriched the World* (Chicago: University of Chicago Press, 2017), 46.

2. See P. K. Piff and J. P. Moskowitz, "Wealth, Poverty, and Happiness: Social Class Is Differentially Associated with Positive Emotions," *Emotion* (December 18, 2017). Advance online publication. http://dx.doi.org/10.1037/emo0000387.

3. See P. K. Piff, "Wealth and the Inflated Self: Class, Entitlement, and Narcissism," *Personality and Social Psychology Bulletin* 40, no. 1 (2014): 34–43; Paul K. Piff, Michael W. Kraus, Stephanie Cote, Bonnie Cheng, and Dacher Keltner, "Having More, Giving Less: The Influence of Class on Prosocial Behavior," *Journal of Personality and Social Psychology* 99, no. 5 (2010):

771–84. The social dominance literature is also highly relevant. See Piotr Radkiewicz, "Another Look at the Duality of the Dual-Process Motivational Model: On the Role of Axiological Moral Origins of Right-Wing Authoritarianism and Social Dominance Orientation," *Personality and Individual Differences* 99 (September 2016): 106–12.

4. See Katherine A. Decelles and Michael I. Norton, "Physical and Situational Inequality on Airplanes Predicts Air Rage," *Proceedings of the National Academy of Sciences* 113, no. 20 (2016): 5588–91.

5. Christopher J. Boyce, Gordon D. A. Brown, and Simon C. Moore, "Money and Happiness: Rank of Income, Not Income, Affects Life Satisfaction," *Journal of Psychological Science* 21, no. 4 (2010): 471–75.

6. http://www.gallup.com/poll/158417/poverty-comes-depression-illness.aspx.

7. Isaiah Berlin, *The Crooked Timber of Humanity*, ed. Henry Hardy (Princeton: Princeton University Press, 1998), 12.

8. William Graham Sumner, *What Social Classes Owe to Each Other* (Caldwell, Idaho: Caxton Printers, 1989), 87.

Bibliography

Abbadie, Jacques. *The Art of Knowing One's Self; Or A Diligent Search After the Spring of Morality*, trans. P. Hansbury. London: Edward Jones, 1696.

———. *L'art de se connoitre soy-mesme, ou La recherche des sources de la morale*. Rotterdam: Pierre Reinier Leers, 1710.

Abercrombie, Nigel. *Saint Augustine and French Classical Thought*. New York: Russell and Russell, 1938.

Ansell-Pearson, Keith. *Nietzsche Contra Rousseau: A Study of Nietzsche's Moral and Political Thought*. Cambridge: Cambridge University Press, 1992.

Arendt, Hannah. "The Threat of Conformism." In *Essays in Understanding: 1930–54*, ed. Jerome Kohn, 423–427. New York: Schocken Books, 1994.

———. *Love and Saint Augustine*, trans. Joanna Vecchiarelli Scott and Judith Chelsius Stark. Chicago: University of Chicago Press, 1996.

Aristotle. *The Politics*. In *The Basic Works of Aristotle*, ed. Richard McKeon and trans. Benjamin Jowett. New York: Random House, 1941.

Augustine. *Select Letters*, trans. James H. Baxter. Cambridge, Mass.: Harvard University Press/ Loeb Classics, 1930.

———. *Confessions*. Vols. I and II, trans. William Watts. Cambridge, Mass.: Harvard University Press/ Loeb Classics, 1951.

———. *City of God*. Vol. I, trans. George E. McCracken. Cambridge, Mass.: Harvard University Press/ Loeb Classics, 1957.

———. *City of God*. Vol. VI, trans. William Chase Greene. Cambridge, Mass.: Harvard University Press/ Loeb Classics, 1960.

———. *City of God*. Vol. II, trans. Philip Levine. Cambridge, Mass.: Harvard University Press/ Loeb Classics, 1966.

———. *City of God*. Vol. III, trans. David S. Wiesen. Cambridge, Mass.: Harvard University Press/ Loeb Classics, 1968.

———. *City of God*. Vol. IV, trans. Philip Levine. Cambridge, Mass.: Harvard University Press/ Loeb Classics, 1968.

———. *Eighty-Three Different Questions*, trans. David A. Mosher. Washington, D.C.: Catholic University Press of America, 1977.

———. *On the Trinity*, trans. Stephen McKenna and ed. Gareth B. Matthews. Cambridge: Cambridge University Press, 2002.

———. *Ten Homilies on the First Epistle of John to the Parthians*, trans. Rev. H. Browne. London: Aeterna Press, 2014.

Babbitt, Irving. *Rousseau and Romanticism*. New York: Houghton Mifflin, 1919.

Badinter, Élisabeth. *Les passions intellectuelles: Désirs de gloire (1735–1751)*. Paris: Fayard, 1999.

———. *Les passions intellectuelles: Volonté de pouvoir (1762–1778)*. Paris: Fayard, 2007.

Bakunin, Michael. *God and State*. New York: Dover, 1970.

Bathory, Peter Dennis. *Political Theory as Public Confession: The Social and Political Thought of St. Augustine of Hippo*. New Brunswick, N.J.: Transaction Books, 1980.

Bayle, Pierre. *Various Thoughts on the Occasion of a Comet*, trans. Robert C. Bartlett. Indianapolis: Hackett, 2000.

Becker, Carl L. *The Heavenly City of the Eighteenth-Century Philosophers*. New Haven: Yale University Press, 1960.

Beilock, S., R. Rydell, and A. R. McConnell. "Stereotype Threat and Working Memory: Mechanisms, Alleviation, and Spill Over." *Journal of Experimental Psychology*, 136, no. 2 (2007): 256–76.

Bentham, Jeremy. *Introduction to the Principles of Morals and Legislation*. New York: Hafner Press, 1948.

Berlin, Isaiah. *The Crooked Timber of Humanity*, ed. Henry Hardy. Princeton: Princeton University Press, 1998.

———. *Freedom and Its Betrayal: Six Enemies of Human Liberty*, ed. Henry Hardy. Princeton: Princeton University Press, 2002.

Bisson, Thomas N. *The Crisis of the Twelfth Century: Power, Lordship, and the Origins of European Government*. Princeton: Princeton University Press, 2009.

Blackburn, Simon. *Mirror, Mirror: The Uses and Abuses of Self-Love*. Princeton: Princeton University Press, 2014.

Bloom, Allan. *Giants and Dwarfs: Essays 1960–1990*. New York: Simon and Schuster, 1990.

Boswell, James. *Life of Johnson*, ed. R. W. Chapman. Oxford: Oxford University Press, 1994.

Boyce, Christopher J., Gordon D. A. Brown, and Simon C. Moore. "Money and Happiness: Rank of Income, Not Income, Affects Life Satisfaction." *Journal of Psychological Science* 21, no. 4 (2010): 471–75.

Boyd, Richard. "Politesse and Public Opinion in Stendhal's Red and Black." *European Journal of Political Theory* 4, no.4 (2005): 367–92.

Brogan, Hugh. *Alexis de Tocqueville: A Life*. New Haven: Yale University Press, 2006.

Brooke, Christopher. "Rousseau's Political Philosophy: Stoic and Augustinian Origins." In *The Cambridge Companion to Rousseau*, ed. Patrick Riley, 94–123. Cambridge: Cambridge University Press, 2001.

———. "Rousseau's *Second Discourse*: Between Epicureanism and Stoicism." In *Rousseau and Freedom*, ed. Christie McDonald and Stanley Hoffman, 44–57. Cambridge: Cambridge University Press, 2010.

———. *Philosophic Pride: Stoicism in Political Thought from Lipsius to Rousseau*. Princeton: Princeton University Press, 2012.

———. "Rawls on Rousseau and the General Will." In *The General Will: The Evolution of a Concept*, ed. James Farr and David Lay Williams, 429–46. Cambridge: Cambridge University Press, 2015.

Brown, Peter. *Augustine of Hippo: A Biography*. Berkeley: University of California Press, 2000.

———. *Through the Eye of a Needle: Wealth, the Fall of Rome, and the Making of Christianity in the West, 350–550 AD*. Princeton: Princeton University Press, 2014.

Cassirer, Ernst. *The Question of Jean-Jacques Rousseau*. Bloomington: Indiana University Press, 1963.

Chambers, Katherine. "Slavery and Domination as Political Ideas in Augustine's *City of God.*" *Heythrop Journal* 54, no.1 (2013): 13–28.

Charvet, John. *The Social Problem in the Philosophy of Rousseau*. Cambridge: Cambridge University Press, 1974.

Cohen, Joshua. *Rousseau: A Free Community of Equals*. Oxford: Oxford University Press, 2010.

Constant, Benjamin. "The Liberty of the Ancients Compared With That of the Moderns." In *Political Writings*, ed. and trans. Biancamaria Fontana, 309–28. Cambridge: Cambridge University Press, 1988.

Cooper, Laurence D. "Rousseau on Self-Love: What We've Learned, What We Might Have Learned." *Review of Politics* 60, no. 4 (1998): 661–83.

———. *Rousseau, Nature, and the Problem of the Good Life*. University Park: Pennsylvania State University Press, 1999.

Craiutu, Aurelian. *Liberalism Under Siege: The Political Thought of the French Doctrinaires*. Lanham, Md.: Lexington Books, 2004.

Cranston, Maurice. *Jean-Jacques: The Early Life and Work of Jean-Jacques Rousseau, 1712–54*. Chicago: University of Chicago Press, 1982.

———. "Rousseau on Equality." In *Social Philosophy and Policy* 2, no. 1 (1984): 115–24.

———. *Philosophers and Pamphleteers: Political Theorists of the Enlightenment*. Oxford: Oxford University Press, 1986.

d'Alembert, Jean le Rond. *Oeuvres complètes*. Vol. I. Geneva: Slatkine Reprints, 1967.

———. *Oeuvres complètes*. Vol. III. Geneva: Slatkine Reprints, 1967.

———. *Oeuvres complètes*. Vol. IV. Geneva: Slatkine Reprints, 1967.

Damrosch, Leo. *Jean-Jacques Rousseau: Restless Genius*. New York: Houghton Mifflin, 2005.

———. *Tocqueville's Discovery of America*. New York: Farrar, Straus and Giroux, 2010.

Darnton, Robert. *The Literary Underground of the Old Regime*. Cambridge, Mass.: Harvard University Press, 1982.

———. *The Great Cat Massacre and Other Episodes in French Cultural History*. New York: Basic Books, 1999.

Davidson, Ian. *Voltaire: A Life*. New York: Pegasus Books, 2010.

Deane, Herbert A. *The Political and Social Ideas of Saint Augustine*. New York: Columbia University Press, 1963.

Decelles, Katherine, and Michael I. Norton. "Physical and Situational Inequality on Airplanes Predicts Air Rage." *Proceedings of the National Academy of Sciences* 113, no. 20 (2016): 5588–91.

Dent, N. J. H. *Rousseau: His Psychological, Social and Political Theory*. Oxford: Basil Blackwell, 1988.

Dent, N. J. H., and Timothy O'Hagan. "Rousseau on *Amour-Propre*."*Aristotelian Society* suppl. 72, no. 1 (1998): 57–73.

Derathé, Robert. "La place et l'importance de la notion d'égalité dans la doctrine politique de Jean-Jacques Rousseau." In *Rousseau After Two Hundred Years: Proceedings of the Cambridge Bicentennial Colloquium*, ed. R. A. Leigh, 55–63. Cambridge: Cambridge University Press, 1982.

Dewald, Jonathan. *The European Nobility, 1400–1800*. Cambridge: Cambridge University Press, 1996.

Dickey, Laurence. "Pride, Hypocrisy, and Civility in Mandeville's Social and Historical Theory." *Critical Review* 4, no. 3 (1990): 387–431.

Diderot, Denis. *Le fils naturel*. In *Oeuvres de théâtre de M. Diderot: Avec un discours sur la poésie dramatique*. Amsterdam: M. M. Rey, 1772.

———. *Rameau's Nephew and Other Works*, trans. Jacques Barzun and Ralph H. Bowen. Indianapolis: Hackett, 1956.

———. "Art." In *Encyclopedia Selections*, trans. Nelly S. Hoyt and Thomas Cassirer, 3–18. Indianapolis: Bobbs-Merrill, 1965.

———. *Oeuvres complètes de Diderot*. Vol. 18, ed. J. Assézat and Maurice Tourneux. Nendeln, Liechtenstein: Kraus Reprint, 1966.

———. *Oeuvres complètes de Diderot*. Vol. 19, ed. J. Assézat and Maurice Tourneux. Nendeln, Liechtenstein: Kraus Reprint, 1966.

Dieckmann, Hebert. "Diderot's Conception of Genius." *Journal of the History of Ideas* 2, no. 2 (1941): 151–182.

Douglass, Robin. *Hobbes and Rousseau: Nature, Free Will, and the Passions*. Oxford: Oxford University Press, 2015.

———. "What's Wrong with Inequality? Some Rousseauian Perspectives." *European Journal of Political Theory* 14, no. 3 (2015): 368–77.

Doyle, William. *Aristocracy: A Very Short Introduction*. Oxford: Oxford University Press, 2010.

Drolet, Michael. *Tocqueville, Democracy and Social Reform*. London: Palgrave Macmillan, 2003.

Elias, Norbert. *The Civilizing Process: The History of Manners and State Formation and Civilization*, trans. Edmund Jephcott. Cambridge, Mass.: Blackwell, 1994.

Elster, Jon. *Political Psychology*. Cambridge: Cambridge University Press, 1993.

———. *Alchemies of the Mind*. Cambridge: Cambridge University Press, 1998.

———. *Alexis de Tocqueville, the First Social Scientist*. Cambridge: Cambridge University Press, 2009.

Faguet, Émile. *Politicians and Moralists of the Nineteenth Century*. Freeport, N.Y.: Books for Libraries Press, 1970.

Fénelon, François. *Oeuvres complètes,* Vol. I, ed. Jacques Le Brun. Paris: Gallimard, 1983.

Ferguson, Adam. *An Essay on the History of Civil Society*, ed. Fania Oz-Salzberger. Cambridge: Cambridge University Press, 1995.

Force, Pierre. *Self-Interest Before Adam Smith: A Genealogy of Economic Science*. Cambridge: Cambridge University Press, 2003.

France, Peter. *Diderot*. Oxford: Oxford University Press, 1983.

Frankfurt, Harry. *On Inequality*. Princeton: Princeton University Press, 2015.

Furbank, P. N. *Diderot: A Critical Biography*. New York: Alfred A. Knopf, 1992.

Gay, Peter. *The Enlightenment: An Interpretation, Volume II: The Science of Freedom*. New York: W. W. Norton, 1969.

———. *Voltaire's Politics: The Poet as Realist*. New Haven: Yale University Press, 1988.

Geuss, Raymond. *Public Goods, Private Goods*. Princeton: Princeton University Press, 2001.

———. *Philosophy and Real Politics*. Princeton: Princeton University Press, 2008.

Goffman, Erving. *The Presentation of the Self in Everyday Life*. New York: Anchor Books, 1959.

Golder, Herbert. "Sophocles' 'Ajax': Beyond the Shadow of Time." *Arion: A Journal of the Humanities and Classics* 1, no. 1 (1990): 9–34.

Goldschmidt, Victor. *Anthropologie et politique: Les principes du système de Rousseau*. Paris: Vrin, 1974.

Goldsmith, M. M. *Private Vice, Public Benefits: Bernard Mandeville's Social and Political Thought*. Cambridge: Cambridge University Press, 1985.

Goodman, Dena. *The Republic of Letters: A Cultural History of the French Enlightenment*. Ithaca: Cornell University Press, 1994.

Grant, Ruth W. *Hypocrisy and Integrity: Machiavelli, Rousseau, and the Ethics of Politics*. Chicago: University of Chicago Press, 1997.

Greenblatt, Stephen. *The Rise and Fall of Adam and Eve*. New York: W. W. Norton, 2017.

Grimsley, Ronald. *Jean d'Alembert*. Oxford: Clarendon Press, 1963.

Harrington, Michael. *The Other America: Poverty in the United States*. New York: Pelican Books, 1981.

Hartle, Ann. *The Modern Self in Rousseau's* Confessions*: A Reply to St. Augustine*. Notre Dame, Ind.: University of Notre Dame Press, 1983.

Hendel, Charles. *Jean-Jacques Rousseau: Moralist*. Indianapolis: Bobbs-Merrill, 1934.

Hennis, Wilhelm. "Tocqueville's Perspective: *Democracy in America* in Search of the 'New Science of Politics,'" *Interpretation* 16, no. 1 (1988): 61–86.

Herzen, Alexander. *My Past and Thoughts*, trans. Constance Garnett. Berkeley: University of California Press, 1973.

Hirschman, Albert O. *The Passions and the Interests*. Princeton: Princeton University Press, 2013.

Hobbes, Thomas. *Leviathan*, ed. Edwin Curley. Indianapolis: Hackett, 1994.

Homer. *The Iliad*, trans. Robert Fagles. New York: Penguin Classics, 1997.

Honneth, Axel. *The Struggle for Recognition: The Moral Grammar of Social Conflicts*, trans. Joel Anderson. Cambridge, Mass. MIT Press, 1995.

Hont, Istvan. *Jealousy of Trade: International Competition and the Nation-State in Historical Perspective*. Cambridge, Mass.: Harvard University Press, 2005.

———. "The Early Enlightenment Debate on Commerce and Luxury." In *The Cambridge History of Eighteenth-Century Political Thought*, ed. Mark Goldie and Robert Wokler, 379–418. Cambridge: Cambridge University Press, 2005.

———. *Politics in Commercial Society: Jean-Jacques Rousseau and Adam Smith*, ed. Béla Kapossy and Michael Sonenscher. Cambridge, Mass. Harvard University Press, 2015.

Horace. *The Complete Works of Horace*, ed. Casper J. Kraemer Jr. and trans. Francis Howes. New York: Random House, 1936.

Horne, Thomas. *The Social Thought of Bernard Mandeville: Virtue and Commerce in Early Eighteenth-Century England*. New York: Columbia University Press, 1978.

Huizinga, Johan. *The Autumn of the Middle Ages*, trans. Rodney J. Patton and Ulrich Mammitzsch. Chicago: University of Chicago Press, 1996.

Hulliung, Mark. *The Autocritique of Enlightenment: Rousseau and the Philosophes*. Cambridge, Mass.: Harvard University Press, 1994.

Hume, David. *An Enquiry Concerning the Principles of Morals*, ed. J. B. Schneewind. Indianapolis: Hackett, 1983.

———. *Selected Essays*, ed. Stephen Copley and Andrew Edgar. Oxford: Oxford University Press, 1996.

Hundert, E. J. *The Enlightenment's Fable: Bernard Mandeville and the Discovery of Society*. Cambridge: Cambridge University Press, 2005.

Hutcheson, Francis. *An Inquiry into the Original of Our Ideas of Beauty and Virtue*. Rev. ed., ed. Wolfgang Leidhold. Indianapolis: Liberty Fund, 2008.

Israel, Jonathan. *Radical Enlightenment: Philosophy and the Making of Modernity, 1650–1750*. Oxford: Oxford University Press. 2001.

———. *A Revolution of the Mind: Radical Enlightenment and the Intellectual Origins of Modern Democracy*. Princeton: Princeton University Press, 2010.

Jack, Malcolm. "One State of Nature: Mandeville and Rousseau." *Journal of the History of Ideas* 39, no. 1 (1978): 119–24.

———. *Corruption and Progress: The Eighteenth-Century Debate.* New York: AMS Press, 1989.

Jaeger, C. Stephen. *The Origins of Courtliness: Civilizing Trends and the Formation of Courtly Ideals, 939–1210.* Philadelphia: University of Pennsylvania Press, 1985.

———. *Ennobling Love: In Search of a Lost Sensibility.* Philadelphia: University of Pennsylvania Press, 1999.

Jardin, André. *Tocqueville: A Biography,* trans. Lydia Davis with Robert Hemenway. Baltimore: Johns Hopkins University Press, 1998.

Jaume, Lucien. *Tocqueville: The Aristocratic Sources of Liberty,* trans. Arthur Goldhammer. Princeton: Princeton University Press, 2008.

Kaeuper, Richard W. *Holy Warriors: The Religious Ideology of Chivalry.* Philadelphia: University of Pennsylvania Press, 2014.

Kelly, Christopher. *Rousseau as Author: Consecrating One's Life to the Truth.* Chicago: University of Chicago Press, 2003.

———. "Rousseau's 'Peut-Etre': Reflections on the Status of the State of Nature." *Modern Intellectual History* 3, no. 1 (2006): 75–83.

Keohane, Nannerl O. *Philosophy and the State in France.* Princeton: Princeton University Press, 1980.

Kiekegaard, Søren. *Journals,* trans. and. ed. Alexander Dru. London: Oxford University Press, 1938.

Kloppenberg, James T. *The Virtues of Liberalism.* Oxford: Oxford University Press, 1998.

Knox, Bernard. *Word and Action: Essays on Ancient Theater.* Baltimore: Johns Hopkins University Press, 1979.

Kolakowski, Leszek. *God Owes Us Nothing: A Brief Remark on Pascal's Religion and the Spirit of Jansenism.* Chicago: University of Chicago Press, 1995.

Kolodny, Niko. "The Explanation of Amour-Propre." *Philosophical Review* 119, no. 2 (2010): 165–200.

Koritansky, John. *Alexis de Tocqueville and The New Science of Politics.* Durham, N.C.: Carolina Academic Press, 1986.

Kors, Alan Charles. *D'Holbach's Coterie: An Enlightenment in Paris.* Princeton: Princeton University Press, 1976.

Kramnick, Issac. *The Rage of Edmund Burke.* New York: Basic Books, 1977.

Krause, Sharon R. *Liberalism with Honor.* Cambridge, Mass.: Harvard University Press, 2002.

Kristeva, Julia. *Strangers to Ourselves,* trans. Leon S. Roudiez. New York: Columbia University Press, 1991.

Kuehn, Manfred. *Kant: A Biography.* Cambridge: Cambridge University Press, 2001.

Lakoff, Sanford. "Tocqueville's Response to Rousseau." In *Lives, Liberties and the Public Good: New Essays in Political Theory for Maurice Cranston,* ed. George Feaver and Frederick Rosen, 101–20. New York: St. Martin's Press, 1987.

Lamberti, Jean-Claude. *Tocqueville and the Two Democracies,* trans. Arthur Goldhammer. Cambridge, Mass.: Harvard University Press, 1989.

La Mettrie, Julien Offray de. *Man a Machine and Man a Plant,* trans. Richard A. Watson and Maya Rybalka. Indianapolis: Hackett, 1994.

La Rochefoucauld, François, duc de. *Maxims,* trans. Louis Kronenberger. New York: Random House, 1959.

Lefort, Claude. *Democracy and Political Theory,* trans. David Macey. Minneapolis: University of Minnesota Press, 1988.

Levi, Anthony. *French Moralists: The Theory of the Passions, 1585–1649.* Oxford: Oxford University Press, 1964.

Lilti, Antoine. *The World of the Salons: Sociability and Worldliness in Eighteenth-Century Paris*, trans. Lydia G. Cochrane. Oxford: Oxford University Press, 2005.

———. *Figures publiques: L'invention de la célébrité, 1750–1850*. Paris: Fayard, 2014.

Locke, John. *An Essay Concerning Human Understanding*, ed. Peter H. Nidditch. Oxford: Clarendon Press, 1975.

Lovejoy, Arthur. "The Supposed Primitivism of Rousseau's 'Second Discourse.'" In *Essays in the History of Ideas*, 14–37. Baltimore: Johns Hopkins University Press, 1948.

———. *Reflections on Human Nature*. Baltimore: Johns Hopkins University Press, 1968.

Malebranche, Nicholas. *Traité de morale*, ed. Henri Joly. Paris: Ernest Thorin, 1882.

Mandeville, Bernard. *The Fable of the Bees*. Vols. I–II, ed. F. B. Kaye. Indianapolis: Liberty Fund, 1988.

Manent, Pierre. *The City of Man*. Trans. Marc A. Lepain. Princeton: Princeton University Press, 1998.

March, Jennifer. "Sophocles' Ajax: The Death and Burial of a Hero." *Bulletin of the Institute of Classical Studies* 38, no. 1 (1991–93): 1–36.

Marion, Jean-Luc. *In the Self's Place: The Approach of Saint Augustine*, trans. Jeffrey L. Kosky. Stanford: Stanford University Press, 2012.

Marks, Jonathan. *Perfection and Disharmony in the Thought of Jean-Jacques Rousseau*. Cambridge: Cambridge University Press, 2005.

McCloskey, Deidre N. *Bourgeois Equality: How Ideas, Not Capital or Institutions, Enriched the World*. Chicago: University of Chicago Press, 2017.

McLendon, Michael Locke. "Rousseau, *Amour-Propre*, and Intellectual Celebrity." *Journal of Politics* 71, no. 2 (2009): 506–19.

———. "Rousseau and the Minimal Self: A Solution to the Problem of *Amour-Propre*." *European Journal of Political Theory* 13, no. 3 (2014): 341–61.

———. "The General Will After Rousseau: The Case of Tocqueville." In *The General Will: The Evolution of a Concept*, ed. David Lay Williams and James Farr, 402–28. Cambridge: Cambridge University Press, 2015.

Mead, George Herbert. *Mind, Self, and Society*, ed. Charles W. Morris. Chicago: University of Chicago Press, 1967.

Mishra, Pankaj. *The Age of Anger: A History of the Present*. New York: Farrar, Straus and Giroux, 2017.

Montesquieu, Charles-Louis de Secondat. *My Thoughts*, trans. and ed. by Henry C. Clark. Indianapolis: Liberty Fund, 2013.

Moran, Francis III. "Between Primates and Primitives: Natural Man as the Missing Link in Rousseau's Second Discourse." *Journal of the History of Ideas* 54, no. 1 (1993): 37–58.

More, Thomas. *Utopia*, trans. Paul Turner. New York: Penguin, 2003.

Neidleman, Jason Andrew. *The General Will Is Citizenship: Inquiries into French Political Thought*. Lanham, Md.: Rowman and Littlefield, 2001.

———. *Rousseau's Ethics of Truth: A Sublime Science of Simple Souls*. New York: Routledge, 2016.

Neuhouser, Frederick. *Rousseau's Theodicy of Self-Love: Evil, Rationality, and the Drive for Recognition*. Oxford: Oxford University Press, 2008.

———. *Rousseau's Critique of Inequality: Reconstructing the* Second Discourse. Cambridge: Cambridge University Press, 2014.

Nicole, Pierre. *Moral Essays, contain'd in several treatises on many important duties*. 2nd ed., trans. A Person of Quality. London: N.p., 1677.

———. *Oeuvres philosophiques et morales, comprenant un choix de ses essais*, ed. Charles Jourdain. Paris: L. Hachette, 1845.

Nietzsche, Friedrich. *The Will to Power*, trans. and ed. Walter Kaufmann and R. J. Hollingdale. New York: Vintage Books, 1968.

Nussbaum, Martha C. *Upheavals of Thought: The Intelligence of the Emotions*. Cambridge: Cambridge University Press, 2003.

O'Donnell, Oliver. *The Problem of Self-Love in Saint Augustine*. New Haven: Yale University Press, 1988.

Offe, Claus. *Reflections on America: Tocqueville, Weber and Adorno in the United States*, trans. Patrick Camiller. Malden, Mass. Polity Press, 2005.

O'Hagan, Timothy. *Rousseau*. London: Routledge, 1999.

Pascal, Blaise. *Oeuvres complètes*, ed. Jacques Chevalier. Paris: Pléiade, 1954.

———. *Pensées and Other Writings*, trans. Honor Levi. Oxford: Oxford University Press, 1995.

Paton, H. J. *The Categorical Imperative: A Study in Kant's Moral Philosophy*. Philadelphia: University of Pennsylvania Press, 1948.

Pierson, George Wilson. *Tocqueville in America*. Baltimore: Johns Hopkins University Press, 1996.

Piff, Paul K. "Wealth and the Inflated Self: Class, Entitlement, and Narcissism." *Personality and Social Psychology Bulletin* 40, no. 1 (2014): 34–43.

Piff, Paul K., Michael W. Kraus, Stephanie Cote, Bonnie Cheng, and Dacher Keltner. "Having More, Giving Less: The Influence of Class on Prosocial Behavior." *Journal of Personality and Social Psychology* 99, no. 5 (2010): 771–84.

Piff, Paul K., and J. P. Moskowitz. "Wealth, Poverty, and Happiness: Social Class Is Differentially Associated with Positive Emotions." *Emotion*. Advance online publication. http://dx.doi.org/10.1037/emo0000387 (December 2017).

Piketty, Thomas. *Capital in the Twenty-First Century*, trans. Arthur Goldhammer. Cambridge: Harvard University Press, 2014.

Plamenatz, John. *Man and Society: A Critical Examination of Some Important Social and Political Theories from Machiavelli to Marx*. Vol. I. London: Longman's, 1963.

Pufendorf, Samuel. *On the Duty of Man and Citizen*, trans. Michael Silverthorne. Cambridge: Cambridge University Press, 1991.

Radkiewicz, Piotr. "Another Look at the Duality of the Dual-Process Motivational Model: On the Role of Axiological Moral Origins of Right-Wing Authoritarianism and Social Dominance Orientation." *Personality and Individual Differences* 99 (2016): 106–12.

Rahe, Paul. *Montesquieu and the Logic of Liberty: War, Religion, Commerce, Climate, Terrain, Technology, Uneasiness of Mind, the Spirit of Political Vigilance, and the Foundations of the Modern Republic*. New Haven: Yale University Press, 2009.

———. "Blaise Pascal, Pierre Nicole, and the Origins of Liberal Sociology." In *Enlightenment and Secularism: Essays on the Mobilization of Reason*, ed. Christopher Nadon, 129–40. Lanham, Md.: Lexington Books, 2013.

Rasmussen, Dennis C. "If Rousseau Were Rich: Another Model of the Good Life." *History of Political Thought* 36, 3 (2015): 499–520.

Rawls, John. *A Theory of Justice*. Cambridge, Mass.: Harvard University Press, 1971.

———. *Lectures on the History of Political Philosophy*, ed. Samuel Freeman. Cambridge, Mass.: Harvard University Press, 2007.

Reinhardt, Mark. *The Art of Being Free: Taking Liberties with Tocqueville, Marx, and Arendt*. Ithaca: Cornell University Press, 1997.

Richter, Melvin. "Rousseau and Tocqueville on Democratic Legitimacy and Illegitimacy." In

Rousseau and Liberty, ed. Robert Wokler, 70–98. Manchester: Manchester University Press, 1995.

Riley, Patrick. *The General Will Before Rousseau: The Transformation of the Divine into the Civic.* Princeton: Princeton University Press, 1986.

Riley, Patrick, Jr. "The Inversion of Conversion: Rousseau's Rewriting of Augustinian Autobiography." *Studies in Eighteenth-Century Culture* 28, no. 1 (1999): 229–55.

———. "Rousseau, Fénelon, and the Quarrel Between the Ancients and the Moderns." In *The Cambridge Companion to Rousseau*, ed. Patrick Riley, 78–93. Cambridge University Press, 2001.

Rist, John M. *Augustine: Ancient Thought Baptized.* Cambridge: Cambridge University Press, 1994.

Rousseau, Jean-Jacques. *Oeuvres complètes.* Vol. I, ed. Bernard Gagnebin and Marcel Raymond. Paris: NRF Edition de la Pléiade, 1959.

———. *Oeuvres complètes.* Vol. II, ed. Bernard Gagnebin and Marcel Raymond. Paris: NRF Edition de la Pléeiade, 1961.

———. *Oeuvres complètes.* Vol. III, ed. Bernard Gagnebin and Marcel Raymond. Paris: NRF Edition de la Pléiade, 1964.

———. *Oeuvres complètes.* Vol. IV, ed. Bernard Gagnebin and Marcel Raymond. Paris: NRF Edition de la Pléiade, 1969.

———. *Oeuvres complètes.* Vol. V, ed. Bernard Gagnebin and Marcel Raymond. Paris: NRF Edition de la Pléiade, 1969.

———. *The Collected Writings of Jean-Jacques Rousseau.* Vol. 1, ed. Christopher Kelly and Roger D. Masters and trans. Judith R. Bush, Christopher Kelly, and Roger D. Masters. Hanover, N.H.: University Press of New England, 1990.

———. *The Collected Writings of Jean-Jacques Rousseau.* Vol. 5, ed. Christopher Kelly, Roger D. Masters, and Peter G. Stillman and trans. Christopher Kelly. Hanover, N.H.: University Press of New England, 1995.

———. *The Discourses and Other Early Writings*, ed. and trans. Victor Gourevitch. Cambridge: Cambridge University Press, 1997.

———. *The Social Contract and Other Later Writings*, ed. and trans. Victor Gourevitch. Cambridge: Cambridge University Press, 1997.

———. *The Collected Writings of Jean-Jacques Rousseau.* Vol. 6, ed. and trans. Philip Stewart and Jean Vaché. Hanover, N.H.: University Press of New England, 1997.

———. *The Collected Writings of Jean-Jacques Rousseau.* Vol. 8, ed. Christopher Kelly and trans. Charles E. Butterworth, Alexandra Cook, and Terence E. Marshall. Hanover, N.H.: University Press of New England Press, 2000.

———. *The Collected Writings of Jean-Jacques Rousseau.* Vol. 9, ed. Christopher Kelly and Eve Grace and trans. Christopher Kelly and Judith R. Bush. Hanover, N.H.: University Press of New England, 2001.

———. *The Collected Writings of Jean-Jacques Rousseau.* Vol. 10, ed. and trans. Judith Bush and Christopher Kelly. Hanover, N.H.: Dartmouth College Press, 2004.

———. *The Collected Writings of Jean-Jacques Rousseau.* Vol. 11, ed. Christopher Kelly and trans. Christopher Kelly and Judith Bush. Hanover, N.H.: Dartmouth College Press, 2005.

———. *The Collected Writings of Jean-Jacques Rousseau*, Vol. 12, ed. and trans. Christopher Kelly. Hanover, N.H.: Dartmouth College Press, 2007.

———. *The Collected Writings of Jean-Jacques Rousseau.* Vol. 13, ed. and trans. Christopher Kelly and Allan Bloom. Hanover, N.H.: Dartmouth College Press, 2010.

Rosenblatt, Helena. *Rousseau and Geneva: From the Second Discourse to the Social Contract, 1749–1762.* Cambridge: Cambridge University Press, 1997.

Rothkrug, Lionel. *Opposition to Louis XIV: The Political and Social Origins of the French Enlightenment.* Princeton: Princeton University Press, 1965.

Russell, Bertrand. *A History of Western Philosophy.* New York: Simon and Schuster, 1972.

Saint-Lambert, Jean-François de. "Luxury." In *Encyclopedia Selections,* trans. Nelly S. Hoyt and Thomas Cassirer, 203–34. Indianapolis: Bobbs-Merrill, 1965.

Schneewind, J. B. *The Invention of Autonomy: A History of Modern Moral Philosophy.* Cambridge: Cambridge University Press, 1998.

Schopenhauer, Arthur. "Pride." In *The Essays of Arthur Schopenhauer,* trans. Ben Ray Redman. New York: Walter J. Black, 1932.

Sedgwick, Alexander. *Jansenism in Seventeenth-Century France: Voices from the Wilderness.* Charlottesville: University Press of Virginia, 1977.

Sénault, Jean-François. *De l'usage des passions.* Paris: Jean Camusat, 1641.

Shklar, Judith. *Men and Citizens: A Study of Rousseau's Social Thought.* Cambridge: Cambridge University Press, 1969.

———. "Jean-Jacques Rousseau and Equality." *Dædalus* 107, no. 3 (1978): 13–25.

Siedentop, Larry. *Inventing the Individual: The Origins of Western Liberalism.* Cambridge, Mass.: Harvard University Press, 2014.

Simmel, Georg. "The Metropolis and Mental Life." In *The Sociology of Georg Simmel,* ed. and trans. Kurt H. Wolff. Glencoe, Ill.: Free Press, 1950.

Smith, Adam. *Lectures on Jurisprudence,* ed. R. L. Meek, D. D. Raphael, and P. G. Stein. Oxford: Clarendon Press, 1978.

———. "A Letter to the Authors of the Edinburgh Review." In *Essays on Philosophical Subjects,* ed. W. P. D. Wightman and J.C. Bryce. Indianapolis: Liberty Fund, 1980.

———. *The Theory of Moral Sentiments,* ed. D. D. Raphael and A. L. Mackie. Indianapolis: Liberty Fund, 1982.

———. *Wealth of Nations,* ed. Edward Cannan. New York: Random House, 2000.

Solomon, Robert C. *The Passions: Emotions and the Meaning of Life.* Indianapolis: Hackett, 1993.

———. *True to Our Feelings: What Our Emotions Are Really Telling Us.* Oxford: Oxford University Press, 2001.

Solove, Erica, Gwenith G. Fisher, and Kurt Kraiger. "Coping with Job Loss and Reemployment: A Two-Wave Study." *Journal of Business and Psychology* 30, no. 3 (2015): 529–41.

Sonenscher, Michael. *Sans-Culottes: An Eighteenth-Century Emblem in the French Revolution.* Princeton: Princeton University Press, 2008.

———. *Before the Deluge: Public Debt, Inequality, and the Origins of the French Revolution.* Princeton: Princeton University Press, 2009.

———. "Sociability, Perfectibility and the Intellectual Legacy of Jean-Jacques Rousseau." *History of European Ideas* 41 no. 5 (2015): 683–98.

Sophocles. *Aias,* trans. Herbert Golder and Richard Pevear. Oxford: Oxford University Press, 1999.

Starobinski, Jean. *Jean-Jacques Rousseau: Transparency and Obstruction,* trans. Arthur Goldhammer. Chicago: University of Chicago Press, 1971.

———. "Discourse on Inequality." In *Jean-Jacques Rousseau: Transparency and Obstruction,* trans. Arthur Goldhammer, 281–303. Chicago: University of Chicago Press, 1971.

Stendhal. *The Red and the Black,* trans. Burton Raffel. New York: Modern Library, 2003.

Stock, Brian. *Augustine the Reader: Meditation, Self-Knowledge, and the Ethics of Interpretation.* Cambridge, Mass.: Harvard University Press, 1996.

Strauss, Leo. *Natural Right and History.* Chicago: University of Chicago Press, 1953.

Strong, Tracy B. "Seeing Differently, Seeing Further: Rousseau and Tocqueville." In *Friends and Citizens: Essays in Honor of Wilson Carey McWilliams,* ed. Peter Dennis Bathory and Nancy L. Schwartz, 97–122. Lanham, Md.: Rowman and Littlefield, 2001.

Sumner, William Graham. *What Social Classes Owe to Each Other.* Caldwell, Id.: Caxton, 1989.

Swedberg, Richard. *Tocqueville's Political Economy.* Princeton: Princeton University Press, 2009.

Talmon, Jacob L. *The Origins of Totalitarian Democracy.* New York: W. W. Norton, 1970.

Thomas, Keith. *The Ends of Life: Road to Fulfillment in Early Modern England.* Oxford: Oxford University Press, 2009.

Thucydides. *The Peloponnesian War,* trans. Walter Banco. New York: W. W. Norton, 1996.

Tocqueville, Alexis de. *L'Ancien Régime et la Révolution.* In *Oeuvres complètes,* vol. II, parts i–ii, ed. J. P. Mayer. Paris: Gallimard, 1953.

———. *Journeys to England and Ireland,* ed. J.P. Mayer. London: Faber and Faber, 1953.

———. *Voyages en Sicile et aux États-Unis.* In *Oeuvres complètes,* vol. V, ed. J. P. Mayer. Paris: Gallimard, 1957.

———. *Voyages en Angleterre, Irlande, Suisse et Algérie.* In *Oeuvres complètes,* vol. V, parts i–ii, ed. J. P. Mayer and André Jardin. 5th edition. Paris: Gallimard, 1958.

———. *Correspondance d'Alexis de Tocqueville et d'Arthur de Gobineau.* In *Oeuvres complètes.* Vol. IX, ed. M. Degros. Paris: Gallimard, 1959.

———. *De la démocratie en Amerique.* In *Oeuvres complètes,* V vol. I, parts i–ii, ed. J. P. Mayer. Paris: Gallimard, 1961.

———. *Journey to America,* trans. George Lawrence. New Haven: Yale University Press, 1962.

———. *Souvenirs.* In *Oeuvres complètes,* vol. XII, ed. Luc Monnier. Paris: Gallimard, 1964.

———. *Correspondance d'Alexis de Tocqueville et de Louis de Kergorlay.* In *Oeuvres complètes,* vol. XIII, part I, ed. André Jardin. Paris: Gallimard, 1977.

———. *Recollections: The French Revolution of 1848,* trans. George Lawrence. New Brunswick, N.J.: Transaction Press, 1995.

———. *The Old Regime and the Revolution,* trans. Alan S. Kahan. Chicago: University of Chicago Press, 1998.

———. *Democracy in America,* trans. Arthur Goldhammer. New York: Library of America, 2004.

———. *Letters from America,* ed. and trans. Frederick Brown. New Haven: Yale University Press, 2010.

Trollope, Frances. *Domestic Manners of Americans,* ed. Donald Smalley. New York: Alfred A. Knopf, 1949.

Trousson, Raymond. *Jean-Jacques Rousseau: La marche à la gloire.* Paris: Tallandier, 1988.

Van Kley, Dale. "Pierre Nicole, Jansenism, and the Morality of Enlightened Self-Interest." In *Anticipations of the Enlightenment in England, France, and Germany,* ed. Alan Charles Kors and Paul J. Korshin, 69–85. Philadelphia: University of Pennsylvania Press, 1987.

Viroli, Maurizio. *Jean-Jacques Rousseau and the "Well-Ordered Society,"* trans. Derek Hanson. Cambridge: Cambridge University Press, 1988.

Voltaire. *Letters Concerning the English Nation,* ed. Nicholas Cronk. Oxford: Oxford University Press, 1994.

———. *Candide, or Optimism,* trans. Theo Cuffe. New York: Penguin Books, 2005.

———. *A Pocket Philosophical Dictionary*, trans. John Fletcher. Oxford: Oxford University Press, 2011.

Waldock, A. J. A. *Sophocles the Dramatist*. Cambridge: Cambridge University Press, 1966.

Welch, Cheryl B. *De Tocqueville*. Oxford: Oxford University Press, 2001.

Welsh, Alexander. *What s Honor? A Question of Moral Imperatives*. New Haven: Yale University Press, 2008.

White, R. J. *The Anti-Philosophers: A Study of the Philosophes in Eighteenth-Century France*. New York: St. Martin's Press, 1970.

Williams, Bernard. *Shame and Necessity*. Berkeley: University of California Press, 1993.

Williams, David Lay. *Rousseau's Platonic Enlightenment*. University Park: Pennsylvania State University Press, 2007.

———. "The Platonic Soul of the *Reveries*: The Role of Solitude in Rousseau's Democratic Politics." *History of Political Thought* 34 no. 1 (2012): 87–123.

———. *Rousseau's Social Contract: An Introduction*. Cambridge: Cambridge University Press, 2014.

———. "Review Essay: Rousseau on Inequality and Free Will." *Political Theory* 45 no. 4 (2017): 552–65.

Wilson, Arthur M. *Diderot*. Oxford: Oxford University Press, 1972.

Wilson, Edward O. *The Social Conquest of the Earth*. New York: Liveright, 2012.

Wolin, Sheldon S. *Tocqueville Between Two Worlds: The Making of a Theoretical and Political Life*. Princeton: Princeton University Press, 2001.

Woodruff, Paul. *The Ajax Dilemma: Justice, Fairness, and Rewards*. Oxford: Oxford University Press, 2011.

Young, Michael. *The Rise of the Meritocracy, 1870–2033: An Essay on Education and Equality*. New York: Penguin, 1975.

Zawadski, Bohan, and Paul Lazarsfeld. "The Psychological Consequences of Unemployment." *Journal of Social Psychology* 6, no. 2 (1935): 224–51.

Index

Acknowledgments

I would like to thank David Lay Williams for being a great friend, wonderful colleague, and now inspiring mentor. Without his willingness to listen to me struggle with my ideas and his constant stream of encouragement, this book never would have made it to print. To repeat a compliment one of my old professors paid his mentor, David represents all that I admire about academic life. In addition to David, I have greatly benefited from conversations with fellow political theorists and philosophers. Jay Conway and Jason Neidleman are especially worthy of mention. I am also deeply indebted to several of my colleagues at California State University, Los Angeles: Scott Wells for generously assisting me in understanding the development of aristocracy in early modern Europe, Heidi Riggio for directing me toward current social science research that provides empirical support for Rousseau's claims, Gar Culbert for copyediting, and Tim Doran for reading my sections on Sophocles. California State University, Los Angeles, also deserves thanks for providing me a one-semester sabbatical to complete this project.

I would also like to thank all the wonderful folks at Penn Press: Hannah Blake, Gavriella Fried, Noreen O'Connor-Abel, and Otto Bohlmann. My editor, Damon Linker, has been terrific. I do not have the words to express my appreciation for his support of my manuscript as well as his professionalism. It has been a pleasure to work with him.

My final words are for family. My parents, Heath and Judy, have been a constant source of encouragement, as have my siblings Laurie, Eric, Brian, and Christine. Brian has always made time to copyedit my work and offer sound professional advice. My greatest debt of gratitude is reserved for my wife, Barbra, and my two sons, Ian and Andrew. I cannot thank them enough for their patience during the writing of this book. It is to them that I dedicate this book. It is my sincere hope that my scholarly activities have in no way interfered with my much more important roles of husband and father. While I cannot say I am a committed Rousseauist, Rousseau is undoubtedly correct in his belief that conjugal and paternal love are the sweetest sentiments known to humanity.